Zhorna

Zhorna

MATERIAL CULTURE of the UKRAINIAN PIONEERS

Roman Paul Fodchuk

UNIVERSITY OF
CALGARY
PRESS

Published by the University of Calgary Press
2500 University Drive NW
Calgary, Alberta, Canada T2N 1N4

www.uofcpress.com

Library and Archives Canada Cataloguing in Publication

Fodchuk, Roman

    Zhorna : material culture of the Ukrainian pioneers / Roman Fodchuk.

(Legacies shared 1498-2358 ; 20)
Includes bibliographical references and index.
ISBN 13: 978-1-155238-197-7
ISBN 10: 1-55238-197-8

    1. Ukrainian Canadians–Material culture–Prairie Provinces.
2. Ukrainians–Material culture–Prairie Provinces. I. Title.
II. Series.

FC3250.U5F63 2006   971.2'00491791   C2006-905304-9

We acknowledge the financial support of the Government of Canada, through
the Book Publishing Industry Development Program (BPIDP), and the
Alberta Foundation for the Arts for our publishing activities. We acknowledge
the support of the Canada Council for the Arts for our publishing program.

This project has been funded in part by the Ukrainian
Canadian Foundation of Taras Schevchenko.

The University of Calgary Press also wishes to acknowledge the generous
support of The Ukrainian Canadian Professional and Business Association
of Calgary and The Ukrainian Self Reliance Association, Calgary Branch.

Printed and bound in Canada by Houghton Boston
This book is printed on 80 lb. Cougar Opaque and 80 lb. Starbrite Dull
Cover design by Melina Cusano, page design and typesetting by Mieka West

Table of Contents

Acknowledgments

I wish to sincerely thank the following:

Ramona Fodchuk – for her ability to review my early writing, correct my grammar, and check my spelling

Ken Preston, copy editor, now retired from the *Calgary Herald* – for his comments and encouragement

John C. Lehr, Professor of Geography, University of Winnipeg – for his excellent review and all-encompassing introduction

Robert Klymasz, Former Curator of the East European Collection, Canadian Museum of Civilization – for his introduction and for his suggestion that this material be developed into a book

Anna Pidruchney, who, with the help of her granddaughter Linda Irvine, provided much assistance translating passages from the Ukrainian writings of Peter Svarich and various other documents in the Peter Svarich Collection at the Provincial Archives of Alberta

St. John's Institute of Edmonton for permission to use these materials, as listed below:
> Excerpts in English translations from Peter Svarich (1891–1964) PAA Collection no. 82.225 (1934)
> Selected sketches of agricultural buildings, homestead and utensils numbers 75.74: 1265–1284
> Text in Ukrainian on homesteading Accession 75.74 Items 6, 7, 8, –10

Kathryn Fodchuk Dobbin and *Jean Paul Rioux* (students at the Alberta College of Art) – for their wondrous illustrations of various pioneer tools, utensils, and effects

Darlene Quaife and *Faye Reineberg Holt* – for their enthusiastic classes in creative writing and their encouragement during the early stages

The staff members of Roman Fodchuk and Associates, Ltd., who gathered research materials and prepared drafts as time permitted

Dianne Parker – for her persistence through thick and thin in putting the manuscript into a suitable format and preparing the draft

Jo-Ann Cleaver, M.A. (Anthropology), Editor – for her fine support and substantive and copy editing work

The fine editorial and graphic support and encouragement of the staff at the U of C Press.

Stan Humenuk, M.S. Lib.Sc.; Ph.D. History; Certified Translator– for his transliteration of the Ukrainian terms

I also wish to thank the pioneer-era elders like my mother and grandmother, who so deliciously infused this colourful culture in me, as well as the sons and daughters of the pioneers no longer with us who contributed in so many ways towards the completion of this work, among others (some are mentioned in the text).

And last, but not least, this book is dedicated to my three daughters (Kathryn, Laura, Ramona) and my wife Adeline, to whom I am deeply indebted for their preliminary support and their encouragement throughout the continuing demands of this project.

Peter Tymchuk's thatched barn – Lake Eliza

Peter Tymchuk's thatched granary

Preface

Walking a trail through the woods in the Lake Eliza[1] district of Alberta in the mid-1950s, I came upon a clearing and a completely thatched Ukrainian immigrant farmstead.[2] My camera's four remaining exposures were not enough to record the entire scene which was comprised of three substantial granaries, a barn, and a house.

Fifteen years later, I was unable to locate the farmstead. The original settler had passed on and the buildings were gone. The only proof I had of the experience were the photographs, and memories of the homestead haunted me. Its disappearance was not an isolated incident. As a young district agriculturist in the early 1950s, I often admired the rich architectural detail, the structural honesty of the logs, and the substantial scale, quality, and fine craftsmanship expressed in the early pioneer buildings I found on abandoned, overgrown farmsteads scattered throughout the Shandro, Myrnam to Two Hills, and Hairy Hill to Willingdon districts of Alberta.[3] Some of the finest examples had been bulldozed into piles of timber and burned to provide additional farmland or to ease operations as farmers became more dependent upon large, modern equipment. Between 1950 and 1970, the movement in the West towards farm enlargement and agricultural consolidation affected these early historical resources dramatically. At one time, dwellings that housed up to twenty people could be found on many quarter sections. Now, these custodians of our past were few

and far between. Some of the best examples of Ukrainian "folk architecture" withstood the raising of children and much hardship through two world wars, only to fall victim to mechanized progress in agriculture.

Much of the impetus for this book comes from the same desire to arrest time that I'd experienced fifty years ago when I happened upon that homestead. It was written to bring together a lifetime's accumulation of photographs, illustrations, and knowledge regarding a widely dispersed and disappearing material culture, to document the symbols expressed by folk architecture that summon such boyhood memories as tossing mud at log walls (and at my sister) during a plastering bee; sleeping on my grandmother's warm and cozy *pich* (pronounced "peach"; it is a clay oven); savouring the aroma of a fabulous feast of *holubtsi* (cabbage rolls), *pyrohy* (soft-dough dumplings with various fillings such as sauerkraut, potato and cheese, onions, and prunes), and other sumptuous dishes simmering in an outdoor clay oven; participating in the harvest work-fest; admiring the rich patina of my uncles' wooden tools in their original tool chests; or listening to my grandparents[4] recount their escape from the oppression of the *pan*[5] (landlord in the old country).

I have dipped into the past and elaborated upon familial memories using various sources, the first of which is excerpts from the memoirs of Peter Svarich. His expressive ability captures the Ukrainian pioneering period in Alberta sincerely and in rich detail. Svarich's *Spomyny 1877–1904* describes this early period.[6] Years later, on numerous trips to Myrnam and Two Hills to raise funds for the St. John's Institute[7] and other Ukrainian organizations, Svarich would stop by my office[8] in Myrnam to discuss old and new farming practices. Although in his eighties and retired, he had a keen interest in what was happening in agriculture and what, why, where, and when these new ideas were being carried out by the descendants of the original settlers throughout my district, most of which was part of the Ukrainian settlement bloc. We would drive out into the countryside together, and he would point out pioneer farmsteads and relate stories of the original settlers, recalling the heads of these families and the significant events in their lives. I was impressed by the breadth of his knowledge. He knew the family names, knew who had first settled and broken the land, and indicated where and how they built their homes. Because his story is tied in with my own family's history and because this man was such a unifying force within Alberta's Ukrainian community, I have scattered excerpts and paraphrases from his memoirs[9] throughout the book. They amplify points made in interviews with original settlers and my own memories of life "back then."

A familial and friendly connection is also present in this work. My family's roots go back to Tulova, a rural Ukrainian village about five kilometres south of Sniatyn (*mistechko*), which is the nearest town located entirely in western Ukraine. The Svarich "contingent" were all residents of Tulova, and all the neighbours in this small village knew each other well. My uncle Stephan Fodchuk arrived in Canada with the Svarich party on the *S.S. Acadia* in 1900. They stopped over at the Gregoraschuk family's home at Edna, Alberta, where the women and children stayed while the men scouted for land to the east in what became Sich Kolomea, north of the Royal Park district near Vegreville. My grandmother was a Gregoraschuk, and this brother, who preceded her to Canada, was her family. Paul and Marie Fodchuk, my grandparents, and their young sons (including my father, seven years old at the time) were to leave for Canada a few years later, and they stayed for a time in the early home that Peter Svarich built.

When my company was hired to plan the Ukrainian Cultural Heritage Project in 1976 (see Appendix 1 for more on the Village Museum), we were able to access private and public collections of rare and often unique pioneer tools and household utensils. Some of these are in the museum collections at the Shandro Museum and the Ukrainian Cultural Heritage Village.[10] The accumulation of data, photographs, and related materials collected during the master plan studies for that project anchor this book. Also included are interviews with the sons and daughters of pioneers. I believe their firsthand impressions lend a special vitality to the text.

The academic realm is well-represented by the involvement of two renowned professors who have studied this ethnic group extensively: Dr. Robert Klymasz (the former head of Slavic and East European Programmes at Ottawa's National Museum of Man) and Dr. John Lehr, who teaches in the geography department at the University of Winnipeg. Dr. Klymasz wrote his preface in 1982, having read only a couple of preliminary chapters. He details various aspects of the immigrants' folk culture, in addition to referencing previous related works, both textual and artistic. Dr. Lehr offers historic background that explains why and how these Ukrainians came to populate the Canadian West over a hundred years ago and the impact the traditional rivalry between the Orthodox and the Greek Catholics had on settlement patterns in western Canada,[11] among other related materials. Their contributions introduce this text, and both offer background information that sheds light on the historic and folkloric traditions that informed the Ukrainian immigrants' lives, both pre- and post-immigration. I am grateful for their contributions.

Finally, I also included reproductions of some of the drawings Svarich brought with him from Ukraine so long ago. These drawings are accompanied by terms and descriptions that reflect and express the local dialect the settlers spoke a hundred years ago. At least three dialects were common in the study area while I was growing up. The Shandros were Bukovynians from the Hutzal region on my mother's side, the Fodchuks were from Tulova in Halychyna, and there was a large contingent of settlers from Szypenitz all around our farm. Each group spoke their own dialect, yet had no problem understanding each other, as the words' roots were usually the same. For instance, my grandmother was sure to correct me when I used my father's technical terms; *khatyna* had to be *khatchyna* (or *khatchynka*, depending on the building's size). She was a hard Bukovynian from Rus'kyi-Banyliv and insisted that I speak to her in her accepted dialect. Recent visitors, modern Ukrainians from Kyiv, have told me I speak an ancient and archaic Ukrainian that is at least a hundred years old and no longer in vogue (they spoke a Russianized Ukrainian).

I have retained dialectal terms to preserve the authenticity of the materials, written and spoken. They are distinguished by accents and pronunciations more than by the use of distinctively different words, which explains why the pioneers could understand each other so well. The dialectal terms scattered throughout the text in quotations and remembrances are listed in the glossary. They have been transliterated from the Ukrainian alphabet to the Roman (English) alphabet using a standard transliteration table accepted by the United Nations and in Ukraine. Some of the dialectal terms in the glossary are not necessarily found in dictionaries, and it is not unusual

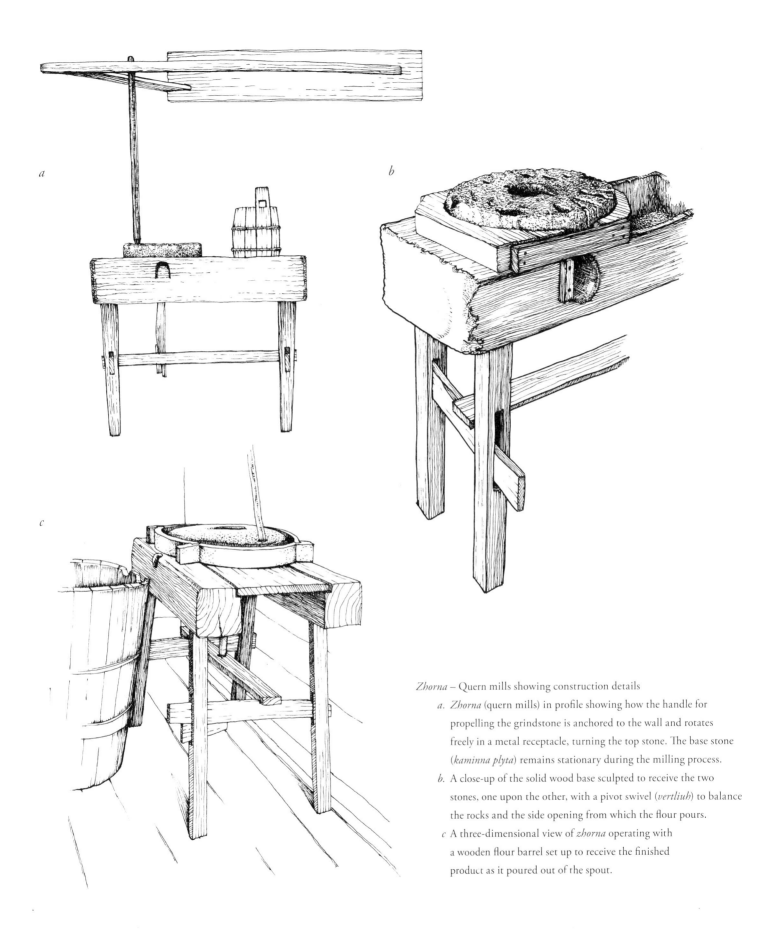

a

b

c

Zhorna – Quern mills showing construction details

    a. *Zhorna* (quern mills) in profile showing how the handle for
        propelling the grindstone is anchored to the wall and rotates
        freely in a metal receptacle, turning the top stone. The base stone
        (*kaminna plyta*) remains stationary during the milling process.

    b. A close-up of the solid wood base sculpted to receive the two
        stones, one upon the other, with a pivot swivel (*vertliuh*) to balance
        the rocks and the side opening from which the flour pours.

    c A three-dimensional view of *zhorna* operating with
        a wooden flour barrel set up to receive the finished
        product as it poured out of the spout.

for words to have a plurality of meanings depending upon the context in which they are used.

My brief association with Peter Svarich further tweaked my interest in pioneer folk architecture. As Terry Jordon[12] notes in the following quote (albeit with respect to settlers in east Texas), the connection between the buildings and the lifeways of pioneers is integral to understanding this historic period.

These buildings, whether dwellings, barns, churches or stores, are based not on blueprints but on mental images that change little from one generation to the next. In this sense, we can speak of "architecture without architects." Folk buildings are extensions of the people and the region. They provide the unique character or essence of each district and province. (1978, 8)

The intent of this project is to illustrate and record the purposeful beauty of this era and of these people. It is the remaining evidence of the vitality and ingenuity of the early Ukrainian settlers in Alberta, a cultural heritage that is rapidly disappearing, that I record within these pages. There is much that is exceptional and worth documenting about their vernacular material culture. By virtue of the geographical, social, and cultural distance between eastern Europe and western Canada, Ukrainian immigrants were completely cut off from their support systems. Most had little money and could bring no more than a few essential possessions to facilitate their new life. Despite the hardships that accompanied settling the Canadian prairies, they endured. Indeed, they prospered. They established a way of life that reflected their cultural and material heritage. This work is dedicated to their spirit and their work ethic.

Once I decided to take on this project, the first task was to somehow choose a title or theme that encapsulated and honoured that pioneering spirit appropriately. Vivid memories again guided me. While walking with my father, we would occasionally see large, flat, pancake-shaped stones with a round hole in the centre, stones that were re-used in various ingenious ways. One set was used as a counter-weight to hold down the corner posts against the pull of the stretched wire of a half-mile-long barbed wire fence. The stones weighed fifty to sixty pounds each, and two provided enough stability to keep the post in the ground. I remember the intricate design of grooves and ridges, almost like a message in a strange language engraved into one side of each of those stones. Upon asking my father about their meaning, I was informed that these were the remnants of disused quern mills (*zhorna*) now serving a new function. This was not their only reiteration, for I also recall seeing worn-out millstones ingeniously used as a step over a rail fence and into a garden, serving both a utilitarian and an aesthetically pleasing function, as did so many of the tools and artefacts used by the early Ukrainian settlers.

Zhorna were often found among the tools the Ukrainian immigrants brought with them in their wooden chests and boxes. A priority in their new homes was to build a quern mill (*mlyn*) in order to mill their own flour as soon as possible (thus saving themselves a six-day-long trip, among other things, as Dr. Klymasz notes in his introduction). At least every second house had *zhorna* in those early days.

The millstone is an ancient symbol of mankind's ability to coax from the earth, through hard work and ingenuity, more sustenance than it freely provides. The grinding of grain is the culmination of a sustaining process that requires human knowledge, energy, and patience, just as pioneering did. I believe that millstones rotating on their wooden axis – strong, stable, and productive – represent a fitting symbol of the pioneer way of life, and thus have titled the work, *Zhorna: Material Culture of the Ukrainian Pioneers*, and dedicated it to the qualities inherent in these people and their material culture.

Introduction
Part One, by Dr. Robert B. Klymasz

Drawing inspiration from one of Europe's richest folk traditions, the folk heritage of Canada's sizeable Ukrainian community has long attracted the attention of the casual onlooker and the informed enthusiast alike. In recent years, this particular legacy has gained added recognition as an important field of scientific research and discovery.

The arrival in Canada of the Ukrainian pioneer immigrants over a hundred years ago and the establishment of their network of settlements on the prairies paved the way for a new, and in some respects more archaic, variant of the European peasant folk cultures that had already taken root elsewhere in Canada. Hailing from various ethnographic regions of western Ukraine, these first groups were very different from other immigrants. Their dress, for instance, included sheepskin coats and richly embroidered shirts and sashes. Their predilection for music-making was betrayed by the occasional tightly gripped *tsymbaly*[1] (dulcimer), old country violin, or *sopilka* (flute) that some of the men would bring along to festive occasions in the new world. Less immediately visible were the talented craftsmen and craftswomen whose assorted trades and abilities were of paramount importance as the immigrant community cleared the land and braced itself for an initial period of toil,

hardship, and adjustment in the new and sometimes harsh environment. Weaving, pottery, woodworking, and traditional Easter-egg ornamentation were just a few of the crafts practised. Indeed, Ukrainian Easter eggs have survived as the most widespread and visible manifestation of Ukrainian folk art in Canada today.

In general, the wholesale transplantation of Ukrainian folk heritage was assisted during this pioneering period by the initial isolation of most Ukrainian colonies from other cultural groups and from Canada's mainstream population. Thus, for some time the Ukrainian pioneer settlement unconsciously retained an authentic, centuries-old, agrarian way of life. It represented the ideal model of a folk culture, one that relies almost exclusively on traditional oral means to transmit its heritage. Function, practicality, and usefulness are the key notes emphasized by the tools, utensils, and various implements that survive as museum relics of the pioneer era. No longer very useful but evoking much nostalgia, many have become collector's items and family heirlooms, tacit reminders of humble but cherished beginnings in a new land.

Anyone in search of a Ukrainian community on the prairies today need only look for the bulbous, onion-shaped domes that mark traditional Ukrainian church architecture.

Another telltale guide is provided by the occasional sighting of a whitewashed peasant cottage – usually in a ruinous state, but sometimes wondrously still inhabited, perhaps by one of the Ukrainian old-timers in the area, or simply maintained by the family for sentimental or historical reasons. "This type of house," reports C.T. Currelly, the first curator of the Royal Ontario Museum of Archaeology, "goes back in the Carpathian Mountains to prehistoric days" (1956, 27). Currelly's autobiography includes the following brief description of a Galician settlement in Manitoba in the 1890s:

They built their houses by driving stakes into the ground and then weaving a huge basket-like structure with the red willows. This was then mudded up. They dug deep down enough to get clay, which was mixed with wild hay and the walls heavily plastered on both sides. … Inside they built a stove of the clay, drew the smoke across near the floor with a horizontal chimney at the other end of the house. On the warm platform thus made they slept. (1956, 27–28)

A great deal has changed since the old days. Modern systems of transport and communications, for example, introduced several undreamt-of luxuries to the Ukrainian immigrant-farmer, who can often recall long hikes on foot to and from his homestead in the virgin bush when necessary to procure provisions from nearby urban centres. The following reminiscence is from an interview I conducted in 1963 in Dauphin, Manitoba:

From Winnipeg, they'd go six days on foot – and hungry because there was no money to buy anything. Those were bad times – they gathered berries and ate them along the way. Right now, it's good. My God, what we went through! If anyone at that time would have said that within sixty-four years there'd be towns, beautiful roads, and aeroplanes here – at that time people didn't know what aeroplanes or cars meant. And if someone would have spoken thus, they'd say, "What are you talking about?"… They'd think he was crazy.

Currently, one of the favourite topics of conversation among Ukrainians on the prairies, as elsewhere in Canada, is life during the early days of pioneer settlement. Perhaps the most characteristic feature distinguishing these accounts is the constant juxtaposition of *then* and *now*, *old* and *new*. With a strange and untamed natural environment providing the backdrop, these stories and personal recollections are very likely to include several asides referring to aspects of the old material culture that have long since disappeared, aspects such as the following:

(1)   And they used to get together. One man from the old country was able to make himself a *sopilka* (a wooden flute). I don't know whether you know what a *sopilka* is. … I recall my father had a big party and that man was playing the *sopilka*. Everyone would fill up on rabbit meat and drink tea …

(2)   So we constructed a kind of oven – I don't know if you've ever seen such an old country oven …

(3)   … and they lit up their *homsha't* – perhaps you heard about the stuff they call *homsha't*? That's a kind of tobacco that used to grow on the farms, and it grew just like rhubarb, and you could smell it for two miles around when someone was smoking it. Well, they began to smoke their pipes …

[excerpts from interviews Dr. Klymasz conducted in Vegreville, Alberta, 1965]

Like the *sopilka*, *pich* clay oven, and *homsha't*, *zhorna* symbolize a period gone by. Made of rock, *zhorna* millstones outlasted many ornaments, tools, and buildings while retaining the skilful marks of the craftsman. In her semi-autobiographical social history of Ukrainians in Alberta, *No Streets of Gold*, Helen Potrebenko provides the following detailed description of *zhorna* in a piece of dialogue between herself and her father:

Do you know what a *zhorna* is?

Well … there was this large piece of rock lying around the farm when I was a kid, but I have no idea how it worked.

That's part of it. What happened to the other pieces?

I don't know. What's it got to do with becoming a Canadian?

I'll get to that eventually if you're still listening. First, I'll explain about the *zhorna*. You start with a *kal'doob*, which is just a hollowed out piece of wood and easy to make. Over this you put a rock which fits tightly over the hole. The rock would be about two and one-half feet in diameter and four inches thick. It can't be too hard because then it can't be worked, not too soft because then you'd get rock chips in the flour. The top of this rock is roughened with a chisel or *molotok*. Then you have to make a hole through the centre of the rock, which you do laboriously with the same *molotok*. Through this hole is stuck the *vertyonok*, which stands on solid wood at the bottom of the *kal'dub*, but with a *klynok* under it.

Klinok?

That's a sort of wedge-shaped piece of wood. The top rock is bigger and again, must be exactly the right kind of rock, not too hard and not too soft – these were difficult things to come by. This rock also had a hole in the centre and under it, a sort of steel nest for the *vertyonok* to rest in.

This *vertyonok* also balances the upper rock. The *klinok* is pushed farther to raise the upper rock for a coarser grind of flour, and lowered for a finer grind.

When you're grinding grain, my father continued, you put your *zhorna* under a hole in the ceiling, which is the right size and height for the pole to rest in. The bottom of this pole is placed on the side of the top rock, and by turning the pole, you turn the rock. With one arm you turn the pole; with the other you pour grain continuously into the central hole. The turning must be done smoothly for an even grind. The flour falls down into the *kal'doob* through the central hole in the bottom rock. The *kal'doob* has a hole in the side of it from which flour pours out with each turn of the rock.

It's women's work, my father said, but as a youth I helped my mother grind. I would take off my trousers, leaving only my shirt on, and it would flap when I moved my arm to turn and blow fresh air on my body. It's hard work and takes a long time. (1977, 7–8)

As suggested by the above excerpt, many objects used in the past are so removed from our present way of life that lengthy explanations are required regarding their original usage and importance. It is understandable that for those who hold this information, these same objects almost always evoke memories of a whole series of bygone events, of personal pleasures and tribulations. Roman Fodchuk, the author/compiler of this book, is one such person.

An Albertan by birth who then trained in design, his Ukrainian heritage is strongly coloured by a strong dose of Bukovynian curiosity, commitment, and pride – characteristics that to a large extent account for his publication of this work after years of study and dedication to the subject matter presented. The material culture of Alberta's early Ukrainian pioneers has attracted the attention of others, as well. In addition to writers such as Helen Potrebenko, John Lehr, a geographer, published his studies on the vernacular folk architecture of Ukrainians in Alberta; Orest Semchishen published an album of striking photographs of pioneer churches in Alberta; Peter Orshinsky – a book of materials relating to his extensive private collection of textiles and apparel items acquired from Ukrainian communities in Alberta; and the late William Kurelek, as well as Peter Shostak, have documented aspects of Ukrainian material culture in Alberta in their art. An appreciation for the beauty and functionality of Alberta's rich heritage of Ukrainian material folk culture permeates the works of all these people. Although this flowering of attention has focused on Alberta, it reflects the Prairie provinces' rich legacy of Ukrainian folk culture, too. It can, in part, be explained by the relatively more rapid pace of economic and social change in Alberta where, almost overnight it would seem, rural interests have been replaced by urban ones, and the closed-in comfort of the Ukrainian farm community has been overshadowed by national and even international concerns. The rapidity of change in Alberta has forced, so to speak, the sons and daughters of pioneering Ukrainian immigrants in Alberta to evaluate, salvage, and document comparatively quickly those aspects of the old culture that warrant attention and preservation before the onslaught of change obliterates all vestiges of their rich heritage. The remarkable culmination of this process of culture sensitivity is reflected in the founding of an impressive outdoor village museum northeast of Edmonton, the Ukrainian Cultural Heritage Village, which serves as a reserve for a range of outstanding examples of material folk culture related to Alberta's early Ukrainian settlements. As one of western Canada's leading landscape architects, Roman Fodchuk was, quite appropriately, involved in the early stages of the planning of this outdoor museum. The illustrative drawings and accompanying documentation he has assembled for publication on the pages that follow reflect his wealth of specialized knowledge and deep personal interest in a remarkable heritage of material folk culture that Canadians of all backgrounds will appreciate as a rich source of instruction, wonder, and pride.

Dr. Robert B. Klymasz currently lives in Winnipeg and is Curator Emeritus of the Canadian Museum of Civilization (Gatineau, Quebec). Prior to his retirement in 2000, he headed the museum's East European Programme. He wrote this introduction in June of 1982, having read only the first few chapters. The author gratefully acknowledges his encouragement and generous support.

Introduction:
Part Two, by Dr. John C. Lehr

Ukrainian emigrants left their homeland by the thousands at the end of the nineteenth century. Propelled by a hunger for land, better economic opportunities, and freedom from oppression, they were drawn to the Americas by the promise of land and work. Thousands went to the United States, but most of these immigrants remained on the industrial eastern seaboard where they toiled in the factories and mines, intending, initially at least, to return to the old country with their savings, acquire more land, and resume life as farmers under improved circumstances. Others were intent on permanent migration, wishing to secure land and remain farmers. Over 170,000 of the latter came to Canada between 1891 and 1914, most of whom settled in western Canada.[1] During the same period, about 80,000 emigrated to Brazil, some 10,000 went to Argentina, and a handful emigrated to Paraguay.[2]

Like many other ethnic groups that settled in western Canada, the Ukrainians were not a homogenous people. They were notable, however, for the degree to which their differences divided them. Although all ethnically Ukrainian and speaking the same language, they were fragmented on the basis of their religious affiliations, political allegiances, and geographical origins (Hryniuk 1991). These closely intertwined divisions were etched deeply into the psyche and landscape of Ukrainian pioneers on the prairies, fading slowly as the generations passed, but nevertheless enduring to a surprising degree.

Almost all who migrated from Ukraine seeking land in the Americas came from the western Ukrainian provinces of Halychyna (Galicia) and Bukovyna. These provinces were then a part of the Habsburg Austro-Hungarian Empire and remained so until the end of the First World War. To the east, most Ukrainian territory lay under Russian Tsarist control, so emigration from there was channelled eastwards to the empty lands of Siberia. Only a handful of emigrants from the Russian-controlled greater Ukraine made their way across the Atlantic.

Those who came from Halychyna mostly worshipped in the Greek Catholic tradition; those from Bukovyna belonged to the Greek Orthodox faith. The two churches shared the Slavic liturgy and both had a married priesthood, but the Metropolitan in Moscow led the Orthodox Church, whereas the Greek Catholics looked to the Pope in Rome for spiritual leadership. Adherents of both mistrusted the other. The Orthodox suspected the Greek Catholics of pro-Polish sentiments and saw the Greek-Catholic Church as a Papist heresy.

For their part, the Greek Catholics saw the Orthodox Church as a Russophilic and anti-Ukrainian, Tsarist organization.[3]

Even though Halychyna and Bukovyna are contiguous and ethnographic divisions do not always coincide with the political border between the two provinces, peasants on each side of the border had firm and generally uncomplimentary opinions about the social characteristics and religious affiliations of the other. In a region that was relatively isolated, loyalties were to family, village, church, and region as much as they were to a vaguely articulated notion of nationality. Some villages that supplied immigrants to western Canada lay within sight of each other on opposite sides of the Dnister River that constituted the boundary between the two provinces, yet the cultural and religious divide that separated them was greater than their geographical proximity would suggest. In Canada these differences were inflamed by the dawning of Ukrainian nationalism and by the religious turmoil that accompanied the move to the new world.

These homeland differences had an immediate impact on the geography of Ukrainian settlement in western Canada. To the bewilderment of Canadian immigration officials working there, immigrants from both provinces often asked to be settled in separate regions. "Verily the Jews not wishing to go with the Samaritans," one bemused official remarked, adding that all were happy when he agreed to settle them in different parts of a township.[4] Chain migration, combined with a natural tendency to favour settlement with those of the same religious persuasion, created the same geographical situation. Until 1896 all Ukrainian settlers in Alberta were from the village of Nebyliw [Nebyliv] and the immediate vicinity in the Kalush district of Halychyna (Galicia), and were all more or less related (Kaye 1964). When immigrants from Bukovyna arrived, the nature of the settlement process changed; it became less orderly because of the increased numbers involved and the greater geographic area that was actively being settled. Settlers from Bukovyna usually kept to themselves, settling north and east of those from Halychyna. Chain migration caused them to cluster together on the basis of family relationships that replicated old country villages and regionally based groupings. For many years the transition zone between the area settled by those from Halychyna and those from Bukovyna remained remarkably narrow and well-defined, especially in the earliest-settled, western part of the colony. Only in the later-settled areas east of Vegreville did competition for land cause any significant inter-mixing of settlers from the two provinces.

This unusual geography had an important effect on the look of the land. Settlers from Halychyna and Bukovyna replicated their own cultural landscape, building houses, ancillary buildings, and churches in the pattern of their homeland area. Similarly, they transferred folk traditions, their agricultural technologies, and other elements of Ukrainian culture from each homeland region to east-central Alberta. Even the more ephemeral elements of non-material culture (such as the dialectal inflexions of language, agricultural terminology, folk rituals, and local social practices) remained remarkably intact, protected by the sheer size of the area settled almost exclusively by Ukrainians and an internal geography of settlement spawned by chain migration and cemented later by religious antipathy.

Ukrainian pioneer immigrants arrived in Alberta over a twenty-three-year period (from 1891 until 1914) when the outbreak of war in Europe effectively terminated further emigration. After the end of the First World War, a further wave of immigrants came from Ukraine, but most went to the cities rather than seek a dwindling supply of homestead land. By then most of the better land had been claimed. That which remained was on the margins of settlement, land that was sub-marginal from an agricultural perspective and not an inviting prospect to even the most determined homesteader. By the early 1920s, when pioneer settlement in east-central Alberta had virtually ceased, Ukrainians, with a few Poles and Romanians intermixed, had settled a block that spanned over seventy townships – well over two thousand square miles – forming a massive Ukrainian bloc settlement where old country life endured without much change for the next two or three decades.

The cultural landscape that Ukrainian settlers created generated comments from curious travellers through the region, most of whom did not, or could not, distinguish Ukrainians from Russians. Miriam Elston travelled through east-central Alberta in 1914; she wrote that when her party penetrated the area some five miles east of Lamont "we entered a district as typically Russian as though we had dropped into Russia itself," going on to comment rather favourably about the neat and tidy, low-browed "Russian" cottages scattered around the countryside (1915, 532). The landscape, of course, was Ukrainian, not Russian, but few outside the Ukrainian community were much concerned with such niceties. Few Anglo-Canadians knew or cared much about the Ukrainian settlements in the Prairie provinces, and the Ukrainian intelligentsia, when it began to document the history of Ukrainian life in Canada, was determined to promote the success stories of Ukrainian immigrants, measuring success in terms of the economic and social progress made within mainstream Anglophone society. Traditional material culture was ignored for a number of reasons but primarily because it was not much valued. It was seen as irrelevant to modern Ukrainian-Canadian life, an embarrassing reminder of pioneer times that many Ukrainian-Canadians saw as an impediment to their social acceptance by the mainstream culture.

Regrettably, by the time attention was directed towards recording and interpreting the Ukrainian pioneer landscape, much of it had disappeared, and the rate at which it was vanishing from the landscape was accelerating. It is difficult to identify what caused this attitude to change, but the initiation of the Canadian Inventory of Historic Buildings by the federal government in 1971 undoubtedly played a significant role, as did an emerging confidence within Ukrainian communities across the prairies that came with the realization that they had played a crucial role in developing the Canadian West.

When Ukrainian emigrants left their homeland before 1914, they left a land that was a rural backwater of the Austrian Empire. But life for the peasants in the villages of both Halychyna and Bukovyna was changing, whether for better or worse is debated by historians of the period. Stella Hryniuk (1991b) argues that conditions in western Ukraine were better than generally portrayed by Soviet historians, but John Paul Himka (1988) disagrees. Certainly western Ukraine was changing in the 1890s: railways were being built linking the principal centres, expanding markets for agricultural products and facilitating the importation of factory-produced products from the industrial centres of Europe. In the villages, houses' fire-prone thatched roofs were beginning to be replaced by newly available corrugated iron: not as aesthetically pleasing, perhaps, but ultimately safer and more durable. Factory-produced textiles, ceramics, and agricultural implements were appearing in the regional markets, competing with and replacing the hand-crafted products of local artisans and farmers.[5] The infiltration of imported manufactures into peasant life was slow but inexorable. Inevitably, the modernization process changed the peasant lifestyle, bringing in its train social unrest and, for some of the poorer and less competitive elements of the population, increased economic hardship.

Those who chose to emigrate from Halychyna and Bukovyna were mostly peasants from the middle ranks. The poorer, landless peasants who eked out a living as day labourers could not afford to migrate, and the wealthier peasants with larger land holdings presumably concluded that emigration made little economic sense for them. To purchase steamship tickets to Canada for a family of five or more people was an expensive proposition. Although many were able to sell their holdings for a reasonable price, by the time they arrived in Winnipeg or Edmonton they had little money left. Canadian colonization agents working to settle immigrants in western Canada suspected that most had more money than they were prepared to admit, owing to a fear of being bilked. Some were clearly destitute upon arrival, not having sufficient funds to pay the ten-dollar entry fee (equivalent to about $200 today) on their homestead.[6] Regardless of when they arrived, almost all

Ukrainian agricultural settlers underwent similar experiences. The material goods that they brought with them were generally limited to a few items that could be crammed into a steamship trunk or carried in a few bags. Clothing, bedding, and seeds were the principal items. Only the smaller implements, without hafts, were brought to Canada: axe and adze heads, hand drills, saw blades, scythe and sickle blades, and perhaps blades for a spade and hoe. With this limited inventory, they tackled the wilderness on what was then the edge of civilization. It was a daunting task.

Lack of capital was an immediate and constant concern for almost all Ukrainian settlers in western Canada. While a few acres of cleared land on the homestead could produce enough to sustain a family, cash was needed to purchase stock, draught animals, and other essentials like salt, nails, and kerosene. Most male immigrants sought off-farm employment, working far from home as miners and loggers, and as railway and farm labourers, where they were brought into contact with the English-speaking community and exposed to North American agricultural and industrial technology (Lehr 1991).

Working in an economic situation where capital was scarce, most immigrants underwent some economic retrenchment in their early settlement years. In the first few years when they lacked the resources that even the poorest could call upon in the old country, pioneers improvised, constructing earthen dwellings modelled on the seasonal dwellings used by shepherds in the Carpathian Mountains (Nahachewsky 1985). Even the first substantial dwellings constructed resembled those of an earlier generation in their simplicity and practicality (Lehr 1976). Folk memory and direct experience of the use of hand-crafted tools and agricultural implements served them well, but it is important to remember that these settlers were not nostalgic romantics; they reached back to their folk traditions only because their circumstances demanded it. When the opportunity was presented to them, Ukrainian immigrants were as agriculturally progressive as any settlers in western Canada. They eagerly adopted manufactured products when they were cheaper or more convenient than those produced in the home, and they showed little hesitation in adapting to their changed environment.

Ukrainians left their homeland at the end of the nineteenth century for many parts of the Americas, but only in Canada did they encounter an environment similar to that of western Ukraine. The climate of western Canada was more extreme; winters were colder and longer than in the old country and the summers were warmer, but the rainfall was comparable and the soils and vegetation, although a little different from that of western Ukraine, were not totally unfamiliar to them. With some notable exceptions, they were able to transplant not only their crops but their agricultural practices, architecture, and building technologies to Canada, whereas in Brazil and Argentina, the altered environment triggered significant shifts in traditional practices and certainly initiated radical changes in the material culture of Ukrainian settlers within a very short time. Paradoxically, in the long term, Ukrainian culture changed less in the Ukrainian settlements in South America because settlements there were more isolated and less linked to the outside world and, perhaps equally importantly, the Ukrainian community was not so fractured by religious or social divisions. Once the initial adjustments to an unfamiliar physical environment were made, there was little impetus for further change.

In contrast, in western Canada, there was at first little obvious impact on Ukrainian vernacular architecture or traditional agricultural practises. Traditional ways of building in wood proved well adapted to western Canadian conditions. The process of transfer and adaptation was facilitated by the immigrants' choice of land, for in the main, they elected to steer clear of the open prairie, preferring to acquire land in the "bush-country" of the aspen parkland. In Alberta, Ukrainians settled in an environment where wood was plentiful. Aspen and poplar could be found in abundance on virtually every homestead, and tamarack and pine were generally accessible to most homesteaders, especially in the country north of the Saskatchewan River in the Smokey Lake area settled by immigrants from Bukovyna.

The shear size of the Ukrainian settlement in east-central Alberta affected the rate at which rural Ukrainian life changed. The division of the community along old country provincial lines further reduced the potential for cultural borrowing and the exchange of cultural practices within the pioneer community. Although English-Canadian Protestant missionaries did their best to introduce Anglo-Canadian social and religious values through the establishment of residential schools and hospitals in the bloc, distance from metropolitan centres served to buffer the community from assimilative pressures, and Anglophone missionaries met with little success in their quest to turn settlers away from their ancestral churches (Lehr 2002).

Elements of pioneer life among Ukrainians thus survived in many rural areas until the 1950s, when rural electrification and improvements in the road system revolutionized agricultural life and sealed the fate of traditional agricultural practices. The older generation, the original pioneers, were perhaps somewhat loath to abandon familiar traditional ways, but few of their Canadian-born children had similar reservations. By the late 1970s, only a few, mostly recently abandoned, traditional-style houses and ancillary farm buildings remained, their contents either rotting or looted by antique hunters. Unfortunately, in the eyes of a generation that was focused on economic and social mobility, these remnants of pioneer life served as unwelcome reminders of the once lowly status of their parents and grandparents. Pioneer buildings were burned or demolished, their timber recycled for fencing or used to fuel stoves on winter nights. The artefacts within suffered a similar fate. A few hand implements were preserved in local "pioneer museums," but the larger agricultural devices were mostly lost forever.

In this book, Roman Fodchuk records this vanished way of life. His work extends the earlier and less complete studies of Ukrainian pioneer culture that dealt either in a more general way with the Ukrainian cultural landscape in western Canada or had a more limited focus on a single element of the wider landscape, such as domestic or religious architecture.[7] Relatively few works have focused on Ukrainian pioneer agricultural technology, and none have done so in great detail.[8]

This book fills this gap in the literature. It is a comprehensive examination of the material culture of pioneer society ranging from the clothing of the immigrants to the wooden kitchen utensils they used. The author's intimate knowledge of Ukrainian rural life in Alberta sets these artefacts in context, specifying how and when they were employed, their geographic and social settings, and the activities that surrounded their use. The book's organization follows the geographic and temporal paths of the settlers. It first examines the journey and the challenges of the first year or two. We then peek ahead to see how these original homesteads, marked with nothing more than a section corner peg, developed over a period of less than thirty years into a community of villages and townsites complete with all the services and amenities that were left behind. The range of tools employed by pioneer carpenters and craftsmen is considered: those brought from the old county and those fashioned anew or imported from the eastern seaboard. The construction of the various forms of housing is chronicled next. Agricultural societies are tied in to a seasonal road of activities that require their own special technologies. These are described and illustrated, followed by a detailed description of the process of homesteading, which involved so much more than clearing land. The chapter outlining domestic life covers types of food, cooking techniques, and the use of kitchen implements as part of a detailed description of the seasonally based social and ritualistic activities that bound this community. Non-material elements are not neglected: a glossary explains terms used by the immigrants to describe specific actions and tools. Many of the names are fading from the lexicon of Ukrainian-Canadians as opportunities for their use became increasingly rare.

From the first of three standpoints from which Roman Fodchuk's work can be viewed, the book is a testament to, and a record of, pioneer tenacity and resourcefulness, demonstrating how settlers fashioned an agricultural technology based on age-old principles, human ingenuity, and the employment of materials available to them on the homestead. Secondly, it clearly demonstrates that when folk culture interacts with the environment, it does so in a harmonious way, creating aesthetically satisfying artefacts that possess an intrinsic beauty of their own. Thirdly, it constitutes an inventory of the material culture of Ukrainian agricultural life in western Canada against which the material culture of western Ukraine (as it was recorded by European ethnographers) can be measured and compared. As such, it is an important scholarly contribution to the ethnography of western Canada and, indeed, to the study of the entire Ukrainian pioneer diaspora.

Dr. Lehr is originally from the United Kingdom, where he earned an Honours degree at the University of Wales before emigrating to Canada and completing his education at the universities of Alberta and Manitoba. He is a historical geographer who began his career as a professor of geography at the University of Winnipeg in 1976. His research interests include agricultural settlement in Western Canada and Ukrainian pioneer settlement in both Western Canada and South America, and he brings a much-valued comparative perspective to this work.

1

The Journey

Leaving the Homeland

As Lehr notes in his introduction, it is tempting to romanticize the pioneering spirit which brought wave upon wave of Europeans to populate the empty plains of the Canadian West. But few people leave their homeland voluntarily. Emigration from known, familiar, and settled villages was often a violent reaction to extraordinary population pressure. Land was scarce. Taxes were heavy. Food was expensive.

In 1895, despite the fact that European industrialized society was peaking, urban cultures were strictly segregated from rural communities. Only a very small measure of material sophistication spilled over from the cities and towns to the villages: Lehr mentions the replacement of thatched roofs with corrugated iron, for example. Peasants in the Carpathian Mountains were rarely touched by the industrial goods that might have enriched their way of life. They could not afford to buy excellent German steel for tools and utensils or refined, manufactured materials for clothing. The economic resources of the peasants of Bukovyna, Halychyna, and Transcarpathia were generally meagre under the rule of the Hapsburg monarchy of Austro-Hungary. The manorial system of land ownership, although it emancipated the serfs through the 1848 reforms, gave the landlords possession of more than half the arable land, as well as *all* the forests and pastures. Remaining lands not held by the Crown were small plots that rarely exceeded half a hectare. The people who owned these plots were often unable to make ends meet because of increasing debts and taxes.

The existing electoral system deprived the indigenous Ukrainian populace of representation in the Austrian Parliament and the Galician *Soim* (provincial parliament). The Hapsburgs had given all possible privileges – land ownership, political representation, and local administration – to the bourgeois, landlord elite. A policy of nationalist oppression was the norm in Transcarpathia at the turn of the century. Laws were enacted to prohibit the use of the Ukrainian language in the schools and the administration. Subsequent decrees forbade Ukrainian residents to speak their mother tongue at all, and they were forced to learn German, Polish, or Romanian[1] to survive. As a result, some of the immigrants spoke more than one language, though few spoke English. Peter Svarich, for example, spoke four languages and was quite proficient in English.

The first wave of immigrants to Canada was made up primarily of peasants whose worldly wealth, consisting of land and all the possessions they left behind, was barely sufficient to cover their journey. Despite this lack of resources, the *Homestead Act* enacted by the newly formed Canadian government was offering inexpensive and abundant virgin land that, compared to circumstances in the homeland, was perceived as "deliverance in the promised land." The Canadian government could not, of course, duplicate the widespread religious and societal order that was the principal mainstay of the immigrants' former lives connecting family to family and parish to parish. Though material conditions were hard in Europe, it would have been impossible for the Ukrainian immigrants to have imagined what life might be like without the social infrastructure they had always known. What a shock it must have been! Before they could address that issue, however, there were other disturbing matters they had to deal with, beginning with a long, difficult sea voyage in less than ideal circumstances: cramped quarters, illness, and worry all added to the strain.

For the promise of new land, the immigrants struggled to overcome the fear of leaving and of risking what little they had. Peasant farmers from the western Ukrainian provinces of Halychyna and Bukovyna faced a journey for which there could be no preparation. Their new experiences began with their stopover in Hamburg, which was the first modern metropolis most had seen. But in addition to the long, arduous voyage by rail and by sea, those planning to emigrate faced numerous hurdles of a different sort. Many were fleeing the requirement to serve in the Austro-Hungarian army. To leave the country, they had to obtain illegal documents from underground sources. As the only alternative, agents (operating freely and shamelessly) demanded money for advice, passports, and help in getting visas, tickets, or fake documents. The authorities persecuted both the agents and their customers. They were literally hunted down and suffered severe retribution for the slightest breach of exit rules. Sometimes the emigrants' goods were confiscated, and all the money they had saved for the trip to Canada was lost.

A well known example was described by Peter Svarich in his 1952 address to the Historical Society of Alberta. There he related the tale of Ivan Pylypiw, a man who returned to his village of Nebyliv in Halychyna from Canada, where he was arrested and sentenced to three months in jail (including days without food) for the crime of enticing his family and neighbours to emigrate. Wasyl Shandro, the author's grandfather, often told the following story of how he came to leave his village and homeland.

Simeon was the oldest of the Shandro brothers, three of whom (Stefan, Nikon, and Sidori) immigrated to Canada in 1899. Simeon also wanted to come to Canada with his three brothers; however, his strong-willed wife Anastasia forbade the thought of such an idea. Simeon's son, Wasyl, was soon to be eighteen years old and eligible for service in the Austrian army under Emperor Frans Joseph. Rather than see his son conscripted to serve in the army, Simeon secretly procured a passport and a ticket for him and saw him off to a train station without Wasyl's mother knowing about it. His last bidding was "Son, I cannot join my brothers in Canada, so I am sending you to join your uncles and make a better life for yourself." Before Simeon returned home, his wife Anastasia had found out what had happened and sent the *shandari* (police) to stop Wasyl from leaving. However, the train was well on the way to Hamburg, and Wasyl, at the age of eighteen, was on the way to a new life in Canada. He was never to see his immediate family again. A year later he met Martha Megley, a young lady whom he had met in Bukovyna who had also immigrated to Canada. They were married in the newly completed Shandro Church in 1907, a church Wasyl helped build.[2]

The Voyage

The unprecedented number of miles these rural Ukrainian folk were about to travel paled in significance compared to the cultural change they experienced. After days and nights of shifting for themselves, negotiating passage, and dodging unscrupulous agents in Hamburg, they boarded ships bound for Canada, then found themselves at last at the end of a one-way journey, far from home in a strange land. Svarich describes the trip to Canada on the S.S. Acadia in his memoirs:

The ocean trip was twelve days long. Ships were overloaded with people. Even on quiet water, people began to be seasick. I told them that to avoid the ocean sickness they must try to come out on deck into the fresh air periodically. They must not overeat.

When the dinner call came, all passengers marched in line through the kitchen where their plates were filled with desired food. Then they sat down to tables in the large dining area. The cooks' helpers filled their cups with coffee. This availability of food was hard to pass up, but an overloaded stomach was apt to resent the rocking of the ship in the waves. An empty stomach could accept cognac, a whiskey, to offset the queasy, dizzy feeling brought about by the constant swaying of the ship.[3]

The women and children found the ocean passage a great hardship. Most would be ill during the whole trip, and then all others would suffer from the stench of the vomit and foul air in cramped quarters. Those who had whiskey, rum, cognac, dills, garlic, and dry whole wheat bread were fortunate, for this alleviated nausea. If only they had brought sauerkraut – raw kraut and its juice, *rosil*, is a relief and it prevents nausea.

Very soon, all offers of cooked food were refused, until they saw salted herrings – the system would accept these and cut the sweet taste of nausea. (1934, n.p.)

Imagine the despair of a nineteenth-century rural family trapped in the hold of a small ship for days at sea. The first glimpse of land and then of the Halifax or Quebec harbour must have brought great joy. After crossing the stormy Atlantic and suffering continuously from exhaustion, weakened stomachs, and emotional and physical strain, these neophyte travelers must have alternated between feelings of excitement and fear when they were once again on solid ground, albeit on an unfamiliar continent, in their new country.

The immigrants felt like strangers, and they were greeted with curious stares as they came off the ships in their native dress. The women and children wore bulky, knee-length coats with the sheepskin turned inward, and the men appeared in

K. Fedchak

Winter Wear

The men's winter headdress was a *kuchma* – a cap – either grey or black, and either fur or sheep's wool. Shown are baggy woolen trousers with a heavy *serdak* and a felt great-coat with *podilian* boots.

The women wore long, cotton undershirts with linen over-blouses. These were decorated with extensive embroidery on the sleeves, and encompassed by woven woolen, wrap-around skirts. Sometimes in cold weather they wore fine leather boots, their headdress, called a *peremitka* (a head towel-kerchief), and a sheepskin *kozhukh* (overcoat).

K.Fedchok.

Bukovynian Festive Wear

Hutsuly (Carpathians); Men wore felt hats adorned with flowers and pea-cock feathers and tunic-style embroidered shirts that included a decorative emphasis on the cuffs and collars. Pants were of homespun fabric, and were folded into moccasins. The long shirt was tightly belted in place with a wide woven decorative band, all encased in a heavy woolen, cape-like coat.

Women wore a heavy woven, woolen skirt with gathers (wool or silk) decorated with embroidery and ribbons. As an overcoat, the women some-times wore a free-flowing, richly-embroidered *mantyia* or *huhlia*.

white, homespun trousers and richly embroidered sheepskin vests and coats (some with colourful panels of iridescent duck feathers). Some wore colourfully stitched shirts and smocks with such accoutrements as beads, homespun and woven sashes, belts, and shoulder bags. The women had an elegant air about them, with their wrap-around skirts, coral beads, and delicately woven linen shawls draped tightly around their heads (similar to a nun's head-dress). Their clothing reflected a love for intricate designs and bright colours.<Fig. 1:1,2,3>

They disembarked to find a sea of strangers who had come specifically to gawk and inspect them as they came down the gangplank carrying their bags and baggage. The staring was not just a one-sided affair, however, for those on exhibit also found the people who had come to greet them unusual and interesting. It was often the Ukrainian children who pointed out the outlandish hats and strange Canadian habits. They might notice that many of the "new" men on the dock seemed to be chewing their cud just as cows might. Who were these strange cud-chewers who spat tobacco juice out the side of their mouths? Were they to become cud-chewers, too? Before long, a childish snicker might ignite boisterous laughter as the comic quality of the event affected newcomers and spectators alike (Romaniuk 1954, 15–16).

All their worldly belongings were in trunks, carpenter's cases, boxes, and sacks, and disembarking mothers herded their children to where these articles had already been as-sembled by the men. The immigrants carried with them only those possessions which they could manage on their long jour-ney from western Europe. The next chapter details the kinds of tools and provisions the settlers brought with them. For now, we note only that the settlers brought possessions they thought would be of use in the new land, plus what little money they had left after paying their passage. In Ukraine, they sold their small holdings to neighbours or passed them on to their families. Some had to borrow money to finance the journey. Others came from families that were relatively well off in their homeland and had the means to buy horses, oxen, wagons, and assorted farming equipment in Edmonton. For example, both the Svarich and the Shandro groups managed to pool their respective family's holdings in Ukraine, thus each had greater resources than most immigrants.

Having disembarked, they all now set off to immigration halls to be sorted, stamped, and approved for entry to Canada. A medical examination and questions concerning their eligi-bility were the order of the day. Some families had to wait in makeshift housing while those who had sickened during the long ocean voyage recovered. The remainder were directed onto trains and made ready for the journey west.

The immigrants traveled by rail through Quebec and Ontario to Manitoba, where some stopped to make their new homes. Some pushed on (the Svarich group, for example) and traveled to the end of the rail, a place called Strathcona on the south side of the North Saskatchewan River, just opposite Fort Edmonton. Upon arrival at Strathcona, the settlers were directed to another immigration hall. This was one of many large, warehouse-like structures located near railway stations in major centres like Winnipeg that offered food and temporary shelter. Here they had a short respite while they made plans to reach their final destination. Their journey was to end as it had begun – on foot, or with a horse and wagon for those who could afford it.

In his memoirs, Svarich maps the physical and emotional landscape they encountered on this leg of their trip:

Fourteen days on the ocean brought them to Canadian shores, in Halifax. They were herded before doctors. A few were held back in hospital quarters. The rest were sent to large immigration units and loaded on trains headed for western Canada.

They were surprised to hear a bell ringing on the train, a bell just like a church bell, as Europe did not have bells on trains. In fact, years later when the Canadian Pacific Railroad (C.P.R.) was discarding these bells, many Ukrainian communities asked for and received them for their churches.

The immigrants found the trains roomy, with seats that made up into beds and upper shelves that also made into beds. Women with small children kept their seats made up as beds for the whole trip and sat cross-legged on them as they nursed, fed, and otherwise ministered to their family.

For twenty-four hours along the St. Lawrence in Quebec and Ontario we gazed out the windows at the rock and forest, each of us hoping to see something to satisfy this magnetic desire to find land – land where our dreams could stretch as freely as our strength and at least give us a chance, a try, at making a good life. Just the sight of land brought forth our questioning fears; Did we do the right thing in leaving our homeland, our relatives, and our villages and thatched, century-old, history-steeped cottages? Would we be able to find happiness in this new land when we knew we would never be able to return to Ukraine?

Such thoughts tired our already exhausted minds as the second night passed. The terrain through Ontario still looked forbidding with its rocks and forests. But the earthy air bolstered our lungs where the salt ocean had eaten away our reserves of strength and anticipation. Another night and day brought a view of huge forests and burned-out patches of stumps – then a trail probably leading to a homestead. The welcome sight of several woodcutters felling and sawing logs for fuel brought fresh interest in the approaching landscape.

Another trail and another house in the woods kept recurring at closer intervals. Wild animals, fox and deer, were surprised in the open, grassy

Bukovynian Summer Wear

The men wore straw hats with coloured coral beads or flashy drake feathers. Men's shirts were rich with ornamentation, for example, an embroidered neck and a deep front-piece. The trousers were white linen *portkynytsi*, sometimes with a series of horizontal pleats or folds running the length of the pant-leg. The vest-coat, a *kiptar*, usually had sheepskin facing in and a rich front piece with a clasped-edge decor.

The women wore a woven, woolen *horbotka* with fine, coloured, horizontal stripes and a wrap-around skirt over a linen long shirt, all girded with a wrap-around, woven woolen belt. The over-blouse was usually homespun with heavily embroidered, puffed sleeves. The headdress was sometimes a fine linen *peremitka* or a silk kerchief. The embroidery and woven designs were specific to the particular village or region of origin, and these patterns were readily recognized.

apertures of the woods. Tiny villages grew here and there along the railroad track, but the train stopped beside them only briefly. All along the Great Lakes, the long hours stretched tiresomely into another night and day. The Fort William[4] announcement was made at night.

The fears of the immigrants began to surface again. Maybe the agents had misrepresented this Canada? I [Peter Svarich] had a map of the Canadian journey which I had drawn myself according to the description of the agents' tour guide advertisements, and I set about to relieve the fears of the families, telling them that we were only one-third of the way, and that now we were entering "the steppes" or "the prairies" of Central Canada – where anyone could detrain and settle. According to my map, we would travel another two days and nights to find the end of these steppes. There we would find wooded lands comparable to Ukraine. Most resigned themselves to the train ride as they had to the ocean journey, but some kept up their worrisome disbelief of all previous and present information. What had prompted them to leave their native land, if their attitude was so unbending? Gold, glitter, the promise of wealth, was not such a deep-rooted acceptance of fate as was the love of a favourable future for one's children, and that difference marked each family of the grouping. (1934, n.p.)

Arrival and Settlement

The new emigrants moved on foot and by wagon beyond Edmonton onto the rolling parkland. Some were accompanied by land agents who explained the survey and lot identification system. These government agents showed them land maps and explained the procedures for filing on a homestead. Every adult male had the right to choose a plot of land measuring 0.5 miles square (or 160 acres, a quarter section) provided by the Canadian government. A fee of ten dollars was required to cover survey and legal costs. The agreement with the government stipulated that the land title would be granted to the colonist after three years as long as the following conditions were met: (1) a dwelling was built, (2) a well was dug, (3) at least thirty acres of land were cultivated, and (4) someone remained on the land for at least six months of the year.

They had survived the ocean voyage, the long train trip, and the perils of crossing roadless prairie and bush land to be welcomed by the only concrete symbol of their new home; survey markers. Under the *Homestead Act* of 1872, this land was theirs if they could tame it and make it support them. These initial years on the land would absorb every ounce of strength, ingenuity, and co-operation these families possessed, while yielding a marginal existence as payment for their sweat. Svarich recounts the conditions that prevailed when his "contingent" of twelve families finally reached friends on a homestead[5] five miles beyond Edna. In 1900, the Svarich party struggled across flooded prairies, swollen rivers, and washed out bridges to reach Edna, eighty miles east of Edmonton. The following quote illustrates the mixed feelings many of the new immigrants experienced when they finally arrived at their destination:

In this area the soil was more sandy and stony, traveling was easier, and in two hours we neared Jacob Porayko's farm where, as luck would have it, Nicholas Gregoraschuk was helping him dig a well.

The wagons emptied their populace and the buildings yielded their numbers of people. Everybody was crying, laughing, and talking. We were muddy, wet, and bedraggled, but we had a reason for our condition. But our hosts were a sorry lot of sunburned, haggard, and ragged people, not unlike our imagination of Indians!

So we cried from happiness at meeting, of course, but also out of bitterness at the misrepresentations of the good fortune in Canada. Is this the paradise they wrote about? Where are the great benefits? But after a while we began to realize that freedom from a *pan* and freedom from a government dictating every hour of the day was worth the hard

toil and harsh living conditions. They had endless acres on which to herd cattle, horses, pigs, and chickens. They had plenty of food already – all raised in their own farmyards. Their children were sunburned and brown but very healthy, given diets rich in milk, butter, and eggs. They were already making feather pillows and quilts instead of the straw mattresses they had in the beginning. They still lived in a sod-roofed log hut, and were hand-digging a second well because they couldn't find water within thirty-five feet. It seemed they had struck mediocre soil in this district, but now this year's settlers could live with them for awhile and search around for better land. Later on, when they have fulfilled their obligations on these homesteads, they will look around to buy some better land.

They asked us in for supper and, true enough, they had milk, eggs, butter, and meat, and now, in the third year, a well and a cultivated garden that yielded enough vegetables to feed family and friends the year round. When we had exchanged news of the old country with news of these parts of Canada, we began to realize that our life as peasants was hard in both places, but here in Canada we could expect things to get better. In the old country, things would get progressively worse. Too many people had divided the land into too small fragments to allow everyone to farm. And these subdivisions would get smaller, because the surrounding countries were also densely populated. We were the first people here. If we worked hard we could add to our land area, and we could buy our sons additional acres instead of subdividing the homesteads. As the hours passed, our faces brightened and we began to realize the truth of their statements that as soon as we settled down a bit and breathed in the expansion of air in Canada and held the acres of soil in our bare hands, we too would write to our families and friends in Ukraine about the free lands in Canada. Here your rewards came from

following page **Map of the Star Colony – Approximately 1910**
This map shows the extent of the Ukrainian settlement bloc in Alberta, largely on a broad band following the southern side of the North Saskatchewan River, from Star (just east of Bruderheim), through to Derwent and Slawa. The southern edge is the Canadian Northern Railway (1906) – now the Canadian National Railway – through Lamont, Vegreville, and Manville, with the northern edge formed by the Canadian National Railway (1920) through Belis, Vilna, and Ashmont. The central corridor, the Canadian Pacific Railway (1927–28) was built through the core of the Ukrainian Bloc well after the settlement was established in a matrix of rural communities. The C.P.R. ties the key "new towns" of Andrew, Willingdon, Hairy Hill, Two Hills, Myrnam, and Derwent to Lloydminster on the eastern bounds of this settlement. Note all the rural schools, with at least one to each of the settled townships throughout the area (a township is six miles by six miles square).

This illustration shows the extent and spread of the Ukrainian bloc settlement: The Star Colony around 1910 from Bruderheim in the west to Myrnam and Slawa in the east was approximately 14 townships long and 8 townships wide, varying in depth. Each township is a square 6 miles by 6 miles.

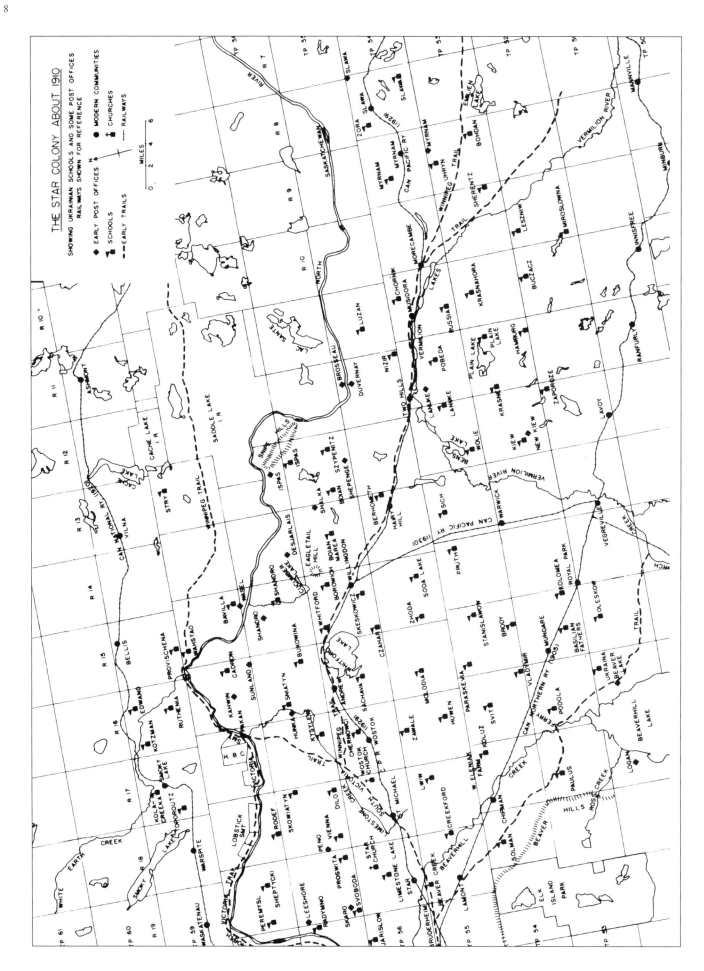

THE STAR COLONY ABOUT 1910

SHOWING UKRAINIAN SCHOOLS AND SOME POST OFFICES
RAILWAYS SHOWN FOR REFERENCE

♦ EARLY POST OFFICES   ● MODERN COMMUNITIES
⚑ SCHOOLS   ⛪ CHURCHES
– – – EARLY TRAILS   ━━ RAILWAYS

MILES
0   2   4   6

Periods of initial construction:

★	1898–1905
☆	1906–1910
✪	1911–1920
✜	1921–1930
✚	1931–1945
✕	Unknown

Notes:

1. Ukranian Labor-Farmer Temple Association
2. Taras Shevchenko Society
3. With General Store & Egg Grading Station
4. Converted First Unknown Hall
5. Second Converted School
6. With Bell Tower
7. Second Floor Above Store
8. With Grotto to Our Lady of Lourdes
9. None Built
10. Additional Communities with No Information: Cadron, Chailey, Cossack, Deerland, Delph, Lac Bellevue, Lake Geneva, North Bank, North Kotzman, Rodef, Stubno, Ukalta & Wahstao

Districts	Post Office	General Store	Combined P.O. & G.S.	Rural School	Ukrainian Catholic	Ukrainian Orthodox	Russian Orthodox	Romanian Orthodox	Roman Catholic	Unkown	Cemetery	Narodniy Dim	ULFTA¹	TSS²	Unknown	Equipment Agency	Blacksmith	Flour Mill	Gas Station
Zawale	☆					✜						✪							
Wasel			★							✕									
Warwick	★																		
Val Soucy	✕								☆										
Sunland	☆																		
Suchava					✜		★												
Stry			★	✪	✕	✚						✜			✕				
Spas Muskalyk					✜				★										
Soda Lake	★																		
Sniatyn	★																		
Skaro	★				✕	✕			★⁸			✜							
Sich-Kolomea			★	☆		✕													
Shepynitz				☆			★					✜							
Shepenge	★																		
Shandro	★			☆			★								✚	☆		☆	
Shalka	☆																		
Pruth				☆		✚						✜							
Plain Lake	☆	✪		☆											✪⁷				
Peno	☆					✕						✚							
Pathfinder				✕	✕⁶														
Pakan	★										✜	✪							
New Kiew				☆	☆				☆			✜							
Mamaesti				✪							✪								
Luzan	✪	✕		✪					☆										
Leeshore	☆	✜																	
Lanuke	☆			☆											✜				
Lake Eliza											✜								
Krakow	★	★			✜⁴						✪	✚			✪⁵				✚
Kahwin	✪					✚													
Ispas	✪						✪			☆									
Hamlin		✕					✕	✕							✕				
Eldorena												✕							
Eastgate	☆	✕		✪	✜		✪								✚				
Duvernay		✕																	
Downing			☆		☆						✜				✕				
Desjarlais	★	✕		☆															
Dalmuir												✕							
Buczacz				✪	☆														
Brosseau	★																		
Borshchiw	☆				☆												✕		
Boriwtsi									☆	★									
Boian		✪		☆				★				★			✕				✪³
Angle Lake			✕		✪														
Amelia	☆	✕		☆															

East-central Alberta Ukrainian Bloc Historical Development

This chart of the East-Central Alberta Ukrainian Bloc outlines the early, pre-railway development of rural communities throughout the Ukrainian Bloc. The matrix outlines the extent and intensity of the historical development of these rural communities. It illustrates six periods (interspersed by railway construction) of the development of community facilities such as post offices, general trading stores, combined post offices and stores, rural schools, churches, cemeteries, community halls, and complementary businesses such as equipment agencies, blacksmiths, flour mills, and gas stations.

When the Canadian Pacific Railway (C.P.R.) was built in 1927–28, many of these rural communities moved to where the newly constructed sidings were built along the new right of ways, thus forming new towns and villages, for example, Andrew, Hairy Hill, Myrnam, Two Hills, and Willingdon, to name a few. The convenience of being located near the sidings where the trains stopped to pick up passengers, cream cans, egg crates, mail, and so on, was the impetus for businesses to move their country stores and services to the new town sites. These towns were all incorporated around the same time (about 1927–28) and their names were changed as well, reflecting the English heritage of the builders of the railway and replacing the original Ukrainian nomenclature.

This chart is reproduced from a three volume report prepared by Roman Fodchuk and Associates, Ltd. in 1977: "The Ukrainian Cultural Heritage Village Master Site Plan."

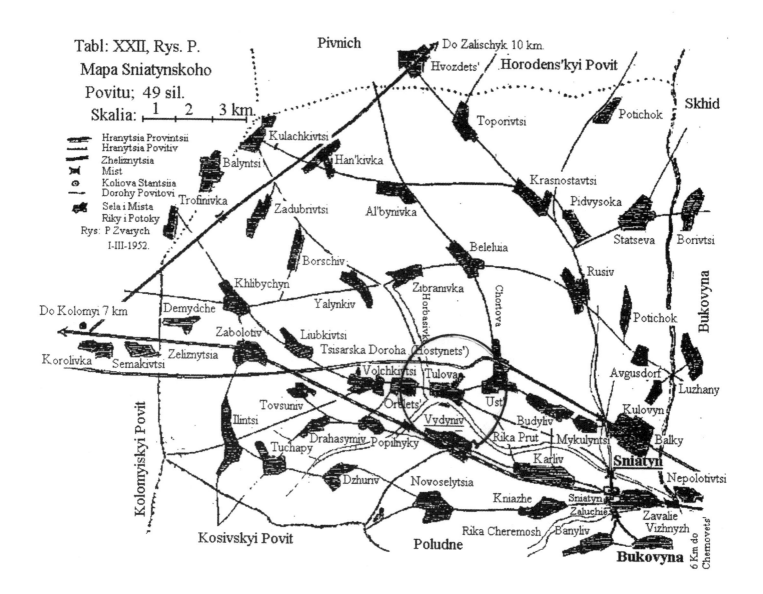

Tabl: XXII, Rys. P.

Mapa Sniatynskoho
Povitu; 49 sil.
Skalia: 1 2 3 km.

Hranytsia Provintsii
Hranytsia Povitiv
Zheliznytsia
Mist
Koliova Stantsiia
Dorohy Povitovi
Sela i Mista
Riky i Potoky
Rys: P Zvarych
I-III-1952.

Pivnich

Do Zalischyk 10 km.

Hvozdets'   Horodens'kyi Povit

Skhid

Toporivtsi   Potichok

Kulachkivtsi

Balyntsi   Han'kivka   Krasnostavtsi

                                              Pidvysoka

Trofinivka   Zadubrivtsi   Al'bynivka

Khlibychyn   Borschiv   Statseva   Borivtsi

Do Kolomyi 7 km.   Demydche   Yalynkiv   Beleluia   Rusiv

                                  Zibranivka   Potichok

Zabolotiv   Liubkivtsi   Bukovyna

Korolivka   Zeliznytsia   Tsisarska Doroha (Hostynets')   Avgusdorf

Semakivtsi   Luzhany

                Volchkivtsi   Tulova   Kulovyn

                Orelets'   Ust   Balky

Kolomyiskyi Povit   Tovsuniv   Vydyniv   Budyliv

Ilintsi   Mykulyntsi

        Tuchapy   Drahasymiv Popilnyky   Rika Prut   Sniatyn

                   Dzhuriv   Karliv   Nepolotivtsi

                            Novoselytsia   Sniatyn

Kosivskyi Povit   Kniazhe   Zaluchie   Zavalie

                            Rika Cheremosh   Banyliv   Vizhnyzh

                Poludne

                                                       Bukovyna

Map of the Small Roadside Villages Surrounding Tulova

Centrally located Tulova is circled on this map. Tulova
was only a short distance from Sniatyn, the regional town
center that provided central government services.

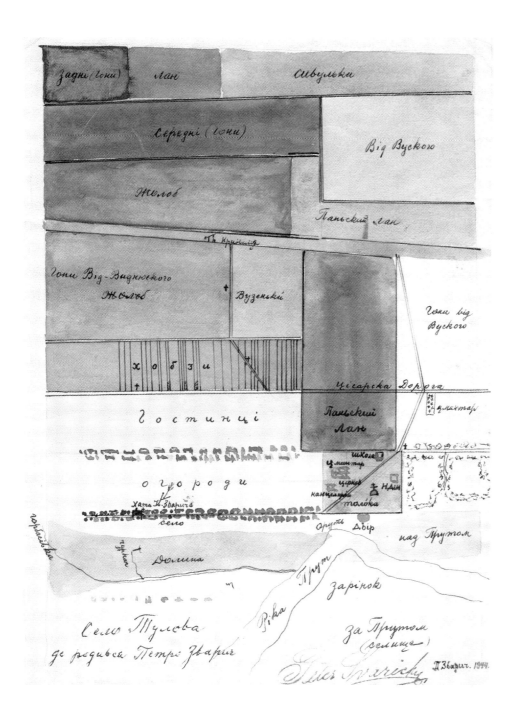

The Village of Tulova Showing Gardens and Agricultural Fields

Tulova was built around a central green commons, with the homes of villagers on either side of two main roads. Shown are the gardens (*horody*) for each house, the larger long lots the families owned, and the large fields to the west owned by absentee landlords for whom the villagers worked. These fields were leased or rented out to villagers. The usual split of the production from the fields was nine parts to the landlord for every one part to the labourer. To the east was a ravine through which the Prut River runs, and at the time of immigration (a hundred years ago), this was the boundary between Romania and western Ukraine. Courtesy Provincial Archives of Alberta, PR. 1975.74/1265.

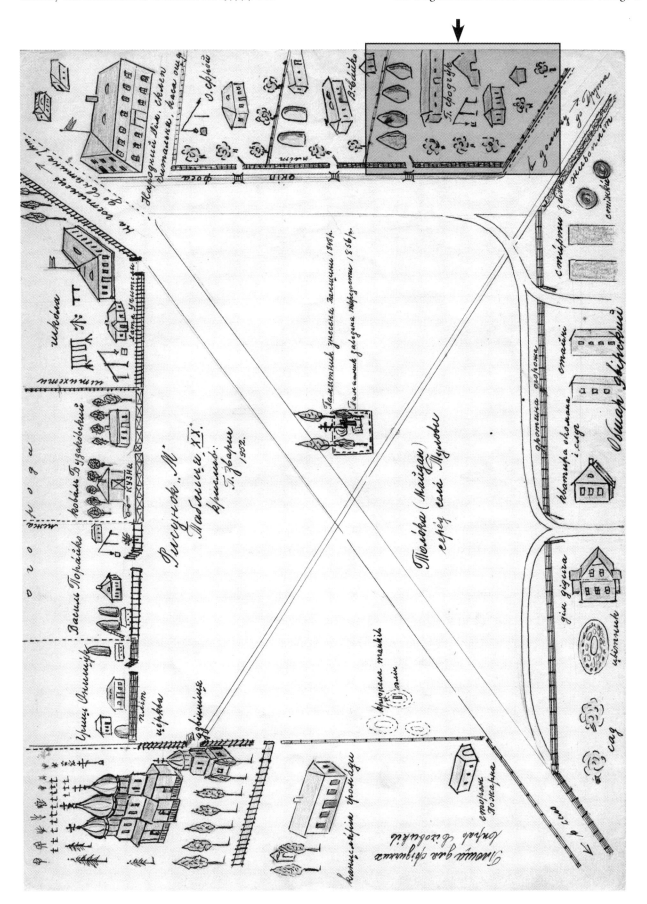

your own hard work, whereas in Ukraine, the *pan* calculated the value of your labour for himself.

Best of all, they enjoyed the freedom of hunting wildlife when and for what their needs were — food or furs. They could cut wood on the C.P.R. land and save their own for building and for future fuel. Wild ducks and geese supplied them with feathers long before they could establish their own flocks. They could hobble their horses on the C.P.R. to save their own meadows for hay or vice-versa.

Although they longed for the church, village, and school companionship, they were pleased that for the time being there were no taxes, police, or taverns. If they had health and strength, they would build a church and school. As they relished the *kapusniak* [sauerkraut soup] and *pyrohy*, they knew that Ukrainians would have strength to conquer the elements, and already they were enough of a family to feel the cheer of human companionship. (Svarich 1934, n.p.)

Central Green Commons of Tulova

This plan details the village (*selo*) of Tulova as it was laid out in the 1890s, when the Svarich group left their homes there in Halychyna, Ukraine, for a new beginning in Canada. This drawing of the village, commons, and surrounds shows various land uses around the commons (starting at the top, from left to right) such as the private holdings of Hryts Onyshchuk, Vasyl Poraiko, and Koval Budakovsky (blacksmith); the school grounds and buildings, the seniors' home, the library, and the private holdings of O. Frei, V. Sajko, and Paul Fodchuk (the author's grandfather). Other public facilities included the children's home, public offices, the local Orthodox Church, the bell tower, and commemorative memorials to the removal of serfdom in 1848 and 1856. Also in the central commons is a memorial to Taras Schevchenko, the National Poet.

The village is centrally split with a green commons, which is diagonally split by the *tsisars'ka doroha* (Caesar's Road) that leads to the regional town center, Sniatyn. Bukovyna is to the east (across the Prut River) and under Romanian jurisdiction. Each, or most, of the linear villages had a central commons that served as the locale of various community and religious celebrations throughout the year.

It was in a central commons such as this in Rus'kyi Banyliv that my maternal grandfather, Wasyl Shandro, met his bride-to-be, Martha Megley, a young lady attending an annual festival. This is where single young men went to meet potential mates, all under the strictest of parental supervision, of course. Wasyl followed Martha to Canada, where they married in 1904 at St. Mary's Russo Greek Orthodox Church at Shandro, Alberta. The drawing is sourced from the Svarich Collection at the Alberta Archives.

German and English settlers had arrived during the 1880s and were already dispersed in settlements near Edmonton. Early French settlers, some Swedes, and a few German families were in the Vegreville, Vermilion, and St. Paul areas. The Ukrainian settlers scattered in all directions. The majority, however, preferred the lands to the northeast along the wooded and fertile valleys and terraces of the North Saskatchewan and Vermilion Rivers. Consequently, east-central Alberta was originally established by predominantly Ukrainian settlers. These people were drawn to farms adjacent to their relations and friends from home, resulting in a relatively clear demarcation between Galician (from Halychyna) and Bukovynian communities. Under Austro-Hungarian and Polish-Romanian rule, land holdings were small, and the people lived in very close proximity to each other. The village community worked on the surrounding manorial lands. This societal, small-village background proved a strong stabilizing factor. The desire to settle near neighbours who came from their home village meant that the old country social and cultural structures were maintained (for better or worse, as Lehr explained in his preface) in the new communities, and it was exhibited in traditional building and farming methods. Place names in Alberta, Saskatchewan, and Manitoba reflect their Ukrainian heritage. Many of the new settlements were given village names from the homeland.

This nomenclature still serves to define the pattern of Ukrainian settlement east of Edmonton, where a distinction between villages established by immigrants from Bukovyna and Halychyna can be identified. This area contains some of the oldest Ukrainian settlements in North America and today is predominantly populated by Canadians of Ukrainian and Romanian extraction. A group of Romanians from Bukovyna settled in the Shalka, Boian, and Desjarlais district east of Willingdon and north of Hairy Hill. The communities in this area have a Romanian background reflected in the old country names attached to post offices, schools, community centres, and churches, for example, Shalka, Boian, and Boian Marea.[6] Such old world, Ukrainian place names as Peremyst, Sheptychi, Zawale, Sachava, Bukowina, Kahwin, Cadron, Sich, Szypenitz,[7] and Kiew brought the homeland a little closer.[8]

The Canadian government considered the Alberta parkland, that transition area between the prairies of the south and the undulating forested lands to the north, to be only marginally suitable for agriculture. Most immigrants preferred the rich prairie lands for ease of farming and grain production. However, the availability of vast areas of woodlands in the Canadian West attracted the Ukrainian settlers to the black soils of the parkland area of the prairies because, though the Ukrainian settlers came from a land of abundant natural resources, forests were privately held in large manorial estates, and peasants did not have access to firewood, game, or wild edibles. They valued this access more than the ease of farming the prairie land chosen by other immigrants. The C.P.R. and the Canadian government were pleased with their choice, as it meant that this otherwise neglected area of Alberta was now being settled and populated.

What a Difference a Generation Makes

We now examine how these settlers (and their familial-based clusters of homesteads), over time and with increasing prosperity, developed community facilities dispersed throughout the rural districts in the span of just over a single generation. By the mid-1930s, these industrious pioneers were able to recreate a virtually complete range of services and amenities very similar to what they had left behind in the old country. The following detailed outline of the progression of the town of Andrew[9] demonstrates the general developmental trend that is representative of any number of urban centres throughout the bloc, for example, Willingdon, Two Hills, Hairy Hill, and Myrnam. Once homesteads were established, the following communal facilities were built[10] (most commonly in this order):

1. General Store
2. Post Office; located either in someone's home or in the general store
3. Church; either Ukrainian Catholic, Ukrainian Orthodox, or Russo-Orthodox
4. Community Hall; used by Ukrainian cultural and educational societies

In Andrew, for example, John Borwich built a half-way house near where the Winnipeg Trail met the Calgary Pakan Trail, and he called it the Andrew Hotel. Shortly thereafter, in 1900, Ed Carey opened a general store. These two establishments were the beginnings of Andrew. The Andrew Post Office was built in March of 1902. This rural community soon expanded to include a blacksmith shop, operated by Johyn Skoreyko and V. Ostopovich. T.J. Matichuk managed a Massey Harris agency that sold tractors, while Andrew Kostiniuk and Pete Ruhalski repaired shoes and made harnesses and canvasses for local farmers. Frank Oliver operated a grist mill and a saw mill from 1906 to 1928. The C.P.R. did not come through Andrew until 1928.

Settlers in surrounding districts and across the Alberta Ukrainian bloc began to establish their own churches, community halls, rural stores, post offices, blacksmith shops, and schools shortly after 1900. A post office established in 1913 just south of the Andrew community was named Luzan.

Some of the services required by the settlers were provided by earlier, better-established immigrants. Nick Ziganash ran a grocery store in conjunction with a post office and a flour mill. Alex Bochanski had a small blacksmith shop on his farm in 1914, and later expanded it into a grocery store. Nick Koruliuk, whose homestead was near the Molodia School, also provided service as an old country blacksmith. The Hameliuks maintained a very important service, an *oliinytsia* (oil press), for the pioneers who grew oil seeds.

School districts were scattered across the Ukrainian bloc shortly after the first settlers arrived. Most townships had one, and given that a township was six miles square, most of the settlers were within walking distance of a school, as they also were from a church. A school was usually built within each township.

The pioneers prospered during the period from 1914 to 1925. Markets improved, and the settlers began to complement their first log houses with buildings of frame construction and sawn lumber. Initially dependent on the Saskatchewan River and the limited trail system, the settlers benefited from the construction of four railways through the area. In 1905/06, a Canadian National[11] railway (C.N.R.) line was built to the south, from Edmonton to Lamont to Vegreville and Lloydminster. In 1910, the Northern Alberta Railway ran along the western boundary of the bloc, later to be connected to the C.N.R. line to the north side of the Saskatchewan River. Finally, in 1927/28, the Canadian Pacific Railway (C.P.R.) placed a track through the middle of the Ukrainian settlement bloc, connecting and establishing towns from Star to Andrew, Willingdon, Hairy Hill, Two Hills, Myrnam, Marwayne, and Lloydminster.

At that point, all of the facilities of a modern prairie town were available to these settlers. In less than thirty years, the bloc went from predominantly bare land with little more than homestead markers to distinguish it, to a thriving, rural area with well-established communities, thus successfully reproducing the social and cultural amenities they had to leave behind in Ukraine. The rest of this book describes the material culture and the tools with which the Ukrainian settlers accomplished this amazing transformation in much detail, but I close this segment with a final reminiscence about the conditions the settlers found upon arrival in the new land, a description taken from my interview with Pearl Svarich Salamandyk, Peter Svarich' youngest sister.

We came to Canada in 1900. On March 20, we arrived in Winnipeg – it was Ukrainian Easter. I was five years old. We came out to Edmonton, and Dad bought a wagon and horses. We drove the wagon all the way from Edmonton to Star and slept under the wagon at night. The mosquitoes were terrible. We had some friends at Star – people from our village who had an empty house – and that is where we stayed. Then my father (Ivan Svarich) and brother (Peter Svarich) went looking for a homestead … as far as what is now Vegreville. (1952)

2
Surviving

The Initial Years

This chapter opens with a discussion of the difficulties faced during the first year or two. Next is a segment describing the various tools and implements immigrants either brought with them or recreated once they arrived, set in the context of the master craftsmen and women who used them, and outlines what became of these cherished items once they were no longer needed for their original purpose.

New arrivals could buy provisions in Edmonton before beginning the trek to the homestead areas if their journey had not depleted their funds entirely. These "store bought" supplies consisted of such staples as flour, sugar, salt, tea, and coffee. If they could manage the price of a cow, this would be one of the first animals bought since it would provide them with milk, butter, and cream. However, families usually climbed down from the train weary, apprehensive, and almost penniless. Some stayed in the immigration hall until they could find work in the coal mines or building the railways and thus finance the last stage of their journey. Established settlers frequented the hall to gather news about the old country and to offer advice, land, or work:

Each had something to gain from the other, and here they could bargain in the Ukrainian language – the locals charging for the wagon trip to the designated land; for lodging at their abode until a shelter was built for that family; for help with ploughing a garden patch, etc. The new arrivals would be relieved of language difficulties when registering their titles and purchasing necessities, and also of worrying about having a roof over their heads for a few weeks, and most of all, supplying food and milk for the family until they bought their own animals.

The emigrants who had money were naturally more desirable to the locals than the poor ones, but even these were worthwhile neighbours, as they would pay back any debts they would incur with the settled pioneers with their labour by clearing the land. (Svarich 1934, n.p.)

The Necessities

As the quote above illustrates, previous immigrants eased the way significantly for newcomers. However, established settlers were not always available to offer support, especially in the early years. If the settlers arrived in the fall, they did not have the opportunity to gather and store wild edibles. The spectre of malnutrition and starvation haunted their winters, especially in the first year. Many new homesteaders had to live on a sack of 4X flour (the lowest grade), sometimes a bag of potatoes or a little tea, along with whatever they could glean from the wilderness.

During the summer, edible wild plants, mushrooms, and berries made up for the lack of fresh vegetables. Mushrooms of various kinds were numerous in the woods, and each variety matured at specific times during the growing season. Puff balls were picked early in their ripening cycle for freshness, then thinly sliced and fried in oil. Mushrooms were sliced into strips, dried, and stored in bags or jars to add to winter meals. As Helen Solowan Boychuk, an early settler I interviewed in 1976, recalled, "The gooseberries were so big and thick in those days. We had big lovely strawberries and nice raspberries and Saskatoon berries along the river. We had a patch of blueberries near the house, and we were waiting for them to ripen fully. The Indians came, and I asked them not to pick. Well, they got there first and picked them all, saying, 'God gives to you and God gives to me.' So, we had no blueberries."

The pioneers were enterprising, and although they cursed the abundant Alberta rose (the prickly rose; *rosa acicularis*)[1] that choked trails and clearings, even this thorny native contributed its petals for use as a fragrant tea. The water for that tea might come from various sources. If there was a stream on their quarter section or a river nearby, the homesteader had a steady source of water. When water was not readily available, and before a well could be dug, Ukrainian settlers often drank slough water filtered through several layers of cloth. Or they might be obliged to haul water from a neighbour's well, frequently on foot. A two or three mile walk to the water source soon inspired the re-creation of the type of wooden yoke used in Ukraine which made two full buckets a bearable load. One of the first of many practical tools and implements the pioneer would make, the yoke was carved from willow or birch with an axe, spoke shaver, and sharp knife (see Fig. 5:5).

Some of the immigrants had the foresight to pack a gun along with their household utensils and farming implements. Despite the fact that wildlife was plentiful, they supplemented their diets primarily with small game, which also could be snared or bludgeoned: "We used to have lots of deer, but nobody killed them because people weren't used to eating deer. Nobody really thought about eating deer, although we ate rabbits, partridges, and prairie chickens" (Boychuk interview 1976).

Ukrainian settlers in western Canada arrived with relatively little in their bags and baggage. What they did bring was fortitude and the strength of their cultural knowledge. Their traditions were quickly imprinted onto their new environment and homes. Forest parklands and adjacent prairies supplied abundant natural resources. Poplar, spruce, tamarack, birches, various cherries, and the abundant willow provided basic structural materials. Prairie slough grasses, rocks, sand, and native clays filled out the craftsman's pallet. Using their adaptations, designs, and ingenuity, they crafted tools, utensils, and buildings uniquely expressive of Ukrainian culture in their homelands.

a

b

d

e

c

Bags and Baggage

The immigrants carried with them only those possessions they could manage on their long journey. Although limited to what they could physically carry onto the ships (from 50 to 500 pounds), the immigrants brought a variety of utilitarian goods. Clothing, farming tools, household utensils, and religious objects were packed in sacks, assorted trunks, wooden crates, and boxes. Many a hardy traveler packed a set of millstones (*zhorna*) in the bottom of their wooden trunk along with pots and pans for cooking and baking, an occasional ceramic pot filled with preserves, and a bottle of hemp oil with which to set up housekeeping in the new land. They left little to chance, and brought seed as well to start their new crops. Rye, buckwheat, corn, and millet were mainstays in the warm climate of their homeland. Cooler crops, such as barley, oats, and wheat,

Settler's Chests; Carpenter's Chest, Dower Coffers, and Blanket Boxes

a. Settler's Chest; an iron bound trunk with a cast-iron padlock, used for shipping all manner of the settlers' effects

d.; b. Wooden Chests (*skrynia*); decorative and beautifully carved, used for storing family heirlooms, festive and ceremonial clothing, and family treasures

c. Wedding Coffer; used as a container for the bride's dowry and for storing all kinds of gifts from her parents and family

e. Utility/Carpenters' Chest; used in the home for storing woven blankets (*vereny*), tablecloths, and other folded materials, including clothing; sometimes used as a carpenter's chest for storing saws, chisels, wooden planes, and other tools

although not as common, were also packed away in precious handfuls amongst bedclothes and pillows. A colourful kerchief containing poppy, hemp, or flax seeds would be opened expectantly later.

Settlers frequently shared their tools with less fortunate neighbours or those who lost their baggage during the trip. A few had the foresight to bring drawings from which they could construct a loom, as well as other hard to construct pieces, such as wooden gears and complex combs.

Chests — Tools and Clothing

Chests for linens and blankets were as old as any form of furniture. These lidded wooden boxes, sometimes with an arched lid for additional strength, were built to stand knee high with an undivided interior. They are highly prized to this day, for their large, undivided space is excellent for storing bulky, foldable linens and clothing. Before closets, they were used for all sorts of household storage, and when the lid was closed, they served as an attractive piece of furniture. By the traditions of the old country, the chests also served as dowry coffers, a gift from the parents to the newly married couple. Made of pine or spruce, they were normally dovetailed at the corners and strengthened artistically with forged iron strapping. They served as excellent containers for the long ocean voyage across the Atlantic and for the train trip from Halifax to the prairies.

Small tools, implements, household articles, packets of grain, and vegetable seeds would have traveled those long miles with them. Importance was placed on such building tools as a felling axe, an Austrian broad axe, a saw, and augers or wooden planes for constructing new houses. A sickle, scythe, spade, flail, whetstone, and spare scythe blades of excellent Austrian steel manufacture were chosen for the new farming venture. Once in Canada, the chests became highly cherished mementos of the homeland. For example, Irene Shandro Hohol, the youngest daughter of Nikon and Anna Shandro, still has the original chest brought to Canada (now well over a hundred years old) as an heirloom in her Edmonton home.

These richly carved wooden chests passed from generation to generation occasionally formed part of a family's belongings (see Fig. 2:1). They often served as furniture until other pieces were constructed. These chests were crafted in Ukraine as part of the preparations for the long journey and packed with cherished mementos and items necessary for homesteading. Simply built but inherently beautiful carved wooden chests were brought from the Carpathian Mountain areas of Ukraine, expressing the traditional designs of the woodsmen carvers, the Hutsuly. The chests were brought by the Shandro settlers from Rus'kyi-Banyliv to the north-west of Chernivtsi. Not only is the body of the chest a simple functional expression, but it also exemplifies the carver's notion of beauty and purpose, with raised panels using mortise and tenon joints. Blending Hutsul motifs with strong Scythian overtones expressed the nomadic feel of the valued treasure chest. This is particularly true of chests with a camel-back lid, rare treasures in themselves. For centuries, chests were built to hold precious contents, and these carved wooden containers exemplified some of the finest works of art. The carver/artist created powerful and ancient designs such as a series of three large rosettes on each side of the top panels symbolizing the "Flower of Life." Using a "chip carving" technique that requires a sharp carving knife or chisel, he removed pyramid-shaped chips from the surface of the wood until a complex pattern developed. The image pattern of the "Flower of Life" symbol in sacred geometry expresses the infinity of life throughout the universe and a oneness with God.[2]

Occasionally, a loom was dismantled, wrapped in a tight bundle, and packed with bedding and clothing. Although carders and a spinning wheel were necessities, only a few families managed to bring these items. The people from the Carpathian highlands, where sheep were raised, brought their knowledge of weaving, along with their *vereteno* (hand spindles). However, once in Canada, it would be some time before they could obtain sheep and the wool which could be woven into clothing and blankets.

Below are two excerpts describing the materials immigrants carried with them. The first outlines the situation of the Lazariuk family, Nikolai and Anna, while the second is taken from an interview with Fred Magera.

They arrived in Edmonton with the clothes on their back, one wooden box with all their possessions, and one dollar in their pockets. The wooden box contained: one white linen tablecloth with red and black cross-stitch embroidery (the diamond design); two pillows stuffed with chicken feathers finely chopped with an axe; two pillowcases with an embroidered red and black design in the centre; two white linen shirts (mid-calf); two knee-length, sheepskin coats with two sheepskin vests with curl embroidered trim; one black kutcha [*kuchma*] (wool cap); two flowered, woolen kerchiefs; a six-foot-long, linen peramitka (turban); and one sickle.

Nikoloa wore white baggy pyjama-type porkanatsi [*portkynytsi*] (pants). In winter, he wore black *koloshi* (woolen pants) tied at the waist with a belt made of braided thread. Anna wore a white blouse and a long skirt. They had matching wedding rings, each set with a "black eye" that cost fifty cents a piece in Austria. Anna wore several necklaces – a choker beaded on horsehair girdan [*gyrdan*], eight strands of pearl beads, a necklace of shiny wine beads, and a necklace of white round beads and red elongated beads. In Austria Anna sold one chicken egg to buy a necklace. She wore gold hoops in her ears, which were pierced shortly after her birth. (Semeniuk 1980, 421–22)

My grandfather brought two tons of luggage from north Galicia [Halychyna]. He had two axes, a fork, scythe, tanning tools, mill stones, and clothes. This was enough to last some time and to supply his two sons and two daughters. Being conditioned to the hard life, they brought all they needed. (Magera interview 1955)

John Zelisko's Violin, *Tsymbaly* Tools

Tools and Specialty Services

These Ukrainian settlers brought more than their tools and possessions; they brought their skills and training. Many of the pioneers who came to Canada from the lands of the Hapsburg Empire of Frans Joseph were tradesmen. They came from villages where they had close relationships with large landholders who employed them to do various tasks ranging from ironwork, to cabinetry, to cooperage (a specialized form of carpentry associated with building round, wooden containers) and other specialized carpentry jobs. Some became very skilled tradesmen and brought their expertise and tools with them.

A master craftsman, or cooper, was reverently called a *maister* by those who recognized his capabilities. John Zelisko of Andrew was one such *maister*-craftsman. Born in 1884 in Eastern Europe, he immigrated to Canada in the early nineteenth century and settled in Andrew, where he lived the rest of his life. He was a talented musician, carpenter, and businessman. This gentleman was a great optimist and always went about his work with a cheerful attitude. He had a curious nature and was extremely courteous. His greatest attribute in life was his capability for making violins, hammer dulcimers, and music. He had a great love and devotion for these instruments and would produce music from the soul of each of them. He was one of the first Ukrainian musicians in the Andrew area. Not only a violin and *tsymbaly* maker, but a fine cabinet maker and cooper as well, John was a skilled carpenter with a full set of various block planes, a jointer, and a cooper's *croze* (a special cooper's tool used to groove staves for holding the churn's bottom). He also had a complete set of wooden block planes, shaving draw knives, and special adzes. With these specialized tools, he produced an astonishingly wide range of goods, from the musical instruments already noted, to various kinds of household furniture, including wooden butter churns, as well as children's cradles and funerary coffins.

On a trip to Andrew with Fred Magera in 1955, we visited John's workshop. He employed two apprentices who crafted a variety of wooden furniture pieces. He showed us his recent creations, a violin and a new frame he was preparing for *tsymbaly*. Zelisko also pointed out that many of the more elaborate tools came from the eastern Atlantic ship-building shops, and that he would acquire them wherever and whenever he could.[3]

Another equally talented *maister* was Prokip Lynkowski, who lived near Myrnam. Lynkowski made wooden cream skimmers, butter paddles, wooden bread troughs, bowls, dishes and spoons, *tovkachi* (mortars and pestles), as well as wooden

John Zelisko's Woodworking Shop in Andrew

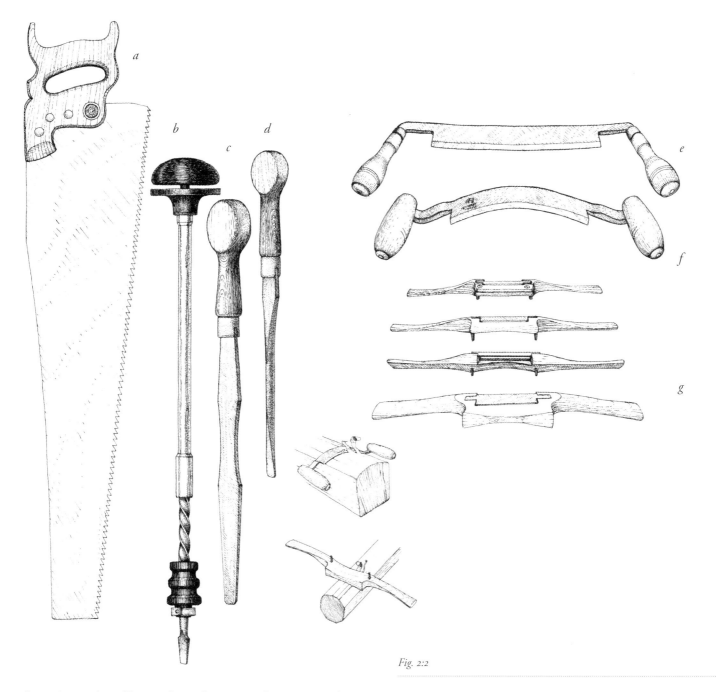

Fig. 2:2

flutes (examples of his work can be seen in figures 6:1 and 6:2 in the final chapter). His work as a cooper was second to none. Lynkowski devoted much of his time in winter to making a variety of wooden articles, including milking buckets, feeding buckets, tubs, and butter churns. The wooden butter churn found throughout the Ukrainian settlement blocs, for example, is an excellent expression of the cooper's craftsmanship. He was also a *tsymbaly* maker and had specialty tools, some of which he crafted himself while others were made to his specifications at the local blacksmith shop (*kuznia*) operated by Bill Demchuk (his building was moved to the Ukrainian Cultural Village[4] and restored as a period blacksmith shop).

Lynkowski explained how he would carefully select seasoned wood, preferably dried over a period of two years. The wood

Drawings of Coopers' and Carpenters' Tools

 a. Cross-cut Saw (*pyla*, pl. *pylka*)

 b. Drill, Archimedian, also used as a screwdriver (*vyretnok*) if with a chuck

 c. London Pattern, Flat-blade Screwdriver (*vykrutok*)

 d. Cabinet Pattern, Round Blade Screwdriver

 e. Cooper's Drawing Knife (*bondars'kyi struh*)

 f. Cooper's Hallowing Knife (*bondars'kyi ohnutyi nizh*)

 g. Series of Spoke Shaves (*tesliars'kyi struh*); used to make tapered and squared legs and to shape staves for furniture. Coopers would have an assortment of special shaves of different sizes and forms used to shape the inside and the outside of staves that were then combined to form wooden buckets (*pyila*), butter-churns (*maslynka* [*maslorobka*], and barrels (*bochky*)

Zhorna – Used to Grind Grain

loom for making cloth, sashes, and mats from Bukovyna. Ivan Zaporozan had a homemade wooden press used to extract oil from hemp seeds for his personal use and for his neighbours (the process of pressing oil is detailed in chapter five). Other immigrants brought small millstones (*querns/zhorna*) with them for grinding grain and making flour.

Carpentry was a common trade, and its practitioners brought the tools needed to construct buildings and implements to till the soil. These carpentry hand tools were usually packed in amongst their baggage. The pioneers also used them to supplement their income in the early years, before the homestead could support the family, and to assist them in purchasing what they needed that they could not produce themselves, as this quote from *Dreams and Destinies* illustrates:

Fred Orydzuk would go out and supplement the family income by building houses, erecting barns and granaries, and doing many other things which required his skills as a carpenter.

Winter transportation depended on the horse and sleigh, and Fred would build runners for sleighs from birch lumber. Fred also built a spinning wheel, which Maria used to spin wool into yarn. … Many a cold winter night was spent spinning wool and knitting it into woolen socks which were sold to surrounding settlers at fifteen cents a pair. (Semeniuk 1980, 478)

Homesteads were built with hand tools like those described above that the immigrants brought with them. These tools, although few in number, included axes, saws, mallets, augers, chisels, and planes and were an indispensable part of the meagre baggage of these early settlers. To augment the need for additional tools, some of these simple instruments were created by the few blacksmiths scattered throughout the Ukrainian settlement bloc. Nykolai Topolnicky, who settled in the area, was one such skilled resident blacksmith and area metal worker. These tools were essential to the building of homes and other farm buildings as well as making implements and useful conveniences such as the quern mill, loom, grain crusher, kitchen utensils, and various farm tools.

The axe was perhaps the earliest and first tool used by nearly all pioneers. It was used for felling trees, chopping felled logs, making joints in log walls for homes and barns, splitting out stock for various tool handles, making legs for stools and benches, and other miscellaneous uses about the homestead. Two types of axes were used in the initial framing work: the broad axe and the adze. The broad axe was one of the principal tools used for fine beam and rafter hewing. The cutting edge was only bevelled on one side like a chisel, so the back of the broad blade would lay flat to the timber being hewn. The broad axe was used to cut in the vertical plane, with work on

had to have a straight, even grain with few or no knots. From a selected wedge of wood, he would rive a large number of staves using a froe and a wooden maul. They were cut to width and given a slight taper on the sides. Two drawknives or spoke shaves were used, one a flat and the other a convex hollowing knife. Next, the staves were bevelled and held in place on a shaving horse. A jointer plane was used to put a finishing edge on both ends of the assembled bucket (butter churn), and a bottom was fitted. Hoops were made of split green spruce or split willow branches from which the bark was removed. Butter churns were entirely made of wood, using neither nails nor metal. These receptacles were a work of art.

Theodore Kushniriuk was an experienced tanner who tanned sheep pelts for fashioning men's and women's coats. Kushniriuk's neighbour, Ivan Machney, brought a weaver's

Fig. 2:3

Maister Carpenter's Tool Set of Various Planes

Illustrated is a set of wooden planes found in the tool chest of a *maister* carpenter in the Andrew district. All the "horn-handled" planes were brought over from Ukraine, which was under Austro-Hungarian rule at that time. These were common to carpenters in Eastern Europe.

    a. long "Pointer Planes"

    b. "Trying Plane" with a double handle and the incised
        decorative pattern at the mouth of the blade

    c. three "Jack Planes," all with replacement handles

    d. a series of five East European planes, also known as "Continental Jack Planes" (*hymbli*). These have the prominent front "horn handle," easily recognized as being of Germanic origin, and sometimes called the "Bismarck Roughing Plane"

    e. a fine "Smoothing Plane" with a tapering iron set well towards the heel

    f. a series of three "Molding Planes"

    g. a set of "Rabbet Planes"

    h. a set of "irons" for wood surface design

    i. three "Compass Planes," one with a convex-shaped sole to shape curved surfaces that might later be used by wheelwrights and other tradesmen the horizontal plane being done with the adze (a two-handed tool with a curved handle and a cutting edge at right angles to the handle). It was used to remove surplus wood from a log which would later be squared with a broad axe. The adze was used to fit logs snugly on top of each other (with the assistance of a chalk line, of course) and to score the log or to make a series of cross cuts in the round log. Scoring cuts were carefully cut to a uniform depth, and then the broad axe was used to put a smooth face on the top and sides of logs.

Logs were pegged with hardwood pegs at regular intervals. Pegged joints required drilled holes, and augers were an essential tool in the erection of log buildings. The augers usually had a cross-bar handle made of hardwood and were used in boring all the holes for the pegs that held framing timbers together. The builder may have had a variety of augers of different sizes and mallets for firmly setting the pegs, some of which penetrated a three-log depth. Pegs were made of birch, wild cherry, or saskatoon berry trees: all were dense, native hardwoods that facilitated constructing all wood buildings with no metallic connectors. Nails were scarce in the rural pioneer community, and were expensive and hard to get. In addition, the traditional methods of building without them generally worked better than nails, so they were rarely used.

The wood saw is one of the earliest cutting tools, going as far back as early Egypt and Greece. Some pioneers brought steel saw blades with them from Ukraine, Romania, Hungary, and Austria. When they arrived on their homesteads, they would fashion a frame from seasoned wood to fit the particular blade they had with them. The settlers possessed a variety of buck-saw types, the design dependent on the skills of the craftsman who fashioned the frame and the nature of the steel blade that was available. Saws used in the initial stages were the one-man crosscut saw, popular with all the settlers, as well as the two-man hand saw. The corner lap or dove-tail keys on log buildings were usually cut by saw and finished with a chisel. Wedge-shaped keys were sometimes used to provide secure corners, designed to shed rain water and lock the corner walls firmly in place.

Tools for finishing a home might include chisels, a brace with a range of bits, handsaws, marking gauges, and a square, as well as a series of planes. The three basic planes, the jack plane, the trying plane, and the smoothing plane, complemented each other. The jack plane, about twelve to sixteen inches long, was used for rough levelling work. The trying plane would be used for final levelling, and the short smoothing plane would be used whenever an especially smooth surface was required. However, a carpenter rarely had a complete set of planes. The gathering of neighbours to a construction bee usually brought together a collection of tools that complemented one another.

a   *b*   *c*   *d*   *e*

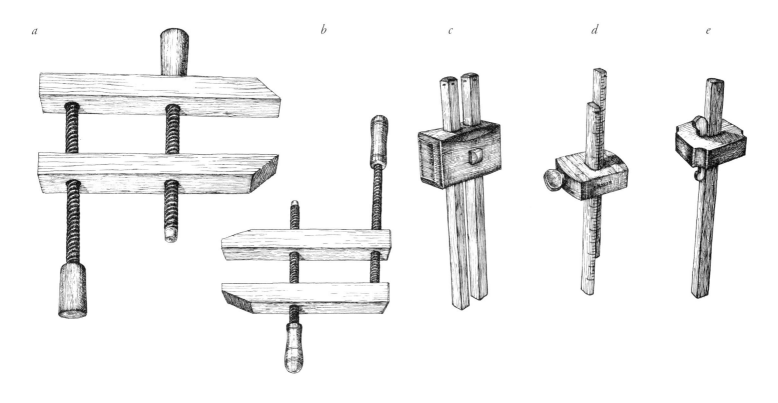

Fig. 2:4

Carpenters' Wooden Clamps and Scribers

a.; b. two different sized "Cramp Hand Screws" (*zatyskach*); consisting of two hardwood blocks connected by two wooden screws, one in the center and the other near the back of the jaws. The work to be cramped is placed in the jaw opening and the two screws adjusted, bringing the blocks nearly parallel, then the outer screw would be tightened. This places pressure on the jaws, bringing them together.

c.; d. two "Combination Gauges" with adjustable spurs on one side for marking mortises, sometimes with a marking or a cutting spur on the other side. The two separate stems are locked in the fence by a wood wedge, a common, east European gauge (*mirka*), while the other is a more modern gauge having two sliding hardwood rules, usually of rosewood with a brass thumb screw.

e. this last "Marking Gauge" is dense rosewood with a simple sliding wedge that locks in the fence. It has a sharp brad that places a deep score across the wood grain.

These old turn-of-the-century farms were not only a repository of wood-working and agricultural tools originating in eastern Europe, Austria-Hungary, and the two provinces of Bukovyna and Halychyna, but also of tools of American and British origin. Tools were judged for their excellence in performing a task and quickly became part of the settlers' tool kits. American and English block planes and various other tools were borrowed from other settlers and sold by general traders in Edmonton. Many of these tools were brought from the east by the builders of the railway stations and the prairie/grain elevators. As construction projects expanded, the required tools were shipped by train from the east, where they were commonly used for ship building. In the west, they were used for building railroad stations and elevators.

Figure 2:2 illustrates a complete carpenter's set of tools. I recall John Zelisko explaining how a fully-equipped European craftsman usually used five planes, whereas an American cabinetmaker normally used only three bench planes. Each of the five planes was sharpened and the depth and angle set for the particular job for which it was intended. A finely set smoothing plane was not used for anything but finishing. Of course, not many of the Ukrainian immigrant craftsmen had a full set of cabinet-making tools. They made do with what they had.

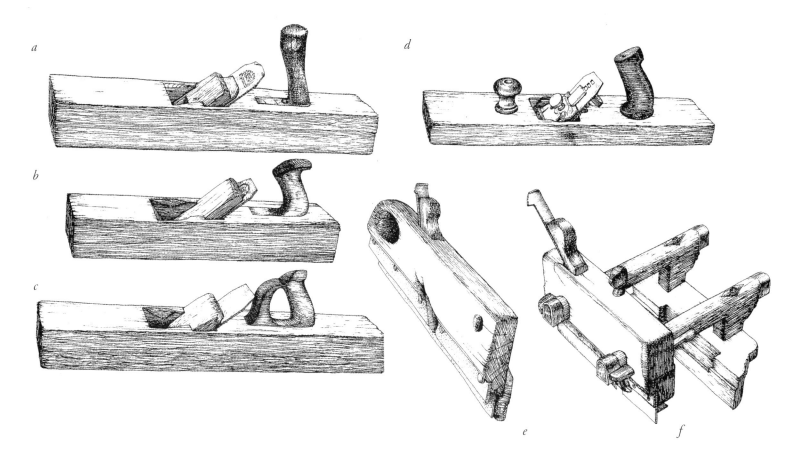

a

b

c

d

e   *f*

Fig. 2:5

Wooden Hand Planes

    Illustrated from the top, down:

a.; b.; c. all are "Jack Planes" (*hybli*), common in all wood
workshops and used for the preliminary preparation of
surfaces before truing up with a "Trying Plane."

d. This plane was intended for joinery and cabinet (*kabinet*) work, having
a device for the lateral and longitudinal adjustment of the iron.

e. a "Grooving Plane" (*vyimchastyi hybel'*) was used in
conjunction with a matching "Tonguing Plane" for
producing tongue and groove boards or joints.

f. the "Plow Plane" was used where a fully adjustable tool was required
for grooving joints and panel work. These have an adjustable fence
with brass thumb screws bearing on each stem, and a bridge joining
them. The two stems are 'D' shaped in section, and the ends are
tipped in brass. Some more extravagant models would have handles of
solid ebony stock and an ebony stem carrying a movable fence. Fine
collectors' pieces would have ivory adjusting screws or wooden nuts.

A few craftsmen/carpenters brought their tools in chests
made specifically for that purpose (see Fig. 2:1). These chests
were externally plain, strong, and usually built of pine, weath-
ered and/or covered in ship's enamel paint. Some of them had
substantial frame and panel construction, using hardwood
pegs to hold the panels in place. The interior was subdivided
into two main compartments with a series of grooves to hold
separators, subdividing the interior to hold tools of varied
dimensions. Often the chest would feature two smaller trays
stacked on top and holding small, specialized items such
as measuring rules, pencils, callipers, scribing and marking
gauges, and other interesting accessories. The chest provided
orderly storage of wood block planes, saws, drill bits and drills,
chisels, a draw knife, and measuring tools. The workmanship
on the chest was usually a very good indicator of the tradesman's qualifications. A single glance into most chests indicated
whether or not the owner was organized, efficient, respectful
of his tools, and knew how to use them. Metal hardware such
as lid hinges, carrying handles, and locking mechanisms were
usually hand-forged by a blacksmith. The chest was the craftsman's calling card, and work was often awarded on the basis of
this display.

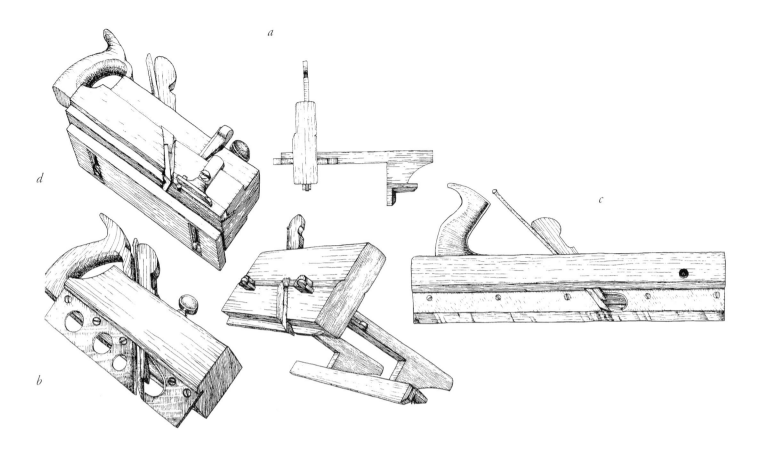

a

c

d

b

Fig. 2:6

More Wooden Hand Planes

Tools of this calibre would be found in a specialist's tool box, such as the *maister* house builder or a carpentry workshop in the town that supplied window sash to local home builders. Depicted is a series of four specialized planes, from the top right;

- *a.* a "Moving Fillister," with an adjustable fence, a brass adjustable depth stop, and a shaving discharge at the side; used for cutting recesses of differing widths on the edge of a woodwork piece
- *b.* a "Wooden Fillister Plane" (*hybel' na vikonnu ramu*) with a right-hand cutter; usually used for cutting window sashes
- *c.* b can be compared to the "Jack Plane Sized Fillister" at the bottom; both would have been included in an advanced house builder's tool kit
- *d.* the last plane (on the upper left) was also used for cutting rebates and could be used on either left- or right-hand sides of the wood; the fence could be changed to function on either side to bear on the face of the wood

Svarich brought with him a complete set of drawings, showing in specific detail and to scale, all the major tools that a pioneer farm family might need to achieve self-sufficiency in the untamed prairie. He also made drawings[5] of traditional hand tools and complex farm tools such as a *stupa* (grain crusher), *oliinytsia* (hemp seed oil press), *vavka* (skein winders), *terlytsia* (flax fibre crusher), *oslin do priadyva* (bench for spinning), *pluh* (plough), oxen yoke (see Fig. 4:4a), *zhorna* (quern mill), *tkats'kyi verstat* (weaving loom), *borony* (harrows), a draw knife bench, a wagon and the gear and harnesses that go with it, and a special chopper for silage and thatching. In 1909, Martha Megley Shandro's[6] father, Michailo Megley, made a loom from sketched plans he had brought with him.

The illustrations on the following pages are all specific drawings Peter Svarich brought with him on his voyage from the Ukraine.

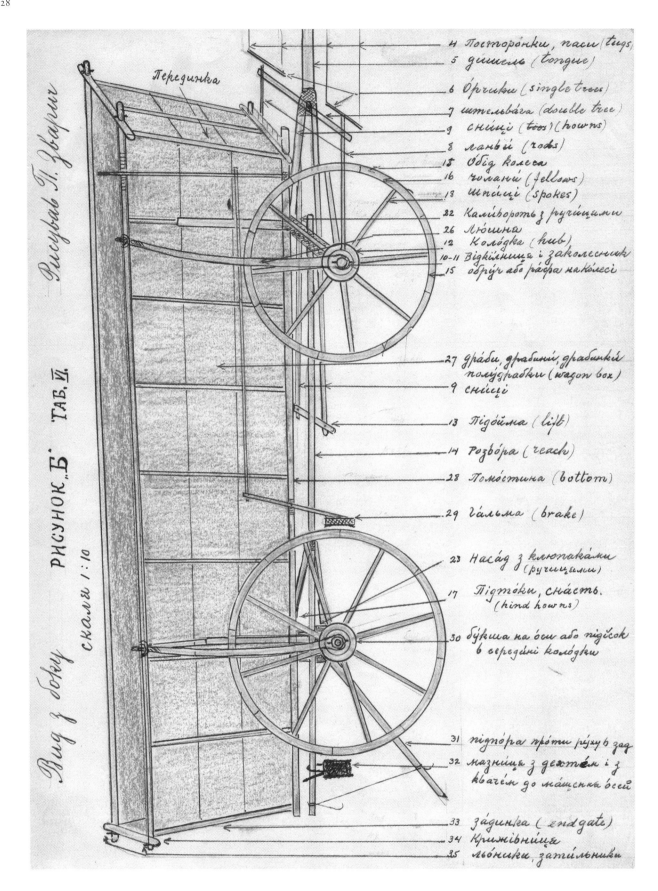

Вид з боку   РИСУНОК „Б"   ТАБ. ІІ.   Рисував П. Зварич

скаля 1 : 10

Перединка

4 Посторо́нки, паси (tugs,
5 ди́шель (tongue)
6 О́рчики (single tree)
7 штельва́га (double tree)
9 сни́ці (toes) (howns)
8 ланьи́ (rods)
15 О́бід колеса
16 чоманьи́ (fellows)
18 шпи́ці (spokes)
22 Калі́ворот з ручи́цями
26 Лю́шина
12 Коло́дка (hub)
10-11 Відкі́лниця і заколе́сник
15 обру́ч або ра́фра на колесі

27 дра́би, драби́ний, драби́нки,
        полудра́бки (wagon box)
9 сни́ці

13 Пі́дойма (lift)

14 Розво́ра (reach)

28 Помо́стина (bottom)

29 Га́льма (brake)

23 Наса́д з клюпака́ми
        (ручи́цями)

17 Підто́ки, сна́сть.
        (hind howns)

30 бу́кша на о́си або піді́сок
        в середи́ні коло́дки

31 підпо́ра про́ти рі́хув зад

32 мазни́ця з дехтём і з
        кваче́м до ма́щенка о́сей

33 за́динка (endgate)
34 Крижівни́ця
35 льо́ники, зати́льники

Fig. 2:7 Wagon – Side View. Svarich Collection.
Courtesy Provincial Archives of Alberta, PR. 1975.74/1266.

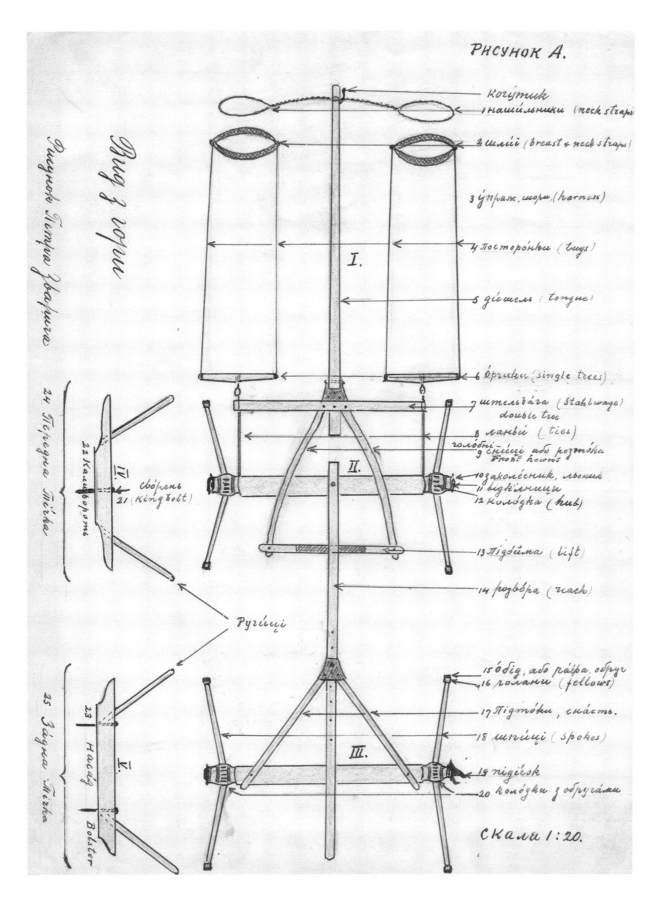

Fig. 2:8 Wagon Gear and Horse Harness with Collars. Svarich Collection.

Courtesy Provincial Archives of Alberta, PR. 1975.74/1270.

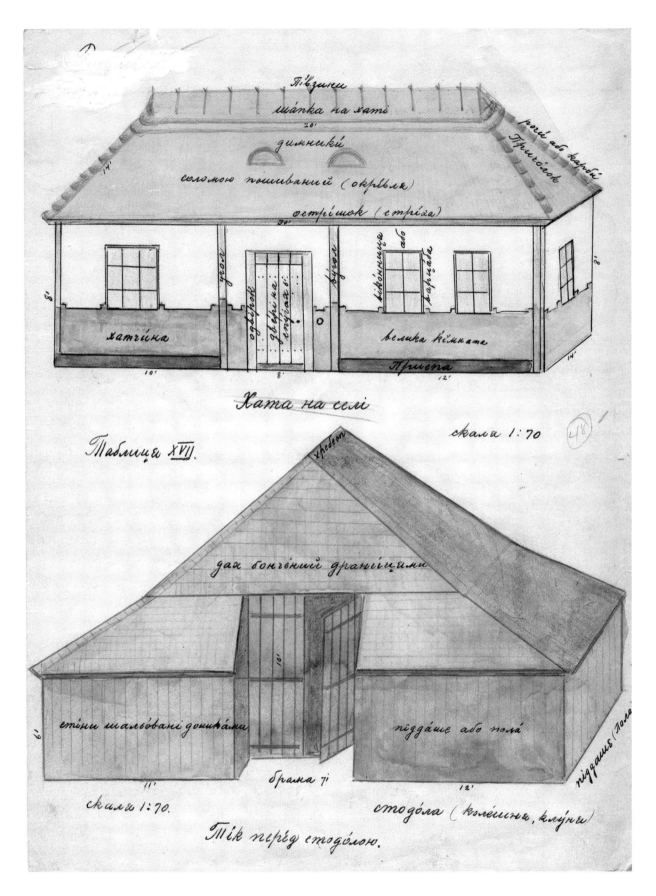

Fig. 2:9 Two Building Sketches; the House (*Khata*) and Storage Barn (*Komora*).
Svarich Collection. Courtesy Provincial Archives of Alberta, PR. 1975.74/1276.

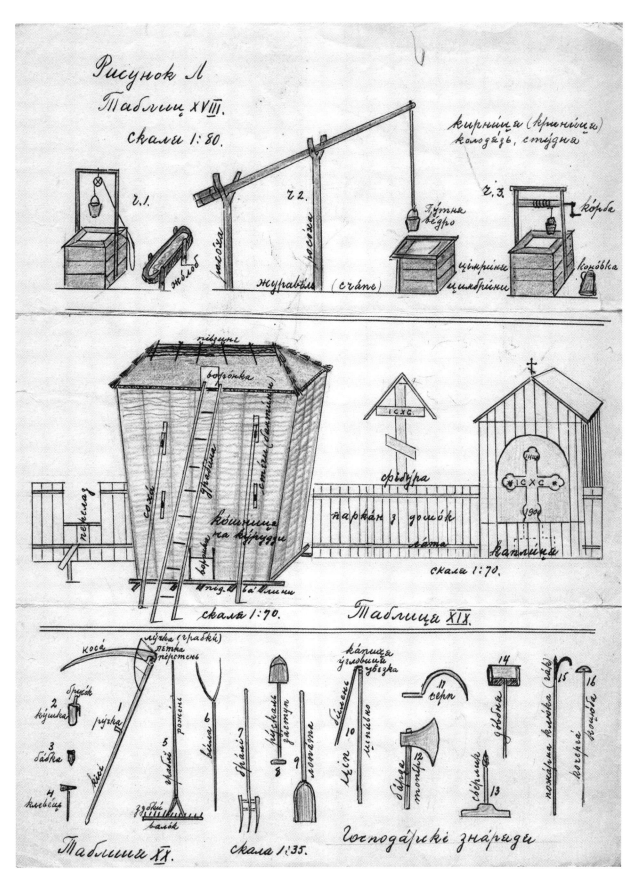

Fig. 2:10 Farm Tools: Corn Crib, Small Chapel, and Three Wells (top). Svarich
Collection. Courtesy Provincial Archives of Alberta, PR. 1975.74/1278.

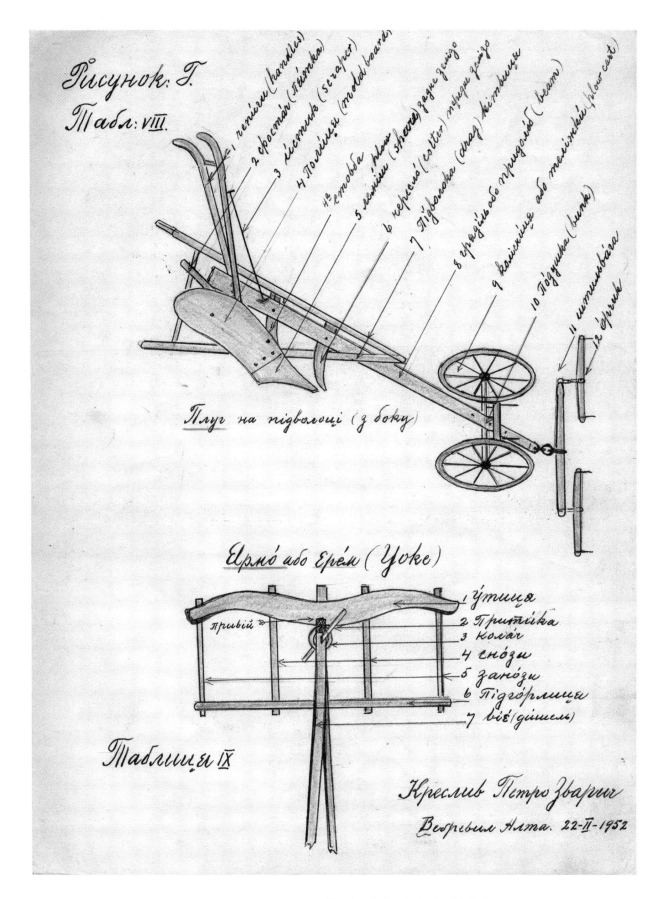

Fig. 2:11 Plough and Oxen Yoke. Svarich Collection.
Courtesy Provincial Archives of Alberta, PR. 1975.74/1271.

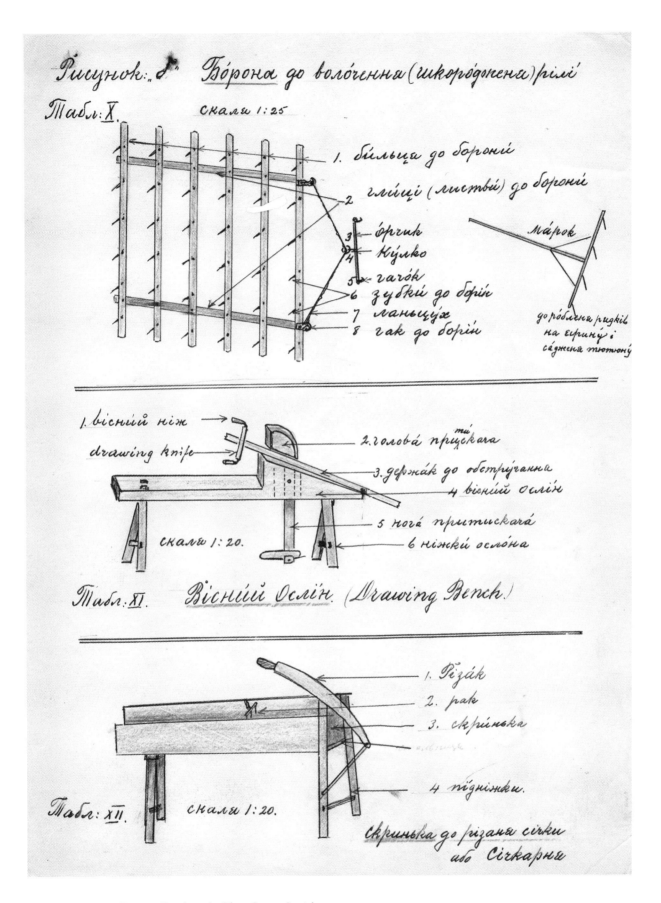

Fig. 2:12 Harrows, a Drawing Bench, and a Silage Cutter. Svarich
Collection. Courtesy Provincial Archives of Alberta, PR. 1975.74/1272.

34

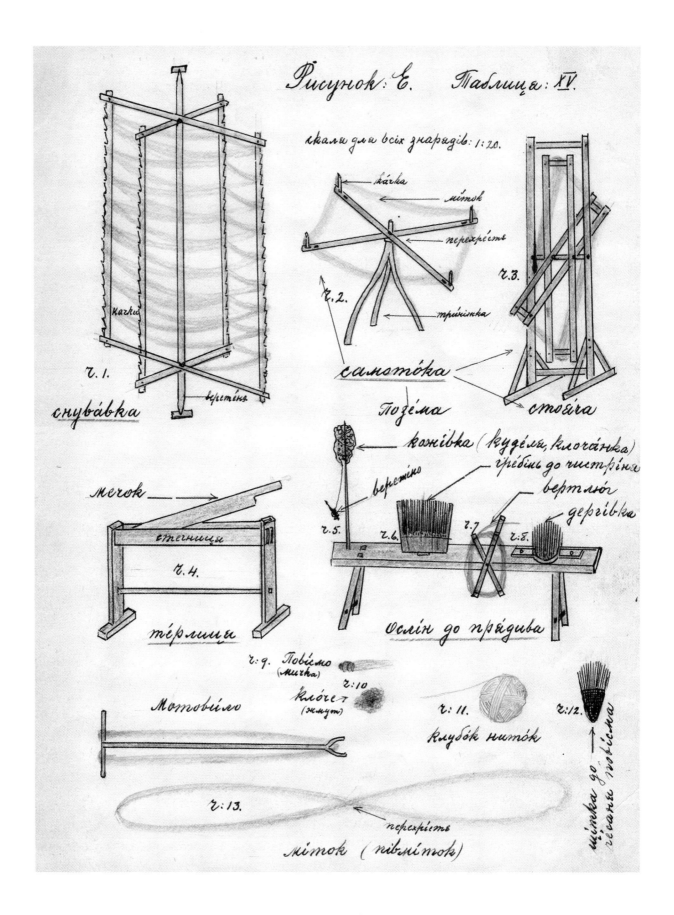

Fig. 2:13 Tools for Preparing Skeins of Thread for Weaving. Svarich Collection. Courtesy Provincial Archives of Alberta, PR. 1975.74/1274.

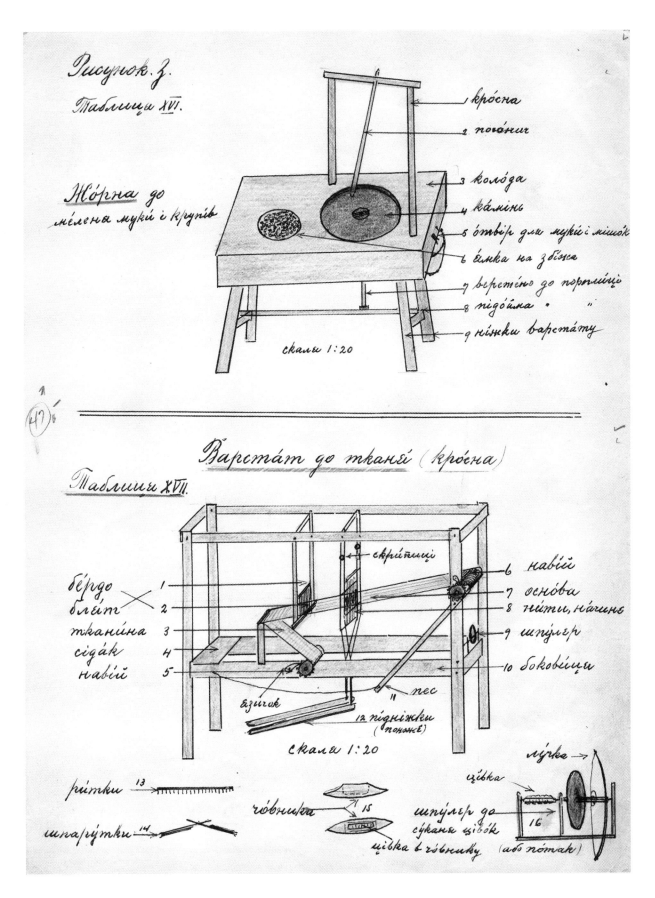

Fig. 2:14 Plans for a Loom and a Quern Stone Grinder. Svarich
Collection. Courtesy Provincial Archives of Alberta, PR. 1975.74/1275.

Collection of Austrian-style Axes

Collection of Wood Block Planes at the Shandro Museum

The End of an Era

I had the opportunity to purchase a wide selection of pioneer tools at farm auctions across the Ukrainian bloc settlement during my sojourn as district agriculturalist from 1954 to 1957. The tools were expressive of the crafts that were practiced by these farmers. They were now in their eighties and were retirees, having moved to larger urban centres. This collection of tools has served as the basis for many of the illustrations in this book. However, thousands of tools were destroyed, passed on, or scrapped. Many of these tools were abandoned or destroyed because they were obsolete, at least in the eyes of the owner. New tools manufactured from lightweight materials such as plastics and aluminium and powered by electric motors and modern craftsmanship were replacing old ones. Metal tools were consigned to the war effort during scrap drives. Some were simply used until they fell apart; others were sold at various farm auctions, collected by antique dealers and sold to collectors in large urban centres. Some of this material found its way to eastern Canada and the United States, mislabelled as being of Doukhobor or Russian origin. These unique tools were quickly picked up by specialist collectors of early primitive and pioneer furniture and tools. Some are preserved for posterity in the Shandro Museum and at the Ukrainian Cultural Heritage Village Museum, at the east entrance to Elk Island National Park.

There is now a growing appreciation for the study of historical information on the use and collection of antique tools. There is a desire to know who made a tool, where and how it was made, and for what purpose. There is also the specialist collector who may have an interest in the fine workmanship, the colour and grain of the wood, and the patina of many years of handling and use. The aging of a traditional finish, such as that created by hemp seed or linseed oil, enhances the colouring of a wooden tool to give it a rich glow. Some of the early craftsmen would use decorative chip carving, particularly on the tops and sides of wooden block planes. These planes were brought from the homelands and expressed the settlers' strong need to enhance their tools with meaningful symbols. The simple and functional design has become a piece of art, a sculpture that would resonate with artistic quality on the wall of any contemporary living room, possessing fine aesthetic values through shape, materials, and sculptural beauty. Every unique tool was crafted by hand, designed for a specific use, and could never be exactly replicated. Most were made with local materials, although some tools were brought from the country of origin, evident by their continental or east European style. For example, hand planes had a prominent upright "horn" instead of a knob, and "Austrian style" broad axes were forged with long and characteristic flaring "goose wings."

3

Building the Little House on the Prairies[1]

Having outlined the range of tools (whether brought over from the old country, or fashioned anew here) and introduced by the craftsmen who built and used them, I now look at one of the first tasks facing the settlers upon arrival: the building of a shelter. Whether immigrants had help or struggled through their first winter alone, they survived and built with what they had. I examine the construction process and the building of pioneers' homes first, noting how they combined prairie resources with Ukrainian customs and techniques to construct their first homes in the same vernacular styles used back home.

Various authors[2] have described pioneer home building, for example, Gwen Dowsett, Michael Ewanchuk, John Lehr, Fred Magera, Peter Svarich, and Wasyl Zazula. The contributions each makes to our understanding of the materials and processes, as well as the symbolic and sociological aspects of building the first Ukrainian homes on the prairies, are gratefully acknowledged. In addition to having grown up with such a family and having some familiarity with the types of homes discussed, I also conducted interviews with descendants of homesteading pioneers Helen Solowan Boychuk, Sidney Pawlowsky, Anna Rycheba Pidruchney, Johnny Shandro, and Harry Zukiwsky, among others. I was fortunate enough to know these interviewees personally. For example: Wasyl and Martha Shandro are my maternal grandparents, and in 1954–55, I was understudy to Fred Magera, a district agriculturist in the western portion of the Municipal District of Eagle and the eastern portion of the District of Lamont. As a student at the University of Alberta, I rented a studio room with board from Pearl Svarich Salamandyk, the daughter of Ivan Svarich (Peter Svarich's father). Portions of my career were also based on the study of pioneer housing, as when my company (Roman Fodchuk and Associates, Ltd.) prepared a field report in the form of the master plan for the Ukrainian Cultural Heritage Village project.

Replica *Burdei* at Shandro Museum   Abandoned *Burdei* in Smoky Lake District

Temporary Housing

The first major task the new settler had to address was the construction of a temporary shelter. There were basically three types commonly used. The choice of which to build depended upon the type of materials available and how much time there was before the weather changed.

The first type examined is a primitive dugout, or *burdei*. It was quickly and easily constructed, but generally inadequate for most needs, as it was considered a temporary shelter only. Nonetheless, it offered protection from the oncoming winter. A *zemlianka*, or sod house, was much more substantial, having four square walls, but it also had a leaky sod roof. If there was enough time, a more permanent, single-room settler's home,

a *khatyna*, might be built of logs. Each of these three types of shelters is described in the following paragraphs.

Burdei

A partially dug-out *burdei* could be constructed in three days if every member of the family pitched in (they subsequently lived in the dugout for anywhere from one to five years). In the meantime, the family might lodge with a neighbouring family, but more often than not, they slept under a tent made of blankets or under a wagon or tree. The *burdei* was partially dug

Original Pioneer *Khatyna* in the Dickie Bush Area   Gowrylo of Wasel in Front of his *Zemlianka*

One Room *Khatyna* in the Szypenitz District

Khatyna in the Smoky Lake District

into the ground, frequently on a south-facing knoll or gentle slope. Some of these homes were completely dug into the ground with only the roof visible. As a result, the *burdei* was often used as a cold cellar once a permanent home was constructed. The upper walls consisted of a framework of straight logs closed in with turf and hay. If time permitted, the log walls and slant roof were plastered with hay soaked in mud to eliminate draughts. The roof was constructed in a peaked fashion, resembling the tepee designed by some Aboriginal peoples. Poplar saplings formed an "A" frame and were covered with sod and/or wild hay. The small home usually measured about three metres by four metres. The head room from the floor to roof on the inside was one-and-a-half metres. This was barely tall enough to stand up in. The dugouts were smoky, dark, and cramped, but they provided shelter over the first winter or until it was possible to erect a permanent home.

Zemlianka (hlynobyta khata)

Some of the settlers built a *zemlianka* (also known as a *hlynobyta khata* – a sod house). This was made of turf blocks built up to form four walls. The substantial roof was constructed with sod, straw, and logs, supported by thin poplar saplings. The roof usually leaked during the rainy season, but it was often lived in from year to year as the settlers concentrated on other tasks. The two photographs at left show such a home occupied by an early pioneer throughout his entire life, a shepherd named Gowrylo of Wasel who lived alone and chose never to replace his sod house. This example was found in the Dickie Bush area north of the Shandro Bridge. The following description of how one such house was built is taken from Mykhailo Stashyn's memoirs:

The time came to build the house as winter was approaching. But how does one build a house? Nykola Genik stood us in good stead. He hailed from the Carpathian Mountains and knew how to build shacks. He helped us put up our house. It wasn't much of a house. A ditch three feet deep was dug, and two poles in each end of the ditch were put in, with a log across. Long poplar poles were then leaned onto the log and covered with sod. The end walls were plastered with clay. In one, a pane of glass 10" x 10" was put in, and in the other, a door made from hewn poplar planks. It was a memorable day when we moved into our own house. There was great rejoicing and great delight.

The banks of the walls served us as beds. An old ink bottle was used as a lamp to light the house in the evenings. The fuel did not cost much. The lamp consumed only one quart of kerosene during the whole winter. We made wicks from threads.

We also accepted lodgers into our house. Many people arrived later than we did and had no time to build houses. Seventeen persons lived in our house for a time. … I remember we had a great amount of snow during the first winter … We ran short of money and supplies before spring arrived, the same as other settlers. But we were able to manage somehow. Usually those who had some flour to spare loaned it to those who were short. And thus we carried on, waiting for spring. (Stashyn 1981, 14)

The First "Little" House – Khatyna

The first house the pioneer built was usually a one-room cottage that provided shelter immediately and in time for the long winter. Made of logs with a simple, four-sided, gable roof (*chotyryskkyl'ny dakh*) thatched with readily available, native slough grasses and plastered with a protective clay outer skin, these simple cottages proved durable and exceedingly warm.

The outside walls were whitewashed and surrounded by a *pryz'ba* (a bench-like structure of densely pressed clay that reinforced the outer walls of the structure). The single-framed door was fashioned from roughly sawn boards, usually built with leather hinges and secured by wooden locks. The threshold (*porih*) was quite high, perhaps consisting of the base log that held the four corners of the house together. A tall person would stoop to enter the house. The windows were small, and some were built within a frame that allowed them to slide open in warm weather.

Temporary Housing Interior Design

Fig. 3:1

Drawing of the *Khatchyna* Interior – One Room Dwelling

The *khatyna* plan, a traditional, one-room house with a *pich* to one side of the entrance, was an early first house common throughout the Ukrainian settlement blocs. In the opposite corner adjacent to the entrance (*dveri*), one would find a hanging cupboard (*mysnyk*) containing dishes and cookware. Beside the stove against the north wall (*napilna stina*) there was a wooden shelf, or *pil* (a rough, sawn-plank bed for sleeping). Against the far eastern wall was a wooden table (*stil*) with a bench (*lava*) and perhaps two chairs. Most likely a wooden short bench (*lavka*) would be placed in front of the table. Icons such as Christ and the Virgin Mary along with family photographs brought from the old country were placed on the eastern wall (*pokut*) of honour. The icons were framed with colourful embroidered towels and dried flowers (*barvinok*). The floor in the initial year was of hard-beaten clay that was eventually covered by rough sawn planks. Seasoned black poplar was preferred owing to its ability to withstand wear and rot. This improvement could sometimes take several years, depending on many factors such as proximity to a neighbour with a

This is how this single room log-dwelling (*rublena khata*) looked from the east wall. This would be the first house that a pioneer would rush to erect before winter set in. The windows (*shyba/shyby*) on the right side are south facing, and the door is usually on the western wall. The cabinet to the right of the door would house the dishes (*dizhky* [*posud*]), cups, eating utensils (wooden spoons–*dereviani lozhky*), and cooking utensils (*mysky*). Along the south wall, you would find spinning and weaving paraphernalia next to the windows where the light was good. The earthen stove had a prominent setting with the opening (*cheliust*) just to the right of the entry, with wood and other materials for the fire stacked under its skirts (*potachok*) or next to the wall. Sometimes the smoke would be vented through a flue (*dymar*) to the side, through the wall, and into an outer storage and entry space, a vestibule called *siny*. Pictured is a baby's rocking crib and some bedding (*postil*) on a substantial pole, along with a bed with a woven *verena* coverlet. In the early period, these one-room cottages would house an extended family of at least three generations; and even one or two others who may have had the misfortune of immigrating too late in the year and thus being unable to build a home of their own before winter set in.[3]

Pich in the *Khata* in Elk Island National Park (*left*) and *Pich* in the *Khatyna* on the Dohaniuk Homestead/Hairy Hill (*right*)

plank sawmill, progress in crop production, or the owner's own ability to carry out the project.

Spinning and weaving were important tasks for the long winter nights, and one would find a spinning wheel (*priadka*), paraphernalia (*predava*) used for preparing fibres, and occasionally, a large loom with a colourful blanket underway. Some early households would have a quern mill against a wall, along with a wooden barrel for grain and another for freshly ground flour. This one room cottage was a hive of activity for the entire family.

The *pich* had an oval oven that extended back to the wall. A detailed description of how it was built and used is covered in the section depicting the interior design of the permanent housing. The flat platform top of this oven was covered with hard packed clay. This was often used as an auxiliary bed by the family's young children or for unexpected visitors. The flat top was as large as a full king-sized bed, and a woven straw mat covered with a blanket and a fine feathered quilt made it the cosiest place to sleep on cold winter nights, a bed I often

shared with my brothers. We generally behaved ourselves when allowed to sleep on the *pich*, because there was no other experience that came quite that close to nirvana.

The *prychipok* (the front opening of the stove) was sometimes framed with dressed fieldstone reinforcing its edges. At a later date, the oven might be rebuilt of bricks brought from Edmonton. As bricks were not readily available to homesteads any distance away from Edmonton, this innovation, too, often came much later. A hood-like structure above the oven opening (*kahla*) caught smoke and funnelled it outside. Cottages were lit by kerosene lamps. One can imagine the air quality within these small homes, with smoke escaping from both the earthen stove and the burning lamp. Now there are only a few of these one-roomed khatyny left on the early homesteads in the Ukrainian settlement blocs. When I interviewed Sidney Pawlowsky in December of 2002, he described his father's *khatyna* home:

I remember the *khatyna* at my father's homestead near Spedden, Alberta; it was a one-roomed cottage, his first house, which was built shortly after his arrival in Canada in 1911. Just before Easter he would always give the interior a new coat of sparkling whitewash. This was an annual practice, a sign of the "revival of life" when the old smells and smoke seared walls were once again exuding the fresh, clean smell of lime. Easter also meant a new oil cloth on the kitchen table with its refreshing smell of spring.

Settlement had begun. The settlers had cut a small niche in this unbroken land from which they could carve out, virtually inch by inch, a homestead that would support them. Their next task was to build a permanent home.

A Permanent Pioneer Home — *Khata*

Fig. 3:2

The construction of a settler's permanent home was the first genuine opportunity for full cultural expression in the new land. Generations of experience in building, folk design, and vernacular embellishment was expressed in the Ukrainian character of these homes (Lehr 1976).

The settlers came from a warmer climate and were accustomed to building materials yielded by a hardwood ecosystem of beech and walnut trees in their homeland. On the prairies, however, the frost-free period was only ninety days, and they had to adjust to materials that a northern boreal, coniferous, and deciduous woodland presented. Tall, straight poplars provided logs for the walls of most prairie dwellings. Heavier logs of spruce, brought in from a distance, were usually used as foundation pieces. Spruce was found along river valleys and larger streams. Birch, willow, wild cherry, and saskatoon berry trees provided the harder woods used to fashion various tools as well as the spikes and pins that held the beams together. Floors were rough-sawn planks of black poplar, a resinous timber cured and hardened into a serviceable surface that withstood wear, fungus, and ground rot.

Differences in the appearance of individual homes were primarily variations of ornamentation and size. Some homes had a series of bedrooms or an additional lean-to running along the entire length of the north wall. All housing was strongly expressive of folk architecture from either Halychyna or Bukovyna.

The common practice of orienting the façade southward (*chil'na storona*) had both practical and symbolic implications, and distinguished Ukrainian farmsteads from the homes of many of the other European and Anglo-Saxon settlers

(left) Bukovynian Homes in Alberta

These are illustrations of two substantial homes built in the Szypenitz district just to the east of Hairy Hill and north-west of Two Hills. Both families emigrated from their native village of Shypyntsi, Bukovyna.

The Home of Kiriak and Mary Eliuk

Kiriak and Mary Eliuk came to Canada with their three children in 1902, and upon arriving by wagon, with the help of family (Alexo Ruptash), filed for their homestead, SE 20–55–13–W 4th, only a half mile away. This first home was a "*Burdei*," an "A" frame dugout. The next year Kiriak started construction on the substantial home, the base being round, cured logs using a saddle-notch, wall tie-connection and interior and exterior mud/lime plaster. The original hipped-gable roof was thatched (later to be shingled) and had a wide front overhang covering a porch with carved posts and rails. This was a lovely home that, until recently, withstood the ravages of time extremely well.

The home of Nicholas Mandryk

The second of these illustrations depicts the home of Nicholas Mandryk, built by his father as a homestead on SE 30–55–13–W 4th, about a mile to the west of the Szypenitz Ukrainian Orthodox Church of St. Mary. Both of these families were from Shypyntsi, Bukovyna, and their families were interrelated. The Mandryk home was of squared-log construction, and at the time these sketches were made, was covered with a siding of clapboards. It had the typical hipped-gable roof that expressed the steep slopes originally designed for thatching. Now it carried a healthy cladding of cedar shingles. The entry and kitchen had a large *pich* and an enamelled cast-iron stove. The large parlour room on the east-facing end had a substantial wood-burning, erect heater. Both these homes were solidly built. These outstanding period folk structures were expressive of this pioneer settlement at the beginning of the century.

Hand-carved, Wooden Sun Symbol and detail; "*Dazhboh*"

The above show the sun symbol facing the east and the rising sun in silhouette. Large homes were designed with the end wall of the *svitlytsia* (the largest room, *chysta khata* or *velyka kimnata*) facing east. Religious icons, family portraits, and other treasures brought from the homeland were placed on or against this east wall (*nastinnyi rozpys*). Houses were rectangular and, reflecting the structural nature of building materials, had small openings (some without frames) for windows. Most early dwellings had only one door. Where window glass was unavailable, cloth covered the openings to protect against insects and weather. Window sills were deep enough to hold a selection of carefully-tended house plants. All of these first homes had but one storey and a steeply-pitched roof, providing a wide eave overhanging a porch on the south side. However, the large attics were accessible, and they nearly doubled the size of the usable space. Although built of logs, Ukrainian dwellings took on a sculptured, plastic look with the addition of multiple coats of mud plaster and lime whitewash, all capped with a massive roof of thatch.

As observed by William Pedruchny, Committee Thatching the Ukrainian Pioneer's House at Elk Island Park in 1951

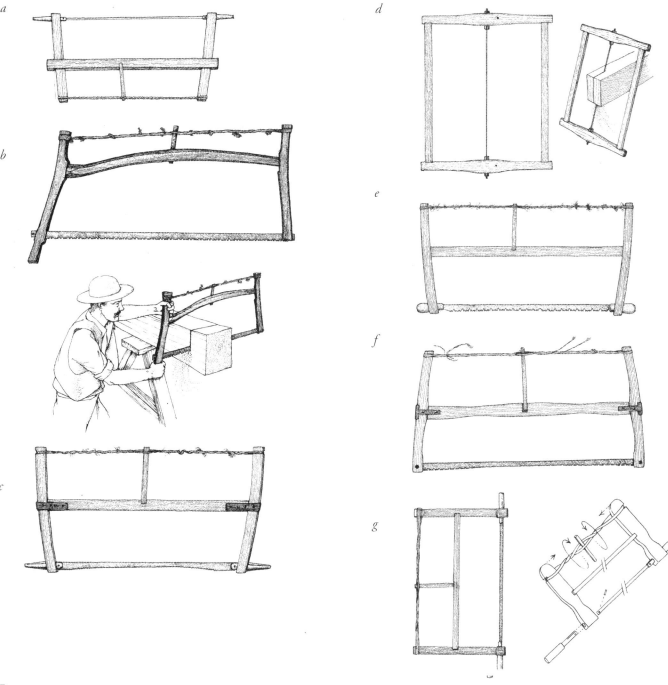

Fig. 3:3

Pioneer Buck Saws

a.; c. These saws are based on the same principle, that is, you can turn the blade as you cut with it. One can cut straight, in a curved line, or around corners, and always see where the blade is. Handles on each side of the blade can be turned to guide the blade in the direction of the cut. This was called a "Turning Saw" (*obtochuval'na pyla*) or a "Chairmaker's Saw" and is recognized by its center "straining" with tension applied at the top against the turning blade at the bottom.

c.; e. These are both "Frame Carpenter's Saws," having the wider and stronger blades.

a.,d.; g. These are finer versions used by furniture craftsmen. They might be called a "Chairmaker's Saw" or a "Fellow Saw," and were used by blacksmiths to cut out "fellows," which are the circular segments of the wooden buggy and wagon wheel.

b; f. These are "Frame Saws," commonly known as "Open Saws," with a longer handle that could be used with two hands. This saw was used primarily for "bucking" wood, meaning to cut logs into proper lengths for the wood stove. This "Buck Saw" (*kozlova pyla*) was the tool of woodsmen and farmers.

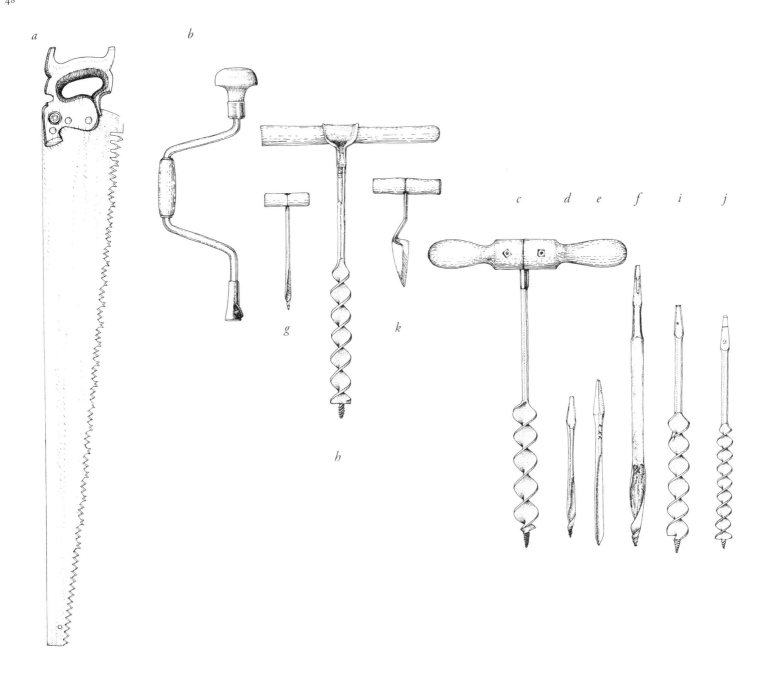

a   *b*

c   *d*   *e*   *f*   *i*   *j*

g   *k*

h

Fig. 3:4

Pioneer Handsaw and Various Augers

    a. A one-man, "Champion Tooth Cross-Cut Saw" (*pyla*).

    b. Brace with Split Chuck; sometimes known as a "Cooper's Brace."

d. e.; f. Two "Shell Gimlets" and a "Farmer's Strong Gimlet." All of these
        were designed for use with a brace, and were not for deep drilling,
        although the Farmer's Strong Gimlet was a substantial drilling tool.

    g. The smallest "Hand Gimlet" was usually used by
        harness makers to make holes in leather.

c. h. i.; j. Boring Drills (*sverdli*), were very important, as the house builder
        used them to drill holes through logs placed in walls in order to
        secure them with hard wooden spikes. Some drills had their own
        handles, whereas others were designed for use with a brace. Some
        of the latter were as deep as four logs in thickness and provided a
        firm, long-lasting anchor for the log walls of the farm building.

    k. The "Cooper's Reamer" or "Wheelwright's Reamer"
        were used to enlarge holes in wood containers or
        craft the wooden hubs of buggy wheels.

Fig. 3:5

Construction Details of Log Building Corner Connections

a.; e. This illustrates the corner detail on a mud/lime plastered home. The upper beams (*platva*) were allowed to extend beyond the walls as a decorative and structural feature. Many of these corners were treated in a more plastic manner, with the outer notching of the logs completely hidden within the sweep of the curve from under the eaves down to the wall itself. This was easily accomplished with the use of the mud/lime plaster, giving the building a strong, sculpted feeling. See Illustration g, which shows this feature.

b.; h. Detail corners showing a "Full-dovetail Notch" (*zamkaiuchyi zarub*). If one examines the bottom beam on h, it was the initial log laid down with a half-notch on the corner.

c. This illustrates the front wall (*perednia stina*) of a substantial home with the foundation beams placed on stone footings. The logs are rough-sawn timbers forming the outer perimeter, facade walls. They are "double-notched" (*vzamok*) on both sides of the building. This was a unique home with a substantial porch (*piddashok*) on the south facade of the house.

The primary tools used in the construction of housing – an axe, saw, auger, and adze, usually of German or Austrian origin – were sufficient. Whatever tools and expertise the settler did not bring from the homeland were garnered from neighbours. Within the extended settlement community, there was usually a carpenter with a chest full of wood crafting tools who would be called in to help with construction. Often, neighbours all pitched in and held a *toloka* (building bee; like many of the events on the pioneer farm, bees were a group affair, wherein neighbours got together to tackle a large project communally).

d. f. g. These show some very interesting techniques such as a Bell Tower (d) where the builders applied a "Square Half-notch" with overlapping log lengths to emphasize the structural integrity of the corner. The detail in f shows how a "Semilinate Notch" together with a "Double Notch" (*podviinyi*) were used for the heavy timber just above the footing, while g shows what appears to be a "Half Notch" in the heavy square timbers used for the foundation logs.

(Fodchuk 1978).[4] First, this orientation served to collect heat and light from the sun and protected the entrance from cold north and north-westerly winds, but it also fulfilled religious traditions. In 1978, while I was selecting buildings suitable for the newly evolving Ukrainian Cultural Heritage Village, I found a "sun motif" on a *khatyna* in the Smoky Lake area. A farmstead near the town had several buildings from the early homestead era. One of these, an early one-room cottage (then being used as a chicken coop), had a hand carved, wooden sun symbol on its east facing façade, in the roof's apex. What a fabulous find! This was a pre-Christian symbol going back to the time when the clans worshipped their own gods, and one of the primal gods was *Dazhboh* (the God of the Sun). (See above, top of page 46.)

Svarich's memoirs describe an incident when Ukrainian house-building incorporated symbolic and sociological processes and religious rituals. At one point during construction, "work was held up until he [the owner] carved out a cross on the southeast end. On this, the owner placed three silver pieces of money, dried flowers, and vegetation from the Thanksgiving basket, which was blessed in church in autumn together with seeds from the cones of the wood used. They sprinkled everything with holy, blessed water as they repeated the Lord's Prayer, then began the next round of logs from this corner" (1934).

A "Hole-in-wall" for a Specialized Locking Mechanism

Wall Construction

For the settler, building the first home began with the straightforward matter of cutting, stockpiling, and curing enough logs to form walls and the roof. Stone foundations kept the structure up off the ground, thus preventing dampness and insect infestations. The foundation also ensured the bottom-most logs would not rot. Logs were scribed lengthwise with a string and marker to duplicate the profile of the lower log upon the upper and were then trimmed with a broadaxe (*topir*) to fit snugly. Some builders trimmed off all four sides; others trimmed only the two that met so the interior and exterior walls had natural, rounded-log surfaces. Successive layers of logs formed the walls, with the corners secured by either dovetailing or saddle-notching the joints. Dovetailing was commonly used on logs hewn flat on all four sides (*vzrub*), thus ensuring a smooth corner with an even surface for plastering. Saddle-notching was commonly used for joining round logs (see Fig. 3:5). The wall's strength was increased by pegging (*tebli*) the logs with long wooden pins. A hole was augured down through several logs and pins made of harder woods (such as birch or willow) were hammered in. None of the early log homes built by the Ukrainian pioneers used metal nails or spikes. Long hardwood pegs (*tybli*) and smaller wooden spikes (*tybli*) hold these structures together to this day.

The building was a simple rectangular box with large areas of unbroken wall interrupted by a few windows. As the walls went up, spaces for the door (*dveri*) and windows (*vikna*) were cut. Window frames (*okesna*) were rough sawn. Some settlers brought window glass in their luggage from Ukraine, others used oiled sailcloth or thick Kraft paper. Forward-thinking settlers brought their own hinges: others fashioned wooden hinges of birch and carved hardwood crotches reinforced with thick remnants of raw cowhide. The settlers often designed ingenious wooden "locks" to secure their doors. Doors were made of rough-sawn boards spiked to a wooden crosspiece that also served as a hinge. They were hung on a carved hardwood hinge pin reinforced with leather braces. Early houses had wooden latches with knobs and a sliding mechanism. One reached through a hole in the wall, then inserted the appropriate key into a wooden lock to unlock the latch and open the door.

a

b

c

d

Fig. 3.6

Details of Courtyard Entry, Doors, Locks, and Hinges

  a. Fenced in courtyard (*grazhda, hrazhda,* or *dvir*) with an outer wall
       that is protected with a lap-board "roof" (*dranytsi*) and gated with a
       double-door reinforced with a "locking beam," as seen from the inside.
       These were more commonly used in Bukovyna, the settlers' homeland.

  b. This shows a leather strap hinge such as was
       commonly found on early pioneer buildings.

  c.; d. Sliding door locks (*kovznyi zamok* or *kliamka*) of various kinds
       were used to secure doorways, some with ingenious locks
       that would only open for one who had the combination.

Fine Old House in the Shalka Area

Kelba Home near Szypenitz Showing Removal of Siding Boards

The south-facing façade was carefully crafted for outdoor living. The front wall was often reinforced with a clay bench (a porch *ganok*) for sitting. This was polished or smeared with sheep dung, creating a stucco-like surface that prevented clay from rubbing off or disintegrating too quickly in the rain and sun. This was entirely protected under a broad roof overhang that sometimes resembled a porch.

Roof Construction

By far the most striking feature of traditional Ukrainian buildings was the roof. The attic space was equal to, or surpassed, that of the ground floor of the house. These large-hipped gable roofs were steeply pitched when thatched, providing a foot to a foot-and-a-half (31–46 cm) of rise for every foot of run. Usually, the height from eave to ridgepole was one to one-and-a-half times the height of the side wall. These dimensions made for an impressive overall visual impact (see the two photographs above).

Bukovyna-style houses had eaves finished with an overhang that varied from two feet (61 cm) in back to five feet (152 cm) in front. Supported by uprights, these wide eaves provided a shady porch (*ganok*) on the south side and protected the clay on the walls from rain wash (forcefully driven rain) capable of damaging the clay finish. Halychyna-style houses tended to have less of an overhang and no porch, and they did not appear as top heavy. Halychyna-style houses usually had an additional overhang at the gable and eave level to protect the lower walls from rain. The end walls, when plastered, were eventually cov-ered with a vertical weatherboard to protect the house from rain damage.

These typically Ukrainian roof forms were developed to permit rapid run-off over the porous thatch. The high roofs and wide overhanging eaves remained a prominent feature of Ukrainian farm buildings even after shingles replaced the traditional thatch material of local sedges and swamp grasses. To construct the ceiling, squared log beams (*svoloky*) were spaced at intervals of about three feet (91 cm) across the top-most wall-log, at right angles to the building. Wooden spikes were driven down through augured holes (*vtsivku*) in the ceiling beams and into the wall logs. An in-fill of poles of smaller diameter was placed every two or three inches (5–8 cm) across the ceiling (*stelyna*) with plugs of twisted slough hay dunked into a slurry of clay. Tufts of slough hay, the soft, lower stem that was dumped into liquid clay mix having a thick, cream-like consistency, were then inserted between the infill ceiling logs (Lehr 1976, 12). Next, a six- to eight-inch (15–20 cm) layer of clay with short straw particles, sometimes strengthened with horse dung, was spread on top of this ceiling, providing excellent insulation against the cold Canadian winters. The large space under the roof (*pid*) was often ventilated through "eyebrow" openings (see photograph on p. 53, top right). These were small, semicircular apertures built into the roof with a thick protective thatch over them. As the space requirements of the household grew, the attic became living space, and eyebrow vents were replaced by dormer windows (Fodchuk 1978).

Although the roofs were structurally sound and made of rigid timbers, rafters were not visible from the outside. The

A Fine Large *Khata* Near Zawale

Completed Replica of a Pioneer Home at Elk Island National Park

undersides of eaves were covered by large fascia boards that hid the rafters and the supporting wall timbers that served as roof supports. The fascias were sculpturally carved to the appropriate shape with a coat of clay plaster and extend to the corners (see figure 3:8). Wherever secondary walls existed to support the overhanging eaves, this was expressed on the façade as a protrusion under the eaves. If covered with plaster, it provided a plastic expression of outward flaring of the topmost wall logs up to the supporting sill timber (see figure 3:5).

Svarich's 1934 description of roof construction in the Ukraine incorporates details about the ritual that traditionally accompanied this stage of home building:

When a wall height of seven feet is reached, then they put on beams (to support the ceiling) which protrude at least one foot over the outside walls. On their ends they place roof rails and nail these (wooden spikes) to beams. Beams and rails must be squared and planed smooth. Under the width-wise beams, sometimes they will fit in a lengthwise beam on which the carpenter carves an artistic three-armed cross, the year of building, and the name of the "*gazda*," or owner. This cross is blackened with candle flame during Epiphany (Jordon January 6 feast) when the priest blesses the new home. "Nests" are cut out at specific spaces on the roof beams (on the roofing beam rails) into which the "heel" of the rafters will fit. These fittings are strengthened with wooden nails. To the rafters are nailed laths, and to these later are tied the straw bundles, as roofing. (n.p.)

Thatching the Roof

Participating in a traditional-style thatching bee was one of the most memorable events of my life as a student. On my way home from the University of Alberta one fall day in the early 1950s, a friend and I took a short cut home. Passing through Elk Island National Park, we noticed a construction project on a stretch of land adjacent to Lake Astotin and drove in. What a fabulous find! A replica of a Ukrainian pioneer house was being fitted with a thatched roof (the thatch consisted of thick sheaves of coarse slough grass, some of which were four to five feet long).

About ten men in their fifties were thatching this log home under the direction of Peter Svarich.[5] We stayed for two or three hours, experiencing the thatching operation as fully as possible. The men below prepared the sheaves and then passed them on to the men on the roof, who crafted the gable end while the master thatcher used a special razor knife to sculpt the eaves. Watching these expert thatchers (*poshyval'nyky*) work synchronously as they always had in the past sparked my evolving interest in folk architecture.

Figure 3:8 outlines the standard stages of the thatching process as they were employed at this *toloka* by Svarich and his crew on the pioneer home in Elk Island National Park. Thatch was the traditional roofing material of the pioneers' homeland. Because tall sedges and slough grasses were free for the

(*following pages*) Series of photographs showing Peter Svarich and the Committee Thatching the Ukrainian Pioneer's House at Elk Island Park in 1951

Zhorna

Chapter 3: Building the Little House on the Prairies

Fine Old Thatched House in the Musidora District
– Now Used as a Granary "*Komora*"

taking, Ukrainian settlers continued their thatching traditions in Canada. In addition to its ready availability, the thatched roof's (*solomianyi dakh*, or *poshytyi dakh*) advantages were its light weight and superior insulation. When the thatch was steeply pitched (*strikha*), generally at about fifty degrees, rain and snow would run off and not permeate and rot the thatch. Gutters were not required. The wide eave overhang carried run-off beyond the walls and out over the porch (*prysinok*). A thick, dense thatch was an ideal insulative material for long, cold, prairie winters.

In Ukraine, rye grass was the preferred material for thatching, but rye was not available until crops were sown and harvested. Prairie grass was too short and was a less effective roofing material than the tall, tough sedges and slough grasses (Zazula 1983). Combinations of species were commonly used as the resourceful settlers made do with whatever was most readily available. Once crops were grown, straws of various cereals were tried. It was not long before rye was specifically grown for thatch, as it was long-stemmed and tough, and it could be used at various stages of growth. Some thatchers chose green rye cut before the kernel had formed, thus eliminating the problem of damage from rodents or birds. Other thatchers advocated the use of ripe, yellow grain, because green thatch had a tendency to dry to a brittle stage and break easily. Some thatchers threshed (*molotyty*) ripe cereals thoroughly to remove kernels. Others left kernels on the stalks, relying on stove smoke to thoroughly permeate the thatch and deter fire-fearing rodents. This was common on early shelters without chimneys (*pidkurna khata*). During my interview with John Stanko in 1956, he recalled how he repaired thatched roofs in Ukraine and then used the same techniques in Alberta.

The straw must be ripe and yellow. If it's green, it will dry and break. Native (slough) grass about four feet tall was good, and we used rye if it was available. The ripe sheaves had to be threshed to remove all grain so mice and birds would not bother the thatch. I made my own knife to cut the straw straight across a sheaf. I did not have the correct blacksmith equipment to curve the knife, so it wasn't exactly like the ones we knew in Ukraine.

Ukrainian settlers in western Canada used several different thatching methods according to the origins (the village and province) and the thatcher's previous experience. Tools were brought from the homeland or fashioned on the homestead, then shared among neighbours. The grass was either cut with a scythe or serrated sickle, or pulled up by the roots. It was laid in straight piles or gathered in sheaves to dry. The cleanest and longest straw was then passed through a coarse wooden comb (*chasivnetsia*) to lay the individual stalks in the same direction and remove tangled leaves and other foreign matter. The thatcher cut the straw into even lengths by putting each small sheaf into a cutting box with a knife hinged onto one end. The sharp knife cut across the butt end and ensured even, finished sheaves.

Sheaves of about sixteen inches (41 cm) in diameter initially were split with a twist, forming a double sheaf. Made pliable by a brief soaking in a barrel of warm water (in the fall, a fire would be lit beneath the barrel to keep it at the appropriate temperature) and joined by a twist of straw, the twin sheaves were bent around the rafter (*krokva*), secured, and tightly tucked in under each other to make a solid, tight bond. The first layer of thatch was laid along the eaves (*ostrishok*) for a trim effect, with the straight-cut, stubble end placed to face downward. The remaining sheaves applied above the eave layer were placed on the rafters (*krovlia*) with the cut-end stubble facing upward. The grain, or top end, of the straw pointed down, creating a smoothly sloping surface by virtue of the irregularly tapered tops. The firmer the thatch's purchase on the roof, the more watertight it became. The thatcher took extra care to ensure a tight roof, employing a special thatcher's mallet to create a tight weave. Successive bundles of thatch provided a thick covering, as each bundle overlaid about three-quarters of the previous layer. At the roof's ridge, another layer of thatch, stubble-end down, was secured in place with a long, tightly-woven, overlay made of hemp canvas (*polotno*), and loose straw was placed over the sheaf tops. The final touch was a row of thin poles (*kizla*) set along either side of the ridge to keep the canvas and thatch in position. These poles, secured together to form an *X (yarno)*, were set over the ridge about every three feet (91 cm), and the roof was then complete. Sometimes a wooden trough (*paluba*) was added to give the roof a finished look.

In 1917 and 1918, a drought in Saskatchewan and southern Alberta created a scarcity of grain and straw. Farmers from southern Alberta and Saskatchewan came up in carts and traded shingles (*dranytsi*) for the straw thatch of the roofs on Ukrainian farmsteads. The southern farmers went home with grain and straw and the northerners had fine, new shingle roofs. That is perhaps one reason why there are so few thatched roofs left in the Ukrainian blocs in these two provinces. Replacing thatch roofs with shingles also reduced concerns regarding the material's susceptibility to fire. Finally, the use of shingles also provided greater flexibility for the builder, who no longer found it necessary to construct the steeply pitched roof required for thatching.

Mud-Plastered Homes

Unlike other settlers from Europe who did not use clay plaster, most Ukrainian pioneers thickly plastered mud on both the inside and outside of their new log homes.[6] Wooden pegs and thin willow laths kept the plaster on the rough log walls. In subsequent buildings, rough-sawn laths were used on squared logs to provide additional purchase (Lehr 1976, 18). Many of the pioneer Ukrainian houses remaining in the Alberta parkland still boast their original coat of mud plaster (comprised of clay, straw, manure, and water). Topsoil was removed from a sizable area to ensure access to clean, humus-free clay. Clay and water were mixed in a shallow pit dug about six inches (15 cm) into the ground. To break down the clay, the settlers trampled it with their feet or led an ox or horse repeatedly through the pit. Straw and dung were added to this mixture. Horse dung was preferred because it was a stronger binder. Finely-chopped straw prevented the plaster from cracking upon drying. The

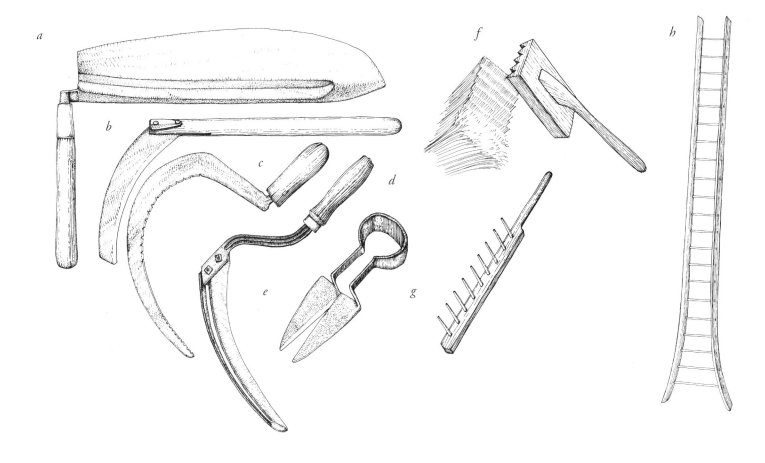

Fig. 3:7

Drawings of Thatching Tools

Pictured are some of the thatching tools used on the replicated Ukrainian settler's home in Elk Island National Park that was a commemorative memorial to early homesteaders. The author had observed Peter Svarich's "*toloka*," whereby a group of seniors undertook the task of thatching the home (*poshyta khata*) the same way thatchers (*poshyral'nyky*) would have done it in the past.

    a. Crofter's (*vkryval'nyk*) Knife; razor-sharp, used for trimming and finishing the thatch

    b. Thatcher's (*poshyval'nyk)* Rough-trim Knife (*nizh do sina*)

    c.; d. Hand-sickles (*serpy*); the serrated edge was used for cutting course, slough hay, while the finer blade was used for softer, stemmed hay

    e. Trimming Shears (*nozhytsi*); used by several of the workers for edge finishing (commonly used for sheep shearing)

    f. Thatcher's Maul; used for tightening up the sheaves both vertically and horizontally

    g. Thatcher's Comb (*chasivnetsia*); removed loose leaves and other foreign materials from the sheaves placed on to the rafter beams

    h. Thatcher's Ladder (*drabyna*); specifically built for stability where climbers cannot steady themselves, for example, when carrying a hod full of sheaves prior to setting them

a

b

f

g

d

c

h

e

i

Fig. 3:8

Stages in the Thatching Process

    a. Sorting uniform bundles of straw for sheaves

    b. Removing the leaves and chaff with a comb (*chashivnetsia*)

    c. Cutting with a sharp straw cutter (*sichkarnia* or *sikach*) and
        providing a uniform base for the butt-end of the sheave

d. e. f. Tying a sheaf (*snip*) with a twist of straw (*pereveslo*) and then
        splitting the sheaf to encompass the rafter and secure it in place

   g.; *h*. Fitting the sheaves securely on to the rafters (*banty*)
        in a weather-proof pattern (*puky na strikhu*).

    i. A *maister* craftsman putting the finishing
        touches to the gable end (*prychilok*)

mixture was thrown by the handful with enough force to wedge it into spaces between logs, and then smoothed with a wet hand. Plaster was applied in three coats. The primary coating was one or two inches (2.5 or 5 cm) thick; the secondary coat was of finer materials (including sand) about one-quarter inch (0.6 cm) thick; and the outer covering was lime.

After the patching of any cracks, the plaster was coated with a mixture of slaked lime and water. Sometimes skim milk and a little washing blue were added (washing blue was a product available in early general stores, used to wash clothing. It functioned like bleach when it was added to the final rinse of white clothing). Lime was brought in large chunks, put into a big container, and warm water was poured over it. The mix would boil and then slacken. The slaked lime formed a thick, smooth paste, almost like butter. This was mixed with sand and water and then brushed onto the walls (Magera interview 1978).[7] An aesthetically pleasing white stucco resulted that served to protect the exterior walls from disintegration from rain wash. Lime also protected the house from insect and rodent invasion. The plaster had a tendency to crack and, although long-lasting when well-maintained, would deteriorate rapidly if neglected. Many houses were later covered with shiplap (*zahata* – boards that overlap) to the level of the window sills to protect against the two greatest hazards, children and poultry (children at play would scratch the finish, and poultry would peck at the walls to get at the grains of sand for their gizzards).

My experience with plastering occurred much later than the initial construction of clay-plastered buildings in the early 1900s. As a young lad growing up on a pioneer farm, I was involved in the repair and refurbishment of these pioneer buildings in the late 1930s and early 1940s. The elders insisted that all able-bodied children participate in the work.

My maternal grandmother Martha Shandro lived about thirty-five miles to the west of us, and she always had the low-down on all our uncles, aunts, cousins, and so on, recalling anecdotes about interesting events in the entire Shandro community. When she came to visit, she would regale us with stories of social events of the past year: weddings; births; who was going out with whom; reviews of all the successes and failures of each member of the extended families, and the neighbours, of course. Grandma was the source of all of this news. We children would listen carefully to catch it all, and we observed her every gesture. Some things were not verbally expressed for fear we might learn too much. She would use her hands showing the huge side of the pregnant one and various facial expressions as a code to my mother, but we soon caught on. These stories became particularly colourful in the evening after supper when we were supposed to be asleep, but early bedtimes did not happen when Grandma Shandro came to visit.

We lived on a turn-of-the-century farm when I was a kid in short pants (cut short to do away with the big holes in the knees). Our farm had evolved as a homestead, and many of the outbuildings were of log construction. Rehabilitation of one or two of the buildings took place every spring. Grandma Shandro initiated this event when she came to visit every year at that time. The day after she arrived, she would go on an inspection tour of the farmstead. She would examine the garden, animals, and farm buildings. She was very perceptive and before you knew it, she had us organized in a plastering bee. She would pick one of the buildings that showed signs of weathering, and that would be our project for the next two days. These buildings were usually used for grain storage and had to be leak-proof so the grain would remain dry and not run out through holes between the logs onto the ground below. The walls were originally all covered with a clay plaster. However, as the years went by, clay chunks fell out, deteriorated, and were perforated, tunnelled through by mice. The granary became porous, rendering it unfit for grain storage.

Our job was to refurbish and restore the buildings to their original condition. This was no problem because Grandma was an expert. She had the key recipe. Clay, straw, manure, and water in the appropriate proportions made up the plaster. My father had previously prepared the necessary ingredients, having brought a load of clay (it had to be the stickiest kind), a barrel of warm water, and some clean, sharp sand. These were all nicely organized in a row together with shredded straw and a small pile of dried horse buns. However, he was busy with spring seeding and left the job to Grandma and the grandchildren. We were her work crew.

We had a shallow pit with the topsoil removed where we placed the clay and added the other ingredients, mixing up the whole mess with our bare feet. My brother, my two sisters, and I, with our pants rolled up, enjoyed the squishy mixture between our toes. Grandma knew exactly what the recipe portions were and when the "dough" had reached the right consistency. She kept adding water, straw, and horse dung. We kept kneading the mixture with our feet and enjoying every minute of it. It was now ready for the next stage, the plastering of the building.

Our job now was to take the thick slurry and close all of the holes between the logs. The wet, sticky plaster was thrown by the handful with enough force to wedge it into the spaces between the logs. (In the process, occasional wet balls of clay would miss the building and go flying into a sibling's head or chest. This always seemed to happen when Grandma was not watching. Of course, this gave her an opportunity to decide who would have to stay after the job was done to clean up the

Clay Plastering of a Small Log Barn

job site. Somehow, I always managed to earn the honour of being part of the clean-up crew.)

Once the cracks were full, one would wet one's hand in a bucket of water and smooth the plaster. The first coat was the rough base coat, the secondary coat was a thin layer of finer materials including some sand, and the final coat was brushed-on slaked lime, which was my grandmother's specialty. She made a thick smooth paste, almost like butter. She would add bluing to the layer on the bottom of the building, as well as a good quantity of some sharp sand. This protected the plaster near the ground from weathering.

Again reflective of the distinctions among the Ukrainian immigrants, the timber walls were occasionally left exposed. These houses were usually built by settlers who came from the mountainous area of the Hutsuls in Carpathia (*Hutsul'schyna*). Traditionally, they built with large diameter trees, so their homes did not need insulating plaster. Hutsul settlers in areas of Alberta where good pine stands were available were able to

maintain their building traditions. Families in the Shandro district of Alberta used the excellent timber found in the North Saskatchewan River valley, and they, too, never plastered the exterior of their buildings. Anastasia Shandro Zazula told me in an interview in 1956 about how her father, Nikon Shandro, built their house without plaster on the walls as was routinely done in the area the Shandros came from (Rus'kyi Banyliv in the upper Carpathians, officially renamed Banyliv in 1947).

It was thatched at first, but the wind blew some of it off, so it was later shingled. Our house had no plaster on the outside because the houses in our village in Ukraine had no plaster. There were many good trees there in the Carpathian Mountains and there was no need for mud. The thick logs did not require additional insulation. So, our house in Alberta just had logs with no mud plaster on the outside. There were no nails, just pegs. Building tools were brought from Ukraine.

Window and door frames were often painted in bright contrasting colours such as yellow, blue, red, or green. Sometimes shingled roofs and trim shared the same colour. The inner and outer walls, when completely encased in earth plaster, provided insulation superior to that produced by the common North American practice of chinking between the logs with mud and moss.

Traditional customs such as these along with the natural resources at hand constituted the basic building practices used by early Ukrainian settlers in Canada. The Ukrainians who settled in the Prairie Provinces used local materials to build their new homes, yet as much as possible, they maintained the building techniques and traditions of Ukraine, particularly the religious ceremony that marked the home's completion, as was conveyed to me by Peter Svarich in an interview in 1956:

A newly-built home was usually blessed and then the priest, dressed in robes, would sprinkle it with holy water, insert into each corner stone space a small picture of a disciple, and seal the pictures in. These holy duties were followed by a dinner at which offerings of bread (the small, round *kalachi*) were handed out as gifts in memory of their deceased ones.

In later years the descendants of the pioneers carried on some of the old traditions. I recall my father placing a blessed "orthodox cross" on the east façade roof gable facing the rising sun. This was a simple cross designed to stick up above the apex formed by the roof rafters. The framing of the new house had just been completed and the sheathing was underway. This cross was to ward off evil and unfortunate events for the duration of the building's construction. When the roof was shingled, the cross was removed.

Permanent House Interior Design — *Khata*

The traditional Ukrainian pioneer home, rectangular and south-facing, was divided into two large rooms, generally separated only by a hallway or vestibule that was usually used as a utility area. Sometimes the ceiling was made of planed and jointed boards. When it was constructed with small poles, it was plastered on both sides like the walls, then the inside ceiling was white-washed together with the walls. The steeply-pitched roof created a large, open attic. Access to the attic was through a hatch in the central vestibule, or through a trap door under the wide, overhanging eave on the outside of the house. In houses where the chimney ended at the attic level, the smoke dissipated into the attic and through vents in the thatch, providing a perfect place to cure hanging meat and fish. Strings of fruit slices and bunches of herbs and flowers were also dried and stored here. Dampness was not a problem, so the attic was used for storing clothes. It also provided extra sleeping space for large families (Pidruchney interview, 1987). Virtually all the early homes had earth floors made of a hard-stamped clay mixture with a solid surface (Mundare 1980, 487).[8] The floor was given a regular coating of a mixture of cow dung and water, which gave a polished effect upon drying – a precursor to modern linoleum. When the reflection of light from coal oil lamps on the new floor mimicked a mirror, the floor was considered finished.

The west room was where the family cooked, ate, socialized, and slept. This warm, busy space was dominated by the clay *pich* that served as stove, oven, heater, and warm sleeping platform. The *pich* was made of the same materials as the house – wood and mud. First, a strong wooden bench about three feet (91 cm) high was constructed in the inside corner of the room. The space under the bench was used to store firewood. The top platform of the bench was built up with a brick-thick layer (sometimes of mud plaster, sometimes with flat stones) over which a cylindrical frame of flexible and interlaced willow branches was constructed. A thick layer of clay mud was spread on and over the interior of the frame, and the whole interior was then reinforced with pleated willow wood (resembling a basket weave) to ensure a sturdy structure. Mud was packed solidly over sand fill and then covered with a thick layer of plaster. The top of the cylindrical structure was filled in and levelled to form a wide bench, providing a warm bed for children or the elderly. All the surfaces were gently but firmly beaten with a wooden mallet to make the clay firm and dense. As the clay dried and cracks began to appear, another coat of

clay would be solidly packed on. At the side of the *pich* opening, a firebox for cooking was built of fired clay brick or stones. A hood in front of the opening of the *pich* collected the smoke. A chimney of pleated willow reinforced with mud was built in front of and above the oven (Dowsett 1986). When the oven was completed, a very hot fire was built inside to fire the clay (Zukiwsky interview 1956) as one would fire ceramics. Once the structure cooled, a finishing layer of mud was smoothed on the oven's inside walls. When the oven was fired for baking, the earthen structure of the *pich* radiated an even heat well into the early morning.

An outdoor *pich* was often built using the same materials and techniques. During the summer, baking was done outside to keep the house cool. This outdoor *pich* was covered with a thatch of grass or hay, or with a tarpaulin to keep the rain from destroying the mud plaster.

To use the *pich* for cooking, a fire was built inside the oven to heat it, and then the coals were cleaned out with a long *kotsiuba* (a wooden, hoe-like implement). The heat was retained for baking by closing the oven door. The chimney, being outside the oven, did not draw out the hot air once the oven door was in place. To regulate heat, the door was opened or closed by degrees. Baking and roasting were done inside the *pich* oven, while boiling and frying were done on the *shparhut*[9] (a cast-iron plate with either three eight-inch [20 cm] lids, or a concave hollow in the cooking surface which fit over the firebox).[10] The women learned through experience how to bring the oven to the desired temperature, building a fire of an appropriate size and intensity to suit the particular food being cooked. After raking the ashes from the hot oven, the cook tested the heat in a number of ways. Some merely reached inside the oven to "feel" the heat. Others scraped the bottom with a *kotsiuba* to see if sparks flew, or they would throw a piece of straw or paper into the *pich* to see if it would singe or flare. If the temperature was too high, the wooden *kotsiuba* would be singed and would send sparks flying as it was rubbed over the hot brick bottom. When the temperature was right, food was placed in the hot oven with a flat wooden *lopata* (spatula). The door of the *pich* was usually a large board propped shut with a stick (meticulous bakers sealed the door with clay). The oven cooked food slowly, much like today's slow-cookers, and allowed women to spend the day in the fields, knowing the meal would be ready and still warm when the family returned in the evening.

Meals were served on tables roughly hewn from planks. Most of the furniture was homemade: a family might spend its evenings sitting on wooden benches and stools and its nights on homemade beds or plank platforms. For the latter, planks were laid across benches and the resulting platform was spread

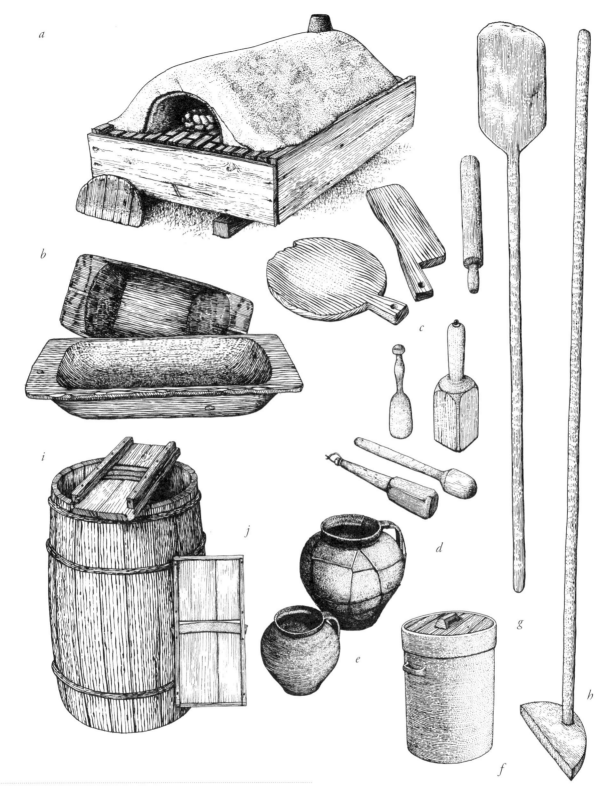

Fig. 3:9

A "*Pich*" with Bread-making Utensils and Sauerkraut Barrel

a. Earthen Peel Oven; a *pich* was usually placed adjacent
  to and outside the home for summer cooking.

b. Wooden Bread Pans (*koryto*, pl. *koryta*); carved out of local woods.

c. Rolling Pin and Wooden Spatulas (*kruzhok*), used
  for removing hot dishes from the *pich*.

d. Meat Tenderizers, Pestles (*makohony*), and miscellaneous kitchen tools.

e. Ceramic Pots (*hornytsi*).

f. Wooden Flour Barrel; containers for food storage.

g.; *h*. Peel Spatula (*lopata*); used to remove hot bread from the
  oven. Also pictured is the oven cleaning tool (*kotsiuba*,
  also *kocherha*) used to clear out the embers and ashes
  prior to placing the loaves in the oven for baking.

i.; *j*. Pickle Barrel with Cabbage Shredder (*shekivnetsia*).

with a woven straw mat. A few pioneers who had served as field soldiers in the Austro-Hungarian army learned how to weave firm, two-inch-thick straw mattresses that were rolled up when not in use. *Peryny* (fluffy feather pillows and quilts) containing wild goose down and duck feathers were common accessories.

Pioneer families hulled and crushed grains used to prepare various dishes. The simplest method was the *stupa*, a mortar and pestle type of grain huller and crusher that used foot power to increase efficiency. This made it easier to prepare the various sizes (coarse to fine cooking grains) from hulled ryes and barleys, to cracked wheat, to ground meal. Flax seed was cracked for use in porridge, and poppy seed was used in the *kutia* (a wheat-honey and poppy seed dish prepared for Christmas). Each of these grains was important in the preparation of various traditional dishes.

The primary component of the *stupa* is the pestle, a hardwood block three feet long, two feet wide, and two feet high, with a sixteen-inch-diameter hole drilled in the middle and a steel plate firmly set into the bottom. The mortar was a swinging wooden mallet which fit snugly into this depression. Sometimes it also had a steel plate. The mallet was mounted on a beam that rested on a fulcrum between two rails attached to the mortar block. Operating much like a see-saw, it swung easily up and down with the application of foot pressure by the person standing on the *stupa*. For the comfort of the operator (usually one of the older children in the family), a rail on each side provided a hand-hold and stabilized the operation. With the patina of hard use and age, these wooden instruments would glow, the wood grains expressing the natural colour pattern of the wood as the result of absorbed oils and waxes from various oilseeds.

The west room might also contain the quern mill or *zhorna*, an ancient hand-milling device. If *zhorna* were not brought from Ukraine in large wooden chests, they were made from specially-selected fieldstones common in the area. Before a quern mill was built or acquired, the early pioneers regularly walked seventy to eighty miles to Fort Saskatchewan to buy sacks of flour, sometimes carrying them home on their backs. For obvious reasons, grinding grain into flour at home was preferable and soon became the custom.

Zhorna consisted of two large stones chiselled into round, flat pieces that fit closely on top of each other. These chiselled stones were carved from hard rock, preferably a solid limestone four to five inches thick and sixteen to eighteen inches in diameter. It was fitted into a gouged-out hole that was about ten inches deep and eighteen inches in diameter, in a three-foot by two-foot by one-inch wooden block (*ktelsok*). The top stone had a four- to five-inch rounded hole into which an iron rod was inserted on the underside. This shaft sat in a hole on a

raised support and provided the "axle" for the top stone that was evenly balanced upon it. The bottom stone was held firmly in place and didn't turn, but it had a hole in the centre through which the iron shaft passed. This held the top stone that could be set to provide a coarse grind such as cracked wheat, or lowered to make a heavy grind of fine, whole-grain flour. To set the grind, the iron bar was moved backward and forward mechanically on its support. This lowered and raised the top millstone.

Preparing millstones was a difficult task, usually requiring the specialized knowledge and experience of a stone dresser or a millwright. Furrows had to be cut on the working face of the stones and the area between them levelled. In milling, the furrow on the top stone breaks up the grain through friction against the bottom stone and guides the meal from the eye of the stone to its skirt, where flour is collected. The millwright marked out selected stones with a "goose" feather brush laying out a furrow spline. This brush was dipped into an "ink" of soot and water. A land spline, a wider strip, is marked beside each furrow spline. The process is repeated until the entire stone is marked all around the centre. The furrow did not follow the true radius, but was instead marked just off-centre below the centre hole.

A hardened steel hammer-head, tapered at each end to form a *molotok* (chisel wedge), was used for dressing the working face of a millstone; this tool was called a "Mill Bill and Thrift" (the English term for a *molotok* used by millwrights). The stationary bed stone on the bottom had to be level. Charcoal was lightly applied to the matching surface of the topmost stone. After the top stone was properly dressed, it was rotated over the surface of the bottom stone. If the stones were properly

Typical Zhorna Found in Old Pioneer Homes

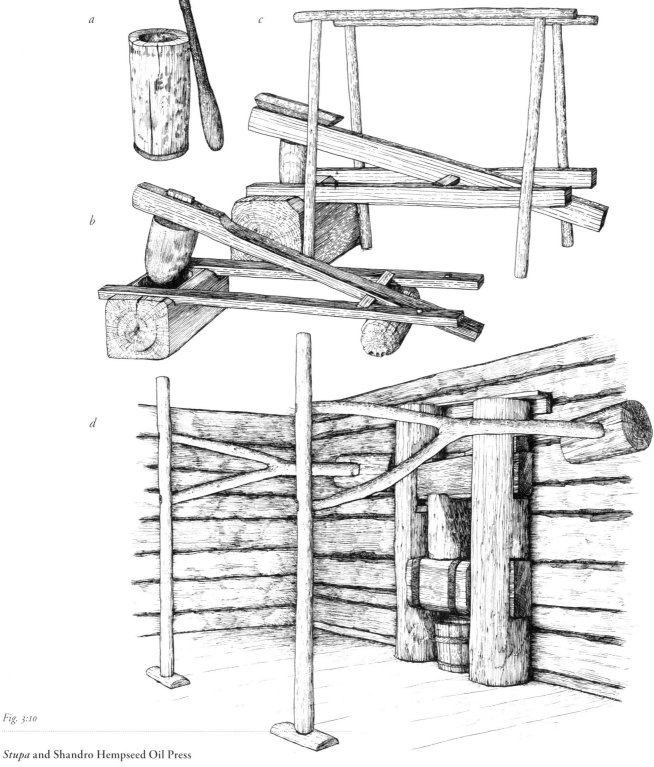

a

c

b

d

Fig. 3:10

Stupa and Shandro Hempseed Oil Press

These were very important tools in the pioneer household, repre-
senting the early stage in the processing of oils; crushing, mash-
ing, pressing, and extracting the desired product.

    a. Mortar and Pestle (*tovkach*); an early form used to pound
        and crush grains, and to hull and crack kernels.

    b. Foot-pedal-style Mortar and Pestle (*tovkach*); this
        model was much easier on the operator.

    c. This mortar and pestle takes the improvements one step
        further, providing arm supports for ease of use.

    d. The Shandro Hemp-seed Oil Press (*oliinytsia*); used to
        extract oil from pre-heated seed-cakes consisting of dried
        and heated seed mash. Flax, sunflower, poppy, and hemp
        seeds were processed by this press. Note the wooden bucket
        under the compression cylinder used to collect the oil.

Dress Clothing Hung On Pegs, including Sheepskin Coats

Tall Clay Heating Oven

aligned, charcoal would be evenly distributed over the whole surface. The craftsman worked the stone until he got a fine, level, matching surface on both stones. Constructing a quern mill required a sensitive feel for setting up a balanced set of stones (Potrebenko 1977, 7–8). The pioneer not only needed to have a "feel" for the mineral (its hardness and the appropriate type of stone), but also had to have some knowledge of the construction of quern mills. These people were craftsmen who knew natural materials and how to use their tools. Considering these factors, it is interesting to note that there were quite a few quern mills spread throughout the pioneer community. Many in the Manitoba Ukrainian blocs used the locally available, tindel limestone for their quern mills.

The wooden bed of the quern rested on four stout legs mortised into the base of the block. These were sometimes strengthened with cross braces. Two arms on either side of the block, connected with a bar, stretched over the centre of the stones. An "arm" (or handle) was affixed to the middle of this bar, with its lever end finished in a steel socket that rested in a hole on the edge of the top stone. The miller grabbed this arm with his/her right hand and turned the stone to grind grains at the desired speed. The miller threw in grain with his left hand from a small reserve cavity on the top wooden block. The milled flour fell through a slot under the millstones. The grain that then passed between the grind stones and the flour poured into a wooden pail below.

When I interviewed Helen Solowan Boychuk in Edmonton 1977, she spoke wistfully about the social, familial aspects that accompanied the grinding of grain in her family. **"We had some wheat and threshed it by hand with a flail. Momma

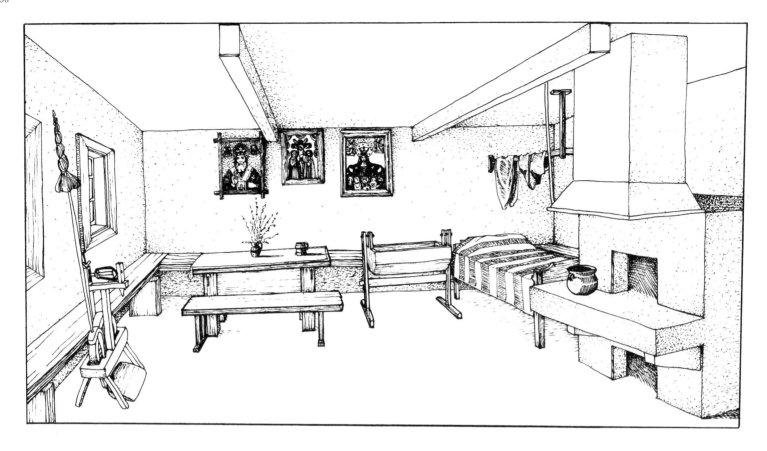

Fig. 3:11

Large Parlour in the Main *Khata* — *Svitlytsia*

The east room was considered special; the best and brightest room where
social gatherings were held and where the family's weaving, sewing, and
woodworking crafts were displayed, along with treasures from the homeland, such as tapestries of wool, hemp, or flax in richly coloured, geo-
metric patterns. *Vereny* covered the beds and benches. Next to the bed,
you might have a baby's crib (*kolyska*). On the east wall hung the icons
of Christ and the Virgin Mary. Here and there you would see a finely
carved wooden chest filled with the best finery. Of course, the large
earthen stove *pich,* with a chimney through the ceiling (*komyn*), occupied
a place of prominence in this large room, also known as a "*svitlytsia.*"

made flour on the stone mill. My sister and I took turns at the
mill. I got so mad that my sister was slow, I turned the wheel
fast. This made the flour coarse. Momma made me grind it all
over again."

Storage

Most homes had a cabinet for dishes attached to the wall next
to a row of wooden pegs on which clothes were hung. The
wooden boxes and chests in which the pioneers carried their
possessions from Ukraine could be found in either the west
or east room, depending upon how ornate the finish. Carved
chests were reserved for the storage of clothing and other finery
(see Fig. 2:1).

Grandparents slept in the east room when they lived with
a married son and grandchildren in an extended family. In
later years, the resourceful settler often passed a long sleeve of
stovepipes horizontally through the dividing wall and into the
east room before directing the smoke through the roof. Later, a
wood stove or an upright heater was introduced to heat it.

4

One Hundred and Sixty Acres

Homesteading

Having addressed the challenges Ukrainian immigrants faced with respect to their lengthy journey and the struggle to secure shelter upon their arrival in Canada, we turn now to a discussion of the yearly farm cycle, from sowing to harvesting, of the fields and the gardens. Homesteading was the only officially-sanctioned way Ukrainians could enter Canada. Whatever trades they may have practised back home, Canada's *Homestead Act* made farmers of them all. This chapter outlines the materials used and the processes developed to adapt traditional farming and gardening methods to the new climate and circumstances encountered in Canada, as well as the socio-cultural aspects involved.

The pioneers began by clearing an initial area of about five[1] acres and planting their first crop. Most had a strong agricultural background, but they found the ruggedness of the Canadian environment and its vigorous climate challenging. They needed to learn about seasonal variations, the suitability of crops, and the nature of the new soils. No longer were they farming on six feet of *chornozem* (the black loam of Ukraine).

Instead, they had only six to twelve inches of precious topsoil breaking the virgin prairies in the Canadian West. Further north were the grey soils of the Peace region. The mild climate of their homeland, suited to growing apples, peaches, grapes, corn, walnuts, and beeches (a *sad*), was but a memory. The new yearly cycle of sharp cold winters that carried well into April, with cool summers and a long Indian summer, demanded new cropping practices, new varieties of grains and vegetables, and new breeds of animals. Their learning period was intensified by the size of their 160-acre homesteads. They must have seemed overwhelming when compared to the small plots they had left behind, usually about one-twentieth that size and sometimes even smaller than that. Although nature was bountiful, they were in a strange land with few tools. The first year challenged the courage of those who braved the wilderness with only the barest of necessities, their skills, and their hardy spirit. It was truly a trial by fire (an ironic phrase, given the deep cold of their first Canadian winter on the plains).

Once the permanent home was built, families began slowly adding to the homestead by constructing new farm

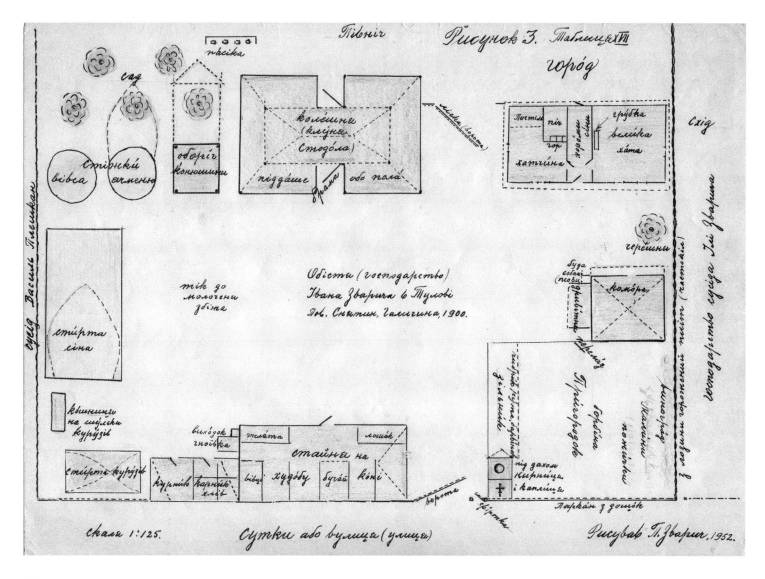

Fig. 4:1

Layout of the Svarich Farmstead in Tulova

This organization is representative of the usual layout, having
a central courtyard with all buildings around the periph-
ery. Farms tended to be organized the same way in Canada.
Courtesy Provincial Archives of Alberta, PR. 1975.74/1277.

buildings. The barn (*stainia*) was of primary importance, followed by the *komora* (a multi-use storage building that served as a summer kitchen and was used for unheated storage during the winter). The large granary *komora* with a drive-through corridor became the hub of operations for grain handling and food storage, and it was needed to hold the ever-increasing crop. However, once the large *khata* house replaced the original one-room *khatyna*, this small, one-room house became the centre of operations for the farm. It housed milking utensils, the cream separator, and storage for crates and for cooling eggs. It was also where workers changed into their work clothes. All laundry and washing was carried out here in the summer, and it was often used as a kitchen during the summer months. Sometimes it housed the large loom and other utensils used for making cloth and for weaving.

These buildings were located some distance to the rear of the main house. This is where most of the farmstead operations took place. The barn, chicken house (*kurnyk*), pig barn (*kucha*), corrals, and haystacks formed an interior parallelogram around a service yard (*grazhda*). It is interesting to note that many of their holdings in the homeland were tight courtyard complexes forming a small, square, central court. Land in Ukraine was scarce and was used very efficiently. Again, the settlers duplicated the old country practices whenever possible, in this case, laying out their buildings similar to the way they were organized in Ukraine.

This was also probably their loneliest year, for the land was sparsely settled. In later years, as old friends and new neighbours arrived and settled adjoining quarters, communities were formed. Neighbours shared the larger tasks faced by each family, making the workload less dreary and more manageable. In the surrounding environs, neighbours included various specialists such as artisans, blacksmiths, and craftsmen who had brought specialized tools and equipment with them. As was noted in chapter two, this kind of specialist was known as a *maister* (master tradesman) in the community, an honorary term conferred by their peers. These specialties were important and some, such as master craftsmen, carpenters, iron-workers (blacksmiths), and thatchers, were quickly and widely recognized. They were soon able to begin trading their services.

Although the farming year began with frost leaving the ground, much preparation preceded the disappearance of snow. Repairs were made to ploughs, harrows, seed spreaders, harnesses and yokes for oxen, axes, forks, and shovels; new handles replaced broken ones; new tools were fashioned for the coming spring; and seed bags and baskets were mended in readiness for the busy planting season. As soon as the snow and frost receded, fields were made ready for planting. In order to use the natural force of frost action, which broke up clumps of soil and made the fields fertile and productive, most fields were turned the previous autumn and harrowed in the spring. Many farmers made their own wooden harrows, but these broke easily and were relatively ineffective. Some resorted to using a heavy drag harrow (made of a beam broad-axed from sturdy timber) trailing a willow-pleated levelling layer to form a smooth seedbed (young, green willow branches were pleated to form a grid that was then attached to a draw-bar for harrowing).

Seeding was done by hand, the traditional method of broadcasting seed over harrowed ground. As birds could scavenge seeds on the surface, a second harrowing was necessary. Where proper equipment was not available, the resourceful tiller used a wooden hand rake fashioned during the winter from birch and willow to lightly cover seeds with rich soil, thus keeping them from birds and encouraging earlier germination.

Many seed varieties brought by the settlers were not suitable for the short Canadian summers. Those that withstood the test of the first season, such as hard spring wheat, became mainstays of the food supply. A very popular and successful prairie wheat, "Red Fife" (*Halychanka* wheat), originally came to Canada from Galacia in Ukraine.[2] Western wheat varieties still contain the Halychanka genes. New strains were later obtained from Manitoba and the Dakotas, producing crops more suited to the abbreviated growing season. Among these were early maturing varieties of rye, wheat, oats, and barley.

Harvesting a Field of Oats with a Scythe   Hand-tied Sheaves Placed in Stooks

Making Hay While the Sun Shines

Producing high quality hay from native grasses using the simplest of tools required the utmost in good judgment, hard work, and a fourteen day stretch of sunny days. Haying operations began in July and were usually completed by the end of August (the harvest began in September). A scythe, whetstone, two wooden rakes, and a fork, along with an abundance of energy, were also needed. Hay was a very valuable energy resource for the sustenance of working draft animals, particularly horses. The settler would put up enough hay to feed a team of oxen or horses, and possibly a cow and calf, over the first winter. As the farm menagerie grew, the one-scythe system became outmoded and was replaced by horse-drawn mowers, such as horse-drawn rakes and racks and the Frost and Wood sickle bar (a reaper-mower with two driving wheels and a sickle cutting bar).

Most of the early hay was native grass found in woodland area openings or in meadows and around ponds or sloughs. The heavy root mat was able to support mowing with a "*kosa*" (scythe) and hand raking; hay was then carted off in horse-drawn racks. The grasses were perennials and provided a thick mass of stems and leaves each year. The expert husbandman knew that the best stage for cutting forage was between the "boot" and "early bloom" stage.[3] The finest hay resulted from knowing when the plants were at the ideal stage for producing easily digested forage. Early in spring, stalks would lengthen and go into flower, attaining the most vegetative stage. This was the time to cut and cure quality hay. The grass floral

organs are usually encased in a leaf covering called a boot. These clustered panicles mature quickly once extended out of the "boot," and the lignin content increases. The longer the grass grows beyond the "bloom" stage, the coarser and less nutritious the hay.

The time to mow was early in the morning when some dew was still on the stalks. This gave the hay stalks time to dry so the swath could be turned with big wooden rakes in the late afternoon. Hay was raked into cocks on the following day. Sedges and tall stands of reed canary grass sometimes required a second day of drying to prevent mould before it could be put into hay cocks. Cocks were round, conical stacks piled as high as a person could conveniently reach with a forkful of fresh hay. Initially, the base of the cock would be formed with some packing by foot and then built up into a peak that would shed rain. The sides and top were combed downward with a fork or rake to provide a rainproof surface that would shed water. Sunlight bleached only the surface so the field-dried hay was fresh, sweet, green, and free of mould and dust. Placing hay in cocks also provided temporary protection while the remaining hay was put up and before all the hay was brought to the farmstead to be carefully stacked in a large, all-season haystack.

Bringing hay to the farmstead involved the entire family. Hay cocks were placed onto horse-drawn racks with three-tined forks and then put up in large stacks next to the barn and the feeding pens. Stacks were carefully built up, layer upon layer. Each was then fed to a stacker, who placed and worked the stack, trampling each forkful into place and building a dense mass with vertical sides and a steeply peaked top. When the last top was in place, a ridge pole would be placed over the stack, weighed down with ropes and held in place with side poles on either side of the stack. Bringing the hay in quickly while it was still sweet smelling and green and then finishing the stack at home marked a time of jubilation. It was an assurance against a winter spent scrounging for scarce feed.

I vividly recall my first scything experience. It was morning, and the long fall rye stalks were up to my waist and still wet with dew, but my grandfather said this was the best time for scything. He had already sharpened the scythe, tapping the sharp cutting edge on a hand anvil to temper the steel, and then using a whetstone to hone it to a fine edge. My grandfather's scythe had a straight snath with a "J" shaped handle on the side and a high tensile, light yet deliciously sharp, Austrian blade. It was a tool that represented a marriage between art and function: a piece of sculpture. The blade was a beautiful sweep of steel, strong yet light, with a finely honed edge. Such a tool has been used since the time of the early Scythians,[4] at least 2,000–3,000 years. I felt that if anyone should know how to use a scythe, a lad of Ukrainian heritage should. I picked up the whetstone in its wooden pouch, filled it half-full of water, and hooked it onto my belt. With the scythe on my shoulder, we set off for the field.

My experience that day increased my respect for those men community seniors boasted could harvest five to ten acres a day. I lasted only four hours my first day, as I had worked up such a sweat that I had to stop. Yet between the "swooshes" of the blade, I enjoyed the leopard frogs, flowers, butterflies, and various grasshoppers and birds throughout the standing rye. Long before stopping for the day, I often paused to lean on the scythe as the breeze cooled my forehead and I took time out to "smell the roses" (or the fresh fallen rye, as the case may be). There was time in those days for work to include pleasure.

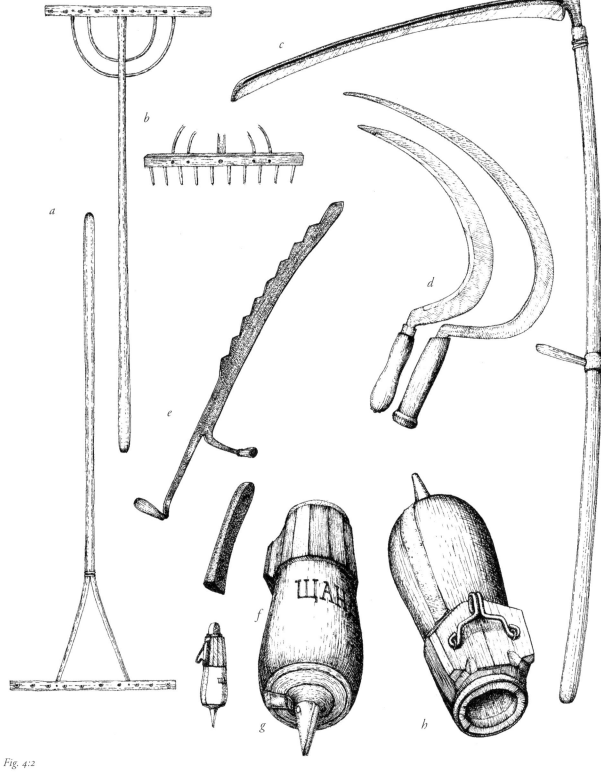

Fig. 4:2

Haying Tools; Scythe, Rakes, Whetstone, and Wooden Pouch

 a.; *b.* Wooden Hand Rakes (*hrabli*)

  c. Bukovynian Scythe (*kosa*); with a straight
   snaith and an Austrian steel blade

  d. Hand Sickles (*serpy*); used to cut long-stalked grains,
   then gather them into bunches to make sheaves

 e. Hay Knife (*nizh do sina*); used to cut stacked hay
  that has settled and is quite compacted

 f. Whetstone (*brusok*); used to sharpen scythe blades

 g.; *h.* Wooden Pouch (*koshka*); used in the field to hold water into
  which the whetstone is placed during hand-sharpening

Shandro Men Performing the Men's Harvest Dance on a Float at the Vegreville Fair

Four Large Stacks of Sheaves Ready for Threshing in the Late Fall

Threshing

The threshing of grain on the Canadian prairies developed in four phases according to the mode of power generation used. The first was hand-wielded flails, still commonly used in many parts of the Third World. The second phase joined horsepower or steam and gasoline power with stationary threshing machines as described below, while the third employed the portable and efficient modern threshing machines, predecessors to the contemporary combine harvester, the fourth and last phase.

Grain threshing, like many of the events on the pioneer farm, was a communal affair. Groups of five or six families would get together for a threshing bee. They would work their way from one settler's farm to the next as a group until the last family's threshing was done. The heads of the families would flail the grain while younger members winnowed the thresh and passed the sheaves. The direct exchange of labour from household to household was integral to the economy of the new community since money was scarce and hired help was unknown. At other times neighbours would help each other with spring plantings or provide several days of labour for erecting buildings or cutting logs. Adjoining neighbours were constantly in touch, exchanging services and stopping by to exchange home-grown vegetables, cooked dishes, or cuts of meat, a common practice after butchering a calf or hog. Women from adjacent farms came along to help with supper preparations for the threshers and all, of course, enjoyed the exchange of local gossip.

The threshing floor was a smoothly polished circle of ground, preferably of hard clay previously moistened and tamped to form a hard, firm surface. As the morning progressed, older boys fed the sheaves from nearby stacks to the threshers. Four experienced senior men wielded flails, standing in a circle and alternatively beating down in a flowing, circular motion. The sequence of flails coming down was like a wave. Soon a smooth rhythm was established. After each batch of sheaves was threshed, the men would change places, moving clockwise. This dance would continue until each had returned to his starting place. Sometimes they would break out into song, accompanying the beat of the threshing. It was thus that the traditional men's harvest dance evolved.

Two or three complete clockwise tours of the threshing floor called for a much-needed respite (a mid-morning break), then back to work! For the men and older children, it was relentless work, hot and dusty, with the continuous throb of the flails coming down on the dry straw. The pile of chaff, rich with kernels of grain, would be swept to a pile on the side and winnowed by the older children so new sheaves could be laid down. Straw was neatly stacked for later use as feed and bedding for the animals through the winter.

In the early years, threshing was done in the winter, as the first threshing machines were relatively slow and inefficient. It took time to move from one farm to the next, and the operation carried on into the winter months. Crops were cut with a scythe and cradle for the first, second, and sometimes even into the third pioneer years. The sheaves were then hand-tied

Steam Engine Operating a Twenty-eight-inch Cylinder Thresher

A Rack of Sheaves Arrives at the Threshing Machine

with a twisted length of straw and placed in stooks of seven or nine sheaves. After the stooks dried in the field, they were brought to the farmstead and, similar to the haying operations, were placed in tall round stacks with the cut-stubble ends to the outside. These stacks were carefully constructed with one of the family experts on top, placing each sheaf as it was pitched up from the horse drawn rack. The stacks looked like large peeled eggs on their flat bottoms, and were spaced to allow a rack to pass between them. Later a stationary threshing machine was pulled between the stacks as sheaves were fed directly into the machine's feeder.

My first role in the harvest season was that of tending the grain pouring into the granary (*shpykhlir*). I was to shovel it away from the spout and see that it was evenly spread as it poured in. By the end of the day, the granary was almost full. I was under the roof, and the opening of the door was quickly becoming a narrow slit. The closing whistle blew not a moment too soon. My escape was through the transom opening above the door and into the arms of my father below. I recall sleeping very soundly that night, and my mother had to poke me to wake me up in the morning. At six years of age, I began gradually increasing my duties during the seasonal harvest.

Before long I was stooking wheat, oats, and barley, then participating in threshing operations, initially as a field pitcher helping the men fill their racks and eventually graduating to having my own team of horses and a rack. When making too sharp a turn with an unbalanced load, I tipped the rack and lost half a load. My fellow workers hooted and cheered loudly: I could do no more than blush at experiencing this traditional rite of passage. At the age of twelve, I was now doing the work of a man. However, it took perhaps two years after being inducted into the farm work group before I was able to keep up

with the men. I looked after a fine pair of Percherons, drove out into the field, and loaded my rack. The days were long and the work tiring, but it was a happy and memorable time. My father and a neighbour, Alex Kusniruk, were partners, and their outfit looked after the threshing for about six other farmers in the vicinity.

The mechanized threshing machine came after the flail. These early machines were stationary, wood framed, and mounted on a substantial frame to stabilize them during operation. Power was supplied either by horse power or by a gasoline engine mounted on a separate frame. Early threshers were simple machines powered by horses hitched to a *kirat*.[5] The *kirat* was an early method used to transfer horse-power into a motive power drive for threshing before the arrival of the steam engine. Teams of horses (as many as six teams) would walk around a large central, cast-iron gear. This was mounted on a sturdy wagon frame, and the motive power was transferred via drive shaft and universal joints to the main drive on the threshing machine. Horse power was erratic, and the energy available varied a great deal. This energy source was also not sustainable over the long work day, thus horses were replaced by engine-powered drive belts as soon as possible. Whether horse powered or machine driven, the twine binding was cut by hand as each sheaf was hand-fed into the machine. As the straw came out of the far end, it was removed and piled using a pitchfork. A pitcher would feed sheaves one by one to the feeder-man, who would cut the twine of the sheaves and hand-spread it evenly as it was fed into the fast rotating cylinders. The straw went through the straw rack, where grain was shaken out, and only the straw emerged at the other end. Here a straw-man would pitch the straw onto a growing stack. The grain emerged at knee height out of a grain-pipe

A Large Grain Tank with a Four-horse Team

A Horse Binder Now Pulled by a Rubber-tired Tractor

into a bagger. Each bag of grain was loaded onto a wagon and taken to the *komora* (the farmstead's granary, usually the first all-purpose farm building that was constructed after the permanent house). The granary was a large building with a drive corridor through the centre and separate bins on each side for wheat, oats, barley, and rye, or for the storage of items such as hemp stalks, barrels of sauerkraut, etc. (see Fig. 4:3). A day's threshing was a thorough workout when you consider that a sack of wheat holds two bushels, weighing in at one-hundred and twenty pounds. The pioneers took freshly harvested wheat to the Mundare or Vegreville flourmill to exchange for flour, bran, and cream of wheat cereal.

These first threshing units were very scarce and were in active use from early fall to almost Christmas. They were mounted on special, heavy wagon gear and drawn by horse from neighbour to neighbour until the entire rural community was harvested. Not all farmers had sawing or chop-making outfits. Usually one farmer in the neighbourhood had the equipment and traveled from farm to farm, supplying the service. The wood-sawing bee was next to threshing. About six men were required, food was extra special, and comradeship was manifest. (Tomyn 1980, 540)

In the next developmental phase, steam engines were used for belt work on the early threshers. As early as 1910, the Shandro brothers, Andrew and Alex, obtained the International Farm Machinery Agency so they could sell tractors and other power machinery. They were one of the first farm families in the Shandro district to have a Case model steam tractor. Andrew Shandro's daughter, Pearl Shandro Landsman, describes the operations:

I remember those days of 1910 to 1913. The steam engine stood beside the house, and the Sawyer Massey separator was about ten feet behind. A wide black leather belt connected them, flywheel to flywheel. When father started the engine, the wheels made the treads of the feeder roll and carry the sheaves into the separators' cutting and sifting machine, sending the grain into the abutting granary and the straw from an elevated pipe directly into the barn loft and then into the corral. The rig was moved into the nearby pasture with the range animals, where the straw stack would feed and shelter them all winter. The grain went into wagons, some into sacks for milling into flour, cream of wheat cereal, and bran at the Mundare mill. The threshing outfit moved to other places during the several-week-long harvest. (Landsman 1999, 233)

Later model threshing machines were mechanical marvels, redesigned and refined, easily portable, pulled by tractors, and set up in the field where the stooks were readily accessible. Farmers combined forces, each farmer providing a team and rack with a teamster (the teamster was responsible for the rack and team) and perhaps a field pitcher (someone who loaded sheaves onto racks in the field). A full-fledged operation would consist of eight to twelve teams with four racks to a side, and two teams for hauling grain to storage bins. A powerful steam engine or gasoline tractor provided the belt power. When steam power was used, two additional teams were needed: one for the water wagon, the other for the hauling of fuel for the burner. Relocated anywhere in the field as needed, these portable machines had a moving self-feeder, a powerful straw blower, and a high grain elevator that poured and measured grain directly into the wagon box.

Later these huge, steam ironhorses were replaced with the more compact McCormick, Deering, and Moline gasoline tractors, all on steel wheels. In 1937 the rubber-tired tractors of

Fig. 4:3

Drawing of a Thatched *Komora* – A Pioneer's Storage House
This was a very important building on the early homestead, serving as an all-purpose storage building. Originally used as a threshing barn (*stodola*), it was usually located close to the house, and in some cases, had wide double doors with a driveway to allow farm wagon access. During the harvest, sacked grains were unloaded into bins on either side of the entryway for winter grain storage (a *shpyklir*). In addition to the storage place of the harvested grains (*korm, kormy*), other products such as broad beans, hemp seed, sorghum, peas and beans, corn cobs, and herbs were also placed here until needed. In winter, a side of beef or pork would be hung from the rafters. Later in the summer, eggs were gathered and placed in crates for shipping to the nearest depot. This building would also be used for separating cream from fresh milk, which would then be shipped to the nearest creamery. This, of course, did not take place till after the advent of the railway.

the Cockshutt, John Deere, Minneapolis, and Oliver tractor models were introduced. Binders were now mounted on rubber with twelve-foot-wide cutter-bars, and a power drive shaft took the place of the bull-wheel on horse drawn binders. Compact, efficient, and expertly designed threshing machines that were almost indestructible soon prevailed. We see them yet, guarding old farmsteads.

Later machines had knives, self-feeding cylinders, and powerful straw blowers powered by belt-driven tractors or steam engines. Modern threshers proved so successful that the next step was to mount them on a moving platform with a long sickle, resulting in the modern, self-propelled, diesel combine harvesters run by microelectronics and including televisions or radios inside comfortable, temperature-controlled cabs.

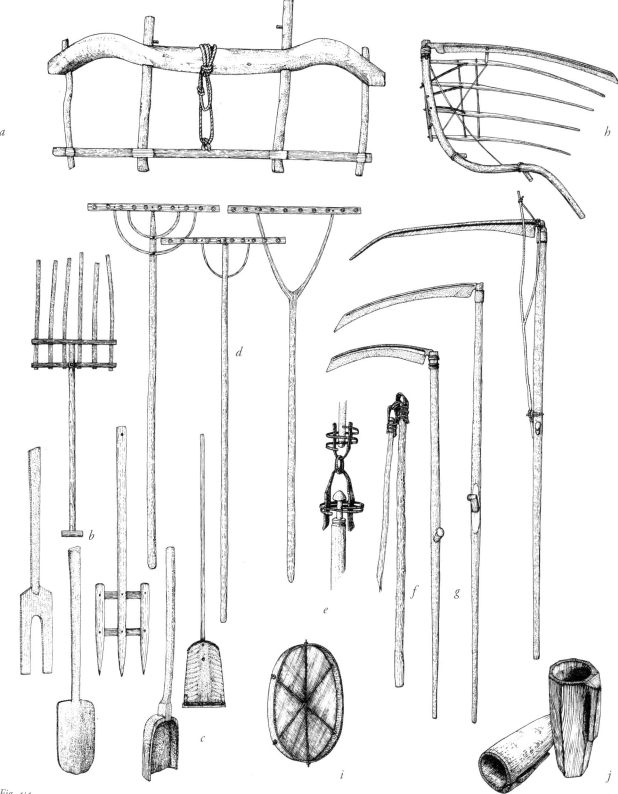

Fig. 4:4

Drawing of Barnyard, Haying, and Harvesting Tools

    a. Oxen Yoke (*yarma, or yarmo dlia voliv*)

b.; *c.* Barnyard Forks (*grali*) and Wooden Shovels (*shukhlia*)

    d. Rakes (*hrabli*)

    e. Flail (*tsip*) and a Rawhide Swivel Joint (*viazy*) and Stout Beater (*bylen*)

    f. Scythes (*kosy*); with straight snaiths

    g. Haying Scythe; used to form windrows

    h. Harvesting Scythe; used with cradle to form a sheaf (*snip*) with each cut

    i. Winnowing Sieve (*resheto, reshitka*)

    j. Wooden Pouches (*kushky*); used with whetstones (*brusok*) in the field during harvest

Gardening

Old habits die hard. In Bukovyna and Halychyna, everyone worked long hours on their garden plots and were thus sustained through lean and bountiful years. Each farmstead had to have a *hradka* (garden). As the days lengthened and once the grain crops had been planted, attention turned to the kitchen garden.

Sometimes gardens were developed in a systematic way. A small area would be fenced to serve as a corral for the livestock. Smudges were used to keep biting insects away. After a year or two, the area was ploughed under (the accumulated manure providing a very fertile garden) and vegetable production was profuse and bountiful. To establish an early crop, the settler's wife might employ a "cold frame" to start many of the cold weather vegetables (cabbages, cauliflower, potatoes, carrots, kohlrabi, etc.). This was usually a simple log frame of three feet by six feet located in a sheltered area that backed onto a wall or a board fence that reflected the sun's warmth. It was carefully located to gain maximum exposure during the day. Seeds started in this hot house would be transplanted to the garden at the appropriate time. The vegetable garden provided food during the heat of the summer when meat products were hard to keep. Leftover root crops were used in the early spring as fodder to supplement remaining hay or straw.

Potato peelings (the potato, for example) were saved to use in planting, and some of the last potato tubers and grain seeds were set aside for the coming year. Surplus plants were exchanged and shared with neighbours. A family short on seed would contact neighbouring families to barter work for valuable seed stock. "Grain and seeds were very scarce, and some were donated to others by earlier arrivals" (Semeniuk 1980, 480) who had arrived in time to prepare seed and tubers before winter set in.

Although gardening was considered by many to be women's work, men spent a great deal of time doing the labour intensive work of preparing the vegetable patch; planting, hoeing, and weeding. The earliest gardens were indeed the domain of pioneer women, but this was often indirectly the result of the men's absence when they were away seeking employment (noted in chapter two).

Gardens were planted with potatoes, beets, turnips, cabbage, onions, and garlic. Cool weather crops became the mainstays. In later years, carrots, parsnips, cucumbers, peas, and beans were added. Large broad beans were brought over from the homeland and became a protein staple.

Children willingly worked on the homestead. They pulled weeds, gathered edible wild plants such as mushrooms, collected eggs, and tended cows at pasture (not to mention plastering walls). From the 1930s to the 1960s, my mother, who had a green thumb, had a garden covering two acres. I remember well the aching joints and soiled knees from weeding rows and rows of onions, garlic, lettuce, cabbages, beets, endives, peas, and corn. We had perennials such as strawberries, raspberries, currants, and gooseberries. Then there was at least a half-acre of three or four varieties of potatoes. Our family was well nourished considering the supplementary eggs, chickens, beef, and dairy products like butter, milk, cream, and various homemade cheeses. Eggs and cream were shipped to the Alberta Dairy Co-op in Andrew, and we ate the surplus. Our cellar was replenished in the fall and the shelves were full for the winter. In retrospect, the task of tending the garden was repaid in a cornucopia of bounty. We were self-sufficient.

After the planting, attention turned to remodelling buildings: replacing leaky thatch on roofs, re-framing or shingling, or perhaps replacing a dirt-packed floor with a new wooden, planked one, projects that were described earlier.

Livestock

A discussion of farming practises would not be complete without a brief survey of the part livestock played in day to day operations. The Ukrainian settlers practiced mixed farming, and the production of livestock played a major role. Milk and beef were the principal commodities, supplemented with swine, poultry, ducks, and geese. Horses were the pride of every farmer, and each tried to own the finest horseflesh in their community as an expression of the pioneer era. The horse was the "king of energy" and the only power available. Percherons were the "kings" on our farm.

Included below are some representative quotes that outline some of the key features of livestock husbandry in the area.

Horses were an important part of farming operations and, with the assistance of the local District Agriculturalist, Fred Magera, Steve Fedorak and other farmers in the community organized the North Willingdon Percheron Stallion Club, the purpose of which was to purchase a registered, purebred Percheron stallion for one thousand dollars in the late 1930s. (Fedorak 1990, 348)

They laughed at Wasyl Zazula when he built his new chicken house. It was too big, they said. Why would anyone want one that size – fifty feet by twenty feet – in 1926? And two hundred chickens in there, too!

That was a reasonable question in Willingdon, Alberta, which as years went by, would often be called the "Poultry Capital of Alberta." For four or five years before that, he had raised a thousand turkey replacements for hatching eggs. In 1962, he had a throughput of 60,000 broiler chickens. He also put through 9,000 chicken broilers by August. Last year, he raised 4,000 turkeys and 9,000 broiler chickens. (Zazula 1983, 179)

For the year 1915, Robert Fletcher, the Supervisor of Schools among Foreigners, included a section on the industriousness and the material progress of the Ruthenians (among many aspects concerned with education and schools) in his annual report to his boss, the Honourable J.R. Boyle, K.C. MMP, Minister of Education. Below is an excerpt from that report in which Fletcher discusses livestock and domestic animals.

The effect of the success of settlers in their farm work is reacting to their ideas in comfort in living, improvements and extension in village operations. The increase in livestock and the improvement in general surface equipment on farms, the raising of hogs is growing to large proportions, and improvement in horse stock is very marked. Their heavy work horses, from Percherons to Clydesdales, have displaced the Cayuse, and the horses invariably show good keep. The settlement is well into the second stage of housemaking. The original shack or hut is being rapidly displaced by the real house. With more room and better floors and adequate lighting, the idea of greater comfort and greater attention to personal conditions is taking hold. (Fletcher 1917, 165)

5
Other Tasks

The settlers never had an idle moment, as anything they could not produce for themselves was generally unavailable due either to a lack of funds, to the distances involved in procuring the items, or to their ability to produce better products at home than what could be purchased. Farming and gardening were the principal activities, but numerous other tasks were required of the men and women (and children) charged with carving out a life on the prairies, tasks such as fencing, oil production, manufacturing clothing, and creating a system of roads, among others.

Fencing

In the early years when the homesteader had only one cow, extensive fencing around a pasture was not necessary. The beast was taken to a good grass meadow and children provided care. As more land was cleared and turned, fields were established and fencing was needed to keep animals out of the grain crops. The first fences erected on the homestead encircled the vegetable gardens and the house to keep stock and game from feasting on precious vegetable crops. These early, rapidly-built structures did not look very sturdy, but many lasted a very long time, and vestiges can still be seen on abandoned farmsteads around the countryside. These lengthy rail fences were commonly made of saplings, either pegged or tied onto upright tamarack or willow posts. Such fences were made quickly and, like wattle fences, were amazingly long-lasting.

Woven willow fences were common, since abundant supplies of flexible willow grew in area wetlands. Stout poles, often of poplar, were secured into the ground, and the willow whips were interlaced to form a solid and aesthetically pleasing wattle fence. This was a simple and effective method of fencing that utilized the local scrub willow, for which the settlers found many uses including baskets, bassinets, and hay-slings, and even wattle walls for farm buildings. However, after the arrival of the railroad, stretched barbwire became the norm for the 160-acre enclaves.

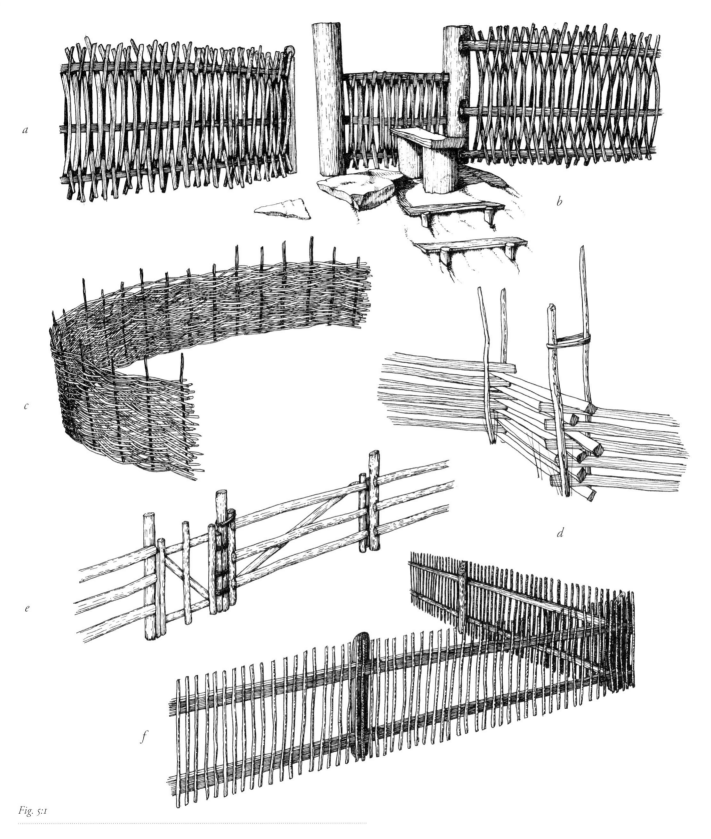

Fig. 5:1

Drawings of Various Fence Details

a. Usually of willow; used for creating enclosures
  (*koshara*) for small animals and poultry

b. A step-over (*perekhid*) leading from the house to the fenced-in garden

c. A tight enclosure of pleated willow (*plit*) for young animals and chicks

d. A pole fence of pine or spruce (*yalyna*) laid in a "snake pattern" (*parkan*) which provided rigidity

e. Post and Rail with nail connections

f. Heavy posts (*shelly*) with incised rails (*shtakhety*); with a fine lath of willow grill

Pressing Oil

Settlers of Ukrainian origin in the Shandro-Willingdon district in east-central Alberta were pressing plant seed oils as early as the 1890s.[1] They brought their seeds and technology with them from a warmer climate[2] where vegetable oils were commonly used in cooking. Most people in the area grew hemp for oil. Neighbours shared their good fortune and the luckier ones whose crops were bountiful would pass over a cup full of clear, fresh, light-coloured, and delicate hemp and sunflower *oliia* for the Christmas and Eastern Lenten cooking. Sometimes an *oliinyk*[3] (travelling, expert oil press journeyman) would tour the village presses one by one, and people waited in line to have their oil extracted. This would normally happen where there was no expert *oliinyk* living in the immediate vicinity.

The pioneers considered the oil press a small community factory. It was housed in an ordinary wooden log shop where the community extracted oil from hemp, pumpkin, rape, sunflower, poppy, and flax seed. Although flax seed did not yield quality cooking oil, it was often used for finishing wood surfaces and oiling machinery. Circumstances like the weather, the microclimate, and the characteristics of local soils played a large role in decisions regarding which grains could be grown and which seeds would be available to produce oil (see figures 5:2 and 5:3).

The unique oil press featured at the Shandro Museum was originally used in the Cadron area, about six miles west of the Shandro Crossing. George Serediuk and John Loliak presented that oil press, a stamping mill, and a unique, foot-operated "mortar and pestle" to the Shandro Museum (Zazula 1983). Hemp oil seeds were thoroughly crushed in the stamping mill, heated, and then pressed to produce cooking oil. There were a number of different presses used in the community, such as the "screw" press[4] that squeezed the block down with every twist of the handle.

Gawrylo Hamaluk, a fine tradesman, settled in the vicinity of Zawale, about six miles south of Andrew. He built and operated an oil press in the early 1900s using a unique crusher powered by four teams of horses via a *kirat*. A large, six-foot-diameter cast iron gear underneath propelled the crusher (by means of universal-joints and a shaft) to a pulley. Four to eight horses on a series of simple drawbars usually powered this assembly. People from as far away as St. Paul came to have their oil extracted at Hamaluk's place.

Bill Hunka (whose farm is now run by his son Orest Hunka), lived fourteen miles north of Vegreville in the Norma district. Bill bought the oil-making equipment from Dizio Rosichuk in the Downing district across the North Saskatchewan River north of Willingdon in 1945 and made oil until 1950. He then sold it to Bill Buzak in the Ispas area. This press is now in the collection of the Ukrainian Cultural Heritage Museum at Elk Island Park.

In 1902 Phillimon Fedoruk, his brother Kost, and their respective families settled on an adjacent homestead in the Szypenitz community north and east of Hairy Hill. Phillimon was a carpenter whose special talent was to make many of the mechanical conveniences found on the pioneer farm. He built one of the first oil presses, as well as a complimentary grinding mill run by a stationary gas engine, also a first in the region. Word of the press spread amongst the pioneers, and Phillimon was also soon established in the oil manufacturing business.

Steve Orleski, who farms near Two Hills, recalled in a letter to me his experience as a boy going with his parents on annual oil-making excursions to the Fedorak homestead. What follows is his verbatim description of that event:

I have vivid and enjoyable memories of going with father and mother [Dmitro and Anna Orleski] on these annual oil-making excursions. Dad and mother, as well as most people in the thirties and early forties, had no money to buy butter, lard, or oil, so they grew their own hemp, flax, poppy, and sunflower seed out of which they made edible oil. The usual time that they made oil was after harvest and before Christmas when the farm work was slacker.

Because help was needed while making oil, usually four families made an appointment with Mr. Phillimon Fedoruk on the same day. We had no cars in those days so we went with horses and sleighs. Many times it was bitterly cold, but when we came to Fedoruk's, the crude stove was fired up already and the place was very comfortable, warm, and cozy. The horses were tied up to the fence, covered with blankets, and fed. The bags of hemp, sunflower, flax, and some poppy seed, were carried into the warm building and the oil-making started.

Mr. Fedoruk would first grind one bunch of seed. While he was grinding another batch of seed, the ladies would put the ground seed into the large pans, put the pans on the hot stove and keep mixing the flour until such time as you could see the oil starting to show and separate. They would then put this hot mash into a cloth and into the base of the screw press, a cavity about twelve inches in diameter. The men would then go to work and turn the press to compress the mash until all the oil was pressed out through a drainage hole at the base of the press.

The aroma of the roasting mash on the hot stove and the fresh warm oil coming out of the press filled the room with an incredibly wonderful smell. It was not all work. There was a lot of camaraderie – jokes, stories, and fun. Mrs. Fedoruk, Phillimon's wife, was a very kind and gracious lady. She was there helping almost all the time. Mr. Fedoruk was a very

Fig. 5:2

Unique Oil Press at the Shandro Museum

The Shandro press[5] had a series of intersecting wedges put in place by levered side hammers that were part of it. As the wedges were pounded in, they applied pressure to the central block and to the "piston" covering the oil cake. With every hit of the hammer, oil would flow into the receptacle below, leaving a dry, oilseed cake. This nutritious fodder was crushed and fed to livestock in late winter and early spring.

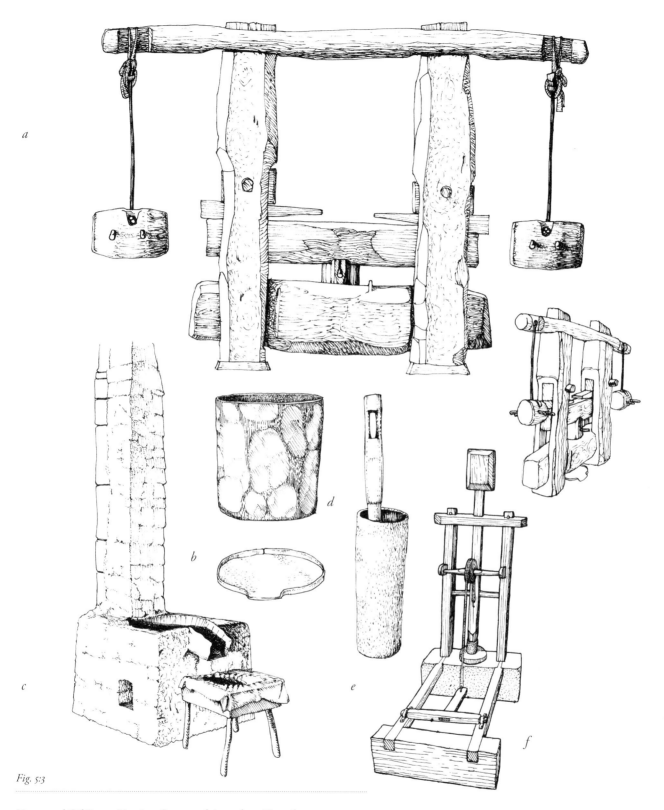

Fig. 5:3

Hempseed Oil Press, Heating Oven, and Attendant Utensils

a. a substantial hempseed oil press (*oliinytsia klynova*) with swinging heavy hammers on ropes; used to drive the wedges and apply pressure to the wooden piston

b. a metal container would be used to collect the extruded oil (*oliia*)

c. an earthen stove (*pich na priazhennia*), usually with a cast-iron plate (*shparhut*) over the fire box; used to heat the mash before it was placed in the compression chamber

d. a wooden barrel contained the seed, which might then be ground with *zhorna*

e. it might also be prepared in a mortar and pestle (*makykh, a makitra*) before it was heated and kneaded into a cake and made ready for the extrusion process

f. the ingenious contraption on the bottom right is a foot-driven mortar and pestle

active and spry man. One time, he came in from outside and told his customers that he could hang upside down by his legs off the log ceiling joist. He did so very easily but unfortunately, his boot slid off his foot and he fell headfirst to the clay floor. He was only slightly hurt, and shortly was up and around, and everyone had a good laugh.

The oil making day was very long. My father and mother would go there at daybreak and come home at ten o'clock at night. The families that came each brought their own lunch and had a potluck dinner and supper. Mother would bring sauerkraut with chopped up fresh onions almost every time. When the first oil was made it was mixed into the sauerkraut. What a treat it was! I do not recall how much the charge was for making the oil, but I know that every family had to give Mr. and Mrs. Fedoruk a cup of oil before leaving at the end of the day. The hardest part of the day, I recall, was driving home six miles with horses and sleigh in bitterly cold weather at ten o'clock at night being very tired – a trip that took an hour.

The oil press shops contained a crusher, mill-stones, an oven to heat the oil mash, tubs for mixing, and heavy tables for kneading the oilseed cake. First the seed had to be dried out. This was done in the *pich* or on top of the stove. When crisp-dry, it was hulled and ground in a *stupa* or in a quern. After being winnowed and passed through a sieve called a *resheto*, the clean grain was ground into flour. A thick, doughy paste was beaten with the addition of some hot water, and then rolled into flat cakes, which were placed in bread pans for the roasting process. The warmer the mash, the better the oil would run, but over-heating or burning would result in dark and bitter oil.

The oil press was basically a large hardwood "piston" which slipped tightly into a sixteen-inch diameter sleeve with a small round hole drilled into the bottom, leading to a spout from which the oil drained. The *oliinyk* stretched a large square of felt over this open sleeve and spread two gallons of the heated oil mash on it. He covered the mash with the four corners of the felting and placed it firmly into the open cylinder. He then covered the seedcake with the hard, thick wooden "piston" and tapped it with a wooden hammer. It was then ready to be squashed down with a series of heavy wooden blocks, the energy supplied by the hammer to a set of sliding wedges on each of the supporting sidebars of the press.

Sewing/Spinning/Weaving

The pioneer women's hands never stopped. Commercially made clothes, fabric, blankets, and towels were not available to Ukrainian settlers, as Edmonton shops were not easily accessible even if the settlers could afford to purchase the goods. Hand-made linen and hemp cloth was extremely durable and, like denim, would last for years, thus the home-made clothing was also a much better product than what was commercially available. Consequently, cloth was manufactured in the home by spinning and weaving. Whether from plants or animals, the short fibres had to be spun into long strands before they could be turned into cloth. It was the women's job to turn wool, hemp, and flax fibres into durable and attractive fabrics and then into warm and comfortable garments. Shirts, jackets, pants, skirts, belts, even underwear, were all produced in the home.

Whenever the women finished the household chores, they picked up their embroidery or knitting. Cross-stitched embroidery formed a colourful, traditional pattern of red and black on white. Some pioneer women raised sheep and spun their own wool to provide yarn for socks, mittens, and scarves, welcome additions to the family's closet. Clothing was usually made in winter. In many households, those men who were not away working in the mines or on railroad construction would spend the long winter evenings spinning wool, flax, or other fibres into long strands in readiness for the weaving process. Wives sewed shirts for the children from flour bags and sugar sacks. Some of the more talented seamstresses sewed for neighbours and even made fully lined coats, enabling them to earn money to buy extras such as a set of dishes or pots and pans, or perhaps a washing board and tub.

Martha Shandro's daughter, Lena Shandro Fontaine, told me stories about how Martha Megley came to Alberta as a young woman with her father, Michailo Megley. She married Wasyl Shandro, and they raised a family of four daughters and four sons. One of their daughters, Anastasia (Nancy) Shandro, was my mother. Her sister, Lena Shandro Fontaine, was my aunt, and it was she who told stories about how her mother "wove for everybody, blankets, bench covers, and many *vereny* [*verety*] (similar to a blanket)."[6] She created beautiful cross-stitch embroidery, crafting complete outfits for both women and men (for women: *peremitka* – headpiece; *sorochka* – blouse; *horbotka* – skirt) (for men: *portkynytsi* – pants; embroidered shirts, and wrap-around belts; and *torbyny* – shoulder pouches).

Hemp

My grandmother and most of her neighbours grew hemp to make both oil and cloth. I remember a patch of about thirty feet square growing on an old straw-bottom on our turn-of-the-century homestead, the old Harry Dohaniuk farm two miles east of Hairy Hill. Some of the families in this area who also grew hemp and used it for cooking oil were Dmitro and Anna Orleski, Myron and Marafta Tkachuk, Stefan and Domka Eliuk, Ivan and Anna Yerichuk, William and Maria Choban, George and Anna Onyfreychuk, Wasyl and Wasylina Mandryk, Petro and Jennie Danyluk, and Bill and Violet Bujak. It was a popular, useful crop.

Apart from producing oil, the settlers used the long hemp fibres to prepare yarn for weaving a sturdy cloth that had many uses on pioneer farms, as cloth made from hemp was extremely durable. The fibres are longer, stronger, and more absorbent and insulative than wool or flax. My grandmother said she could produce a hemp cloth that was as soft as the finest imported silk.

Harvested hemp was dried in stooks, and when brittle-dry, the heads were threshed. The stalks were set aside, requiring further drying. These sheaves were sometimes laid out on rail fences or special racks for drying. Once dry, the stalks were submerged under water until they began to rot, a process that stripped away the ligneous cells binding the fibres. This was known as "retting," and it had to be done carefully to produce the softest hemp fibres. Simple wooden frames were used. They were placed over the stalks and anchored with heavy stones after the hemp bundles were placed in the water. Sometimes nearby streams were used for retting, but wet soil on the shady side of trees together with early morning dew worked just as well. The loose batches or bundles were turned over regularly until the stalks were ready for drying, at which point their fibre could be extracted. Stalks were checked as the retting process continued until the husk showed signs of swelling and cracking. Intuition on the part of the women regarding when the fibres were ready for the next step was essential, and this came only with experience. This retting or steeping process could take three to five weeks, depending on the temperature of the water (the warmer the water, the faster the process). Water quality was also important. Fresh water streams were preferred. The cleaner and purer the water, the lighter and whiter was the colour of the cloth. Svarich described some of the difficulties of the retting process in his pioneer journal:

Often a stream was just filled with hemp stalks, so that the water became dirty and polluted with pod narcotic that was very harmful to the cattle drinking there. As a result, the water would be *salitra* (salty), and the owner would disallow the women to immerse their hemp in that particular stream. But the women could not be denied the necessary immersion and would find other waters or fill shallow dugouts from the stream.

In the odd year, a sudden rainstorm would raise the water level in the stream and carry away all the bundles of hemp. What the people couldn't catch would end up lost in open waters. (1936, n.p.)

In a few days, rows of hemp bundles, like pyramids of war guns, dry and whitened, light and puffy, were carried home and the stems were crushed to eliminate chaff and to clean threads. The hemp bundles were then dried on a rail fence or on racks until brittle dry. The husk was then broken using a scutch or *terlytsia* (both terms describe a primitive wooden board held upright in a recess in a bench). A tough, flat, wooden ladle was used to break the stem core, preparing the fibre to be spun, and the fibres were cleaned, combed, and carefully sorted into bundles in readiness for the weaving process.

These are the techniques that my Grandmother Martha Shandro, in one of our interviews, told me she used to prepare hemp fibres prior to spinning thread for cloth. Cultural practices in the production of hemp fibres were similar throughout the settlement. Because a finer quality of fibre was produced on richer soils, horse dung was often added to sandy loam soil to enrich it.

As a toddler, I would play in my grandmother's hemp garden during family visits to the homestead. I was allowed to roam through her garden and enter her hemp plantation.[7] It was much like entering a deep and dense forest. I was only about two feet tall, and the hemp plants towered over me at eight to twelve feet. One particularly memorable time was during the height of summer, with the hemp in full bloom. As I ran up and down the hemp rows, the golden pollen would float down in clouds all around me as I disturbed the plants. Soon I was in the middle of a yellow cloud that completely engulfed me. The golden fluff was in my mouth, ears, nose, and lungs, and I laid down amongst the plants in a state of euphoria. When I looked up at the sun, I saw an effervescent rainbow completely encircling the golden orb. My run through the jungle that day resulted in a memorable "high." I lay there spread-eagled, making "angel wings" in the garden. Luckily, my grandmother rescued me, or I might be there still.

All kidding aside, I have been fascinated by the integration of plants with their environment and with people ever since, and the development of the hemp industry and the role it played in the pioneers' livelihoods is an interesting one, as the growing of hemp was prohibited by the Canadian Parliament owing to the influence the Duponts and the cotton lobby groups had on the American Congress. Canada soon followed

suit. Hemp growing was prohibited in Canada in 1937–38 under the *Narcotic Control Act* that stated "no person shall cultivate opium poppies or marijuana without a license issued under the regulations." The clause provided for controlled cultivation for medical use.

This impacted the Ukrainian farmers who were advised that they must now destroy their valuable oil seed plantations. These small plantations were scattered throughout the Ukrainian bloc settlements from Edmonton, Alberta, into Saskatchewan, and through to Winnipeg. When I interviewed Steve Orleski in 1956, he recalled a day in 1944 when the family was in the garden. They were visited by Constable Stan Serby of the Two Hills RCMP who warned Dmitro Orleski that hemp was now illegal. He was asked to cut his immature crop. This was the beginning of the end of the oil-making era in the Ukrainian settlement area. This was unfortunate, because this evolving industry could have brought western Canada to the forefront with a well established, flourishing hemp industry after the Second World War. In 1998, the Government of Canada seemingly reversed its position and is now, under the auspices of the Ministry of Health, providing new regulations that enable the growing and commercial production of low-level THC strains[8] of cannabis. Canadian farmers can now grow and sell hemp plant material for fibre and seed for oil processing. Industrial hemp is finally legal in Canada again.

Wool

Wool was first "teased" to remove sticks, leaves, and dirt. It was then carded. Carding employed two boards or paddles with a series of nails or metal wires embedded into their flat surfaces. A small amount of wool was spread on one card and the other card was brushed over it, straightening and aligning the fibres, and loosening any remaining dirt or debris. Carded wool was then spun into thread.

Very few spinning wheels were available around the first of the century when the settlers originally came to Alberta, so a drop spindle, a tool used for centuries in many old world countries, was employed. My grandfather Wasyl Shandro was an excellent spinner (or so my grandmother claimed). The drop spindle was simple to make and resembled a toy top. It consisted of a straight wooden shaft notched at the top and a weight at the bottom called a "whorl." The straightened fibres from the cards were twisted into a continuous length of yarn by the spindle's spinning. Wool was wound onto the spindle shaft as it was spun.

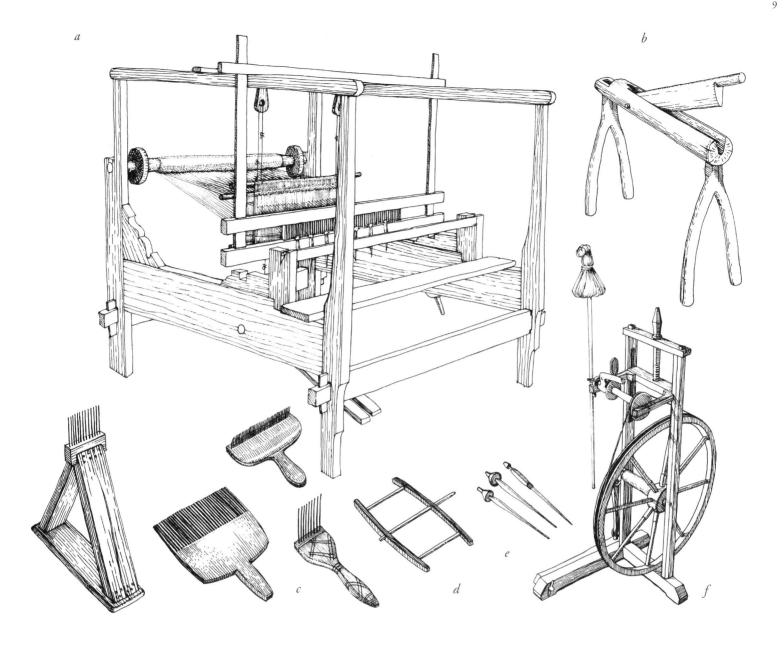

a

b

c

d

e

f

Fig. 5:4

**Spinning and Weaving – A Loom and a Scutch for Breaking
Fibres for Processing and a Spinning Wheel**

a. This illustrates a two-shaft loom (*verstat, krosna*) with a top-slung batten; with a bench seat for the weaver. This loom can be assembled and disassembled easily, with all joints tightly fitted together; slot and tenon with wedged connectors, also of wood. The loom's width is generous and allows for a warp that can be doubled to create blankets or verenya (*vereta*) for bed covers. The comb (*berdo*) for spreading waft threads is hung in a frame from above.

b. The fibres of various plants such as flax and hemp need to go through a retting (soaking) process before they are dried and scutched with a *terlytsia*. This is a breaking, beating, and combing operation (*mechok*) that straightens the longer fibre bundles and separates them from the shorter ones, as well as from the corky stem cells. A subsequent combing process cleans and further straightens the long fibres.

c. This shows a series of various combs (*hrebini*) used to prepare the fibre before the spinning can begin.

d. A yarn winder (*motovylo*) used for storing lengths of yarn as it is finished, spun, and readied for the warp (*nyty; nytka*) preparation.

e. Wooden, hand-carved bobbins (*vereteno*) were used to spin various fibres such as hand-spun wool, which is very resilient and makes excellent clothing.

f. A spinning wheel (*priadka*) with a *kudelia* attached was used in the pioneer home for the manufacture of yarn from wool, flax, and hemp.

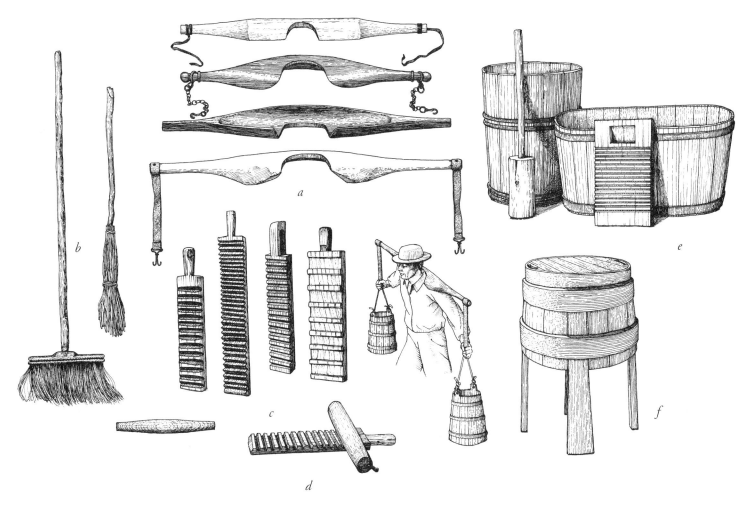

Fig. 5:5

Flax

Yoke for Carrying Water and Washing Paraphernalia

a. These are different yokes (*koromesla*) used for carrying water or other heavy containers with ease over a distance. The size and shape of the yoke had a bearing on just who would feel comfortable using it. It had to be fitted to the individual "wearer," just like a suit.

b. Two types of broom (*mitla*) are illustrated, one (*vinyk*) made with rigid plant fibres (hemp), the other with horse hair.

c. A series of wash boards (*magil'nytsia*). Sometimes the pioneer woman would take her wash to a nearby stream and complete the wash in the wilds. She brought along her wash board, perhaps some soap, and the clothes.

d. This wooden roller and ribbed board was used to prepare the pleats, a series of horizontal creases across the men's linen pants and on the women's long, wrap-around turbans (the *peremitka*). This was a very tedious job, requiring much dexterity and patience.

e. Wash tub (*tsebryk; lata*), wash barrel, plunger (*rubel'*), and scrub board.

f. The forerunner of the modern washing machine.

My grandmother also grew flax because its long fibres could easily be spun into thread without a laborious carding process. Flax grows about three to four feet high, branching at the top and ending in a spray of pale blue flowers. When mature plants are used, seeds can be crushed to produce oil; however, the plants must be harvested before reaching maturity in order to produce the best linens. Yellowing leaves were an indication the flax was ready to be harvested. Stems were stripped of leaves and flower heads and left to dry in thinly spread bundles on the ground. When dry, the stems were retted. After retting, the stalks were dried and then, once brittle, they were systematically crushed, breaking the inner corky core and leaving only the long, flexible fibres. The crushing process was hastened by use of a wooden scutch or *terlytsia* that was hinged into a grooved hardwood "anvil" (see Fig. 5:4). Fibres were slowly pulled through the scutch and crushed until the corky stem core separated from the fibres. Flax was customarily loosely tied onto a distaff before spinning. Fingers had to be kept wet for spinning. The linen thread produced was grey in colour and did not absorb dye.

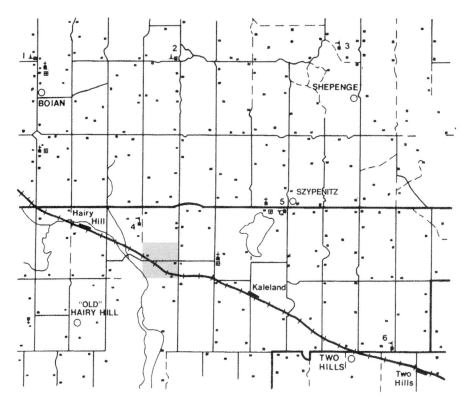

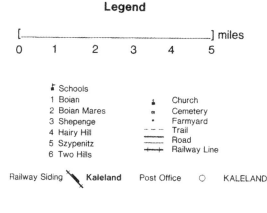

Municipal Map of the District of Eagle, including the Hairy Hill and Szypenitz Areas (and the farms where the author spent his childhood)

This map shows the author's "homestead," two miles east of Hairy Hill in the district of Eagle at the time of the C.P. Railway construction in 1927–1928. This 1927–28 map of the municipality of what is called Two Hills illustrates the density of the homesteads (each is a home) and the land's subdivisions.

(Map reproduced from Manoly R. Lupul, ed. *Continuity and change: The cultural life of Alberta's first Ukrainians.* Edmonton: Canadian Institute of Ukrainian Studies, 1988)

Roads, Bridges and Municipal Services

As the population density in rural Alberta increased due to mass immigration in the 1900s, the need to form a local, organized government became evident. Rural government evolved from the earliest Local Improvement Districts to the present county system. Over the past seventy years, the province changed from a virtual wilderness to a modern agricultural and energy resource entity.

In the early years, the most important municipal service was the provision of roads and bridges. Farmers had to get their produce to market, send their children to school, and attend their place of worship. Some of the first (early 1900s) local government services for the Wostok L.I.D. #38N4 formed in June of 1908 under Chairman Theodore Nemirsky. Mandatory taxes of four dollars and fifty cents on a quarter section of land were assessed: the remainder could be paid with two days of road labour. Chairman Nemirsky was a visionary and an outstanding leader in the pioneer community.

Farmers were able to provide labour entirely in lieu of farm taxes in some improvement districts to the east of Lamont,

such as Sobor Municipality No. 514, now part of Two Hills County, particularly during the Great Depression. The secretary-treasurer at the time was Maxim Tomyn, who was known to bend the rules to suit the conditions and who had a great deal of influence on municipal policies. "Labour in lieu" became an acceptable method of tax payment, particularly where there was a need for roads and bridges. This arrangement proved practical and continued for approximately fifty years, resulting in a grid-work of roads every mile east to west and every two miles north to south. The township was a checker-board of convenience. It is also interesting to note just how important heavy draft horses were to the progress of the pioneer community.

To build and maintain their roads, pioneer farmers used special equipment designed for horse power. A slip drawn by two horses, along with a *fresno* (a larger version of the slip or scoop used to move dirt in early road construction) usually pulled by four horses, were used to move dirt and fill depressions. Farmers working as scrapers needed dexterity for handling horses and managing equipment. A slip could flip and inflict serious injury if it hit a hidden obstacle such as a stone or tree root. This equipment was later replaced by drags with a heavier framework and an angled blade drawn by horses. My father would go to work "on the road" (*sharvarok*, Ukrainianized form of "share work") after spring seeding was completed and just before haying season began. This was an annual affair that took a week to ten days and was well worth the effort. He had a team of Belgians that were anxious to put their backs into the upholstered collars and pull. They were fed a healthy portion of oats every day and showed off with a series of loud, sporadic farts as they dug into the first few heavy loads of the slip. This was his favourite heavy horse team.

Early roads were not built to modern standards and in many cases were only seasonally passable, swamped by spring thaws, runoff, and heavy rains where gravel surfacing was not available. In the late 1930s, we lived two miles east of Hairy Hill along a road built by the pioneers using horse-drawn equipment. We walked to school along the road during the spring, summer, and fall. A railway built in 1928 ran parallel to this road. Some of the more memorable springs were those marked by floods. The runoff would be sudden; the melt appeared to happen in a matter of two to three days. A surge of water would come tumbling down the stream bordering the north side of town, follow the railway grade, and cross under the rail grade to the road between our house and town. This creek was part of the Vermilion River system.

On our way to school we would walk on the tracks, as the railway grade was much higher. The road would now be covered and under water. The bridge, about a mile down from town (or halfway home) had been washed out overnight. By late afternoon, even the railway would be undercut and the gravel washed out for a stretch of the line. All of this could happen in a matter of hours while we were in class. Coming home from school, we surveyed this stretch of rails and attached ties suspended ten feet or more in the air above the rumble of flowing waters. The washout was about fifty feet long. The road parallel to the rail line was completely under water, part of a new, wide lake of spring meltwater spreading to both sides of the railroad. The only way to get home was to walk the intact twin rails held together by the pattern of ties over the surging flood waters. One misstep and one of us would fall into the fast-flowing stream below, just as the occasional missing 12" x 14" x 8' timber tie had. We gingerly tested each of the hanging timbers before quickly stepping from one to the next. Since I had practice in "walking the rail," I used this technique where the missing ties left large open gaps of rumbling and boiling water, but I also watched out for my sisters to make sure we all made it home safely.

The road, which paralleled the railway as well as the railway grade, had to be rebuilt after the flood receded, so we had a week-long holiday from school that year. This gave my brother and me an opportunity to watch the railway construction train and crew repair the break, which was much more interesting than anything going on in the classroom, of course.

6
Food/Celebrations

Having detailed the tools and material culture and processes developed to sustain the pioneers in their adopted country, it would be appropriate to now conclude my portrayal of the lives led by my Ukrainian forbears by expanding upon the societal features mentioned in passing throughout the text. Just as *zhorna* symbolizes, for me, many of the most admirable qualities of Ukrainian pioneer life, so, too, does *toloka* encapsulate the best of the societal/community-building aspects my relatives enjoyed. This, the final chapter, describes the socio-cultural traditions brought from the old country and maintained in the new land, at least until the Second World War.

Toloka

These rural courtesies, perhaps a reflection of the last vestiges of the pioneer era, have long since disappeared, but the memories of that era have not.

The all-encompassing *toloka* was a traditional communal process applied to many large-scale endeavours, everything from grain harvesting to house building, from ice fishing to oil pressing. These co-operative ventures illustrate the communal nature of the pioneers' lifestyle. The Ukrainian pioneers knew they could turn to their neighbours for advice and instruction. These settlers, as noted in John Lehr's introduction, practised chain migration, meaning that they chose homesteads next to relatives and families they knew back in the old country. This communal spirit eased some of the stress of the farming year. Though they had the stubborn tenacity to build their homesteads into self-sufficient and productive "estates" by themselves, help and ready advice was never far away. A hand offered to a neighbour was always returned in kind, and the next opportunity to celebrate together was never too far away. Anna Navalkowsky describes the importance of family and neighbourly ties in two quotes from the book outlining the history of the Shandro family, *The Shandros – Our Story*.

The Shandro settlers brought with them the culture of their native Bukovyna – its language, religion, clothing, housing, and its customs. The word "family" had two meanings in Ukrainian. The first connotation is the unity of parents and children, while the second was relatives that included aunts, uncles, cousins, and in-laws, as well as godparents with their families. All of these relatives, although many are not blood-related, were strongly linked by unwritten customs and mutual obligations which regulated the whole range of life. (1999, 58)

Among Ukrainian customs, the rituals of marriage, birth, burial, and name-day celebrations are most conspicuous. The essential tie is the moral obligation to help one another in every way. If an individual launched an undertaking, he could always count on his relatives for assistance. (1999, 58)

Neighbourliness was accepted without question. Each family helped the next. This was especially appreciated in times of crisis. When a wife had to be taken to a hospital some thirty to eighty miles away to give birth, the neighbourhood wives came over and helped, particularly when it was a young family with the husband busy in the fields. What a joy it was to open the door and be greeted by the aroma of a hot roaster full of browned chicken, roasted potatoes, and a stew of cabbage and carrots brought by one of the neighbour's girls. The dish would be wrapped in a blanket to ensure the food stayed warm. This was a common courtesy extended to less fortunate families.

Celebrations

Although pioneer life was hard, families and friends shared joys and sorrows. Good times were had by all during Christmas, New Year's, the Feast of Jordan holidays, and Easter. Interspersed with these main religious holidays were weddings, funerals, births, and other seasonal holidays, all times when the entire extended family would get together. There were often two and three sittings for a meal, and when the dishes were done, out came the fiddles, flutes, mouth organs, and hammer dulcimers. Singing and dancing began after supper and continued into the early morning hours. The social life of the community was robust and regular, and would take place in their homes or in church halls, and later, in the community centres.

Because food is always an important (some would say integral) component of social events, these two aspects are combined and intertwined in this chapter, along with descriptions and photographs of the tools and other aspects of material culture used in the reproduction of this important aspect of the pioneers' lives in their new country. This material is presented according to the yearly cycle of events and festivities.

Cheese making was a very important food process practiced by the Ukrainian pioneers. Those who had come from the lower Carpathians, as the Shandros did, had sheep and cattle and made excellent processed cheeses. In order to process cheese that can be stored for future use, you need dried curds, which are a soft summer cheese called buz. Buz is the first stage in cheese making. The pioneer woman would use dried, ground-up chicken gizzard in warm milk and set this aside in a crock to ferment, usually in a warm place on the stove shelf. The dried chicken gizzards would provide the appropriate "rennet organisms" to start the fermentation process. In later years, my mother would buy rennet tablets in the general store in preference to using dried chicken gizzards. This cheese, which was processed into "brynza," was a very important dairy food item that could be stored for long periods without spoiling. It was an important part of the winter diet for most of these settlers.

Most of the Ukrainian pioneers were also very adept in preparing and processing distilled beverages such as home-made wines, beer, fruit brandies, or vodka, as their private production and consumption was not considered illegal in their homeland. They brought the practice with them from their homelands.

Spring

As the prior year's cycle swiftly came to a close, the stock of perishables, such as greens, potatoes, and turnips, fell dangerously low. Frozen meats were also in short supply, and the last of the cheese was now being consumed. The butter was long gone. The arrival of spring, however, replenished hope as the pioneers knew they had put up enough feed for the livestock, and they no longer had to worry about the depletion of their own supplies of meat and perishable vegetables. By foraging in the woods, they supplemented staples with partridge, prairie chicken, and wild rabbit. Some of the nearby ponds yielded muskrats for fur and food. A sumptuous dish of muskrat (sometimes called marsh rabbit) in a thick stew provided a much appreciated change in the diet.

With the first signs of spring, the men would organize an ice-cutting bee. Ice on local lakes and/or rivers would be cut into blocks and hauled into icehouses or placed in root cellars, where it would be packed in sawdust to provide refrigerant to cool milk, cream, eggs, meat, and other perishables over the coming summer. The initial dwelling, the *burdei*, was converted into an excellent root cellar (*pohrib*) and icehouse once the settlers moved into their permanent house, as it was built partially underground. The first well, later replaced with a much deeper water supply, also served as an outdoor cooler for storing food.

Summer

Picking berries was a favourite activity in the summer months. Wild fruit was plentiful. We picked and processed saskatoons, chokecherries, strawberries, raspberries, pin cherries, gooseberries, high bush cranberries, and loganberries. We had a native orchard of saskatoons on our farm in Hairy Hill, and chokecherries and pin cherries grew along every roadside. Mother used to send my sisters, my brothers, and me with Roger's Syrup pails to bring home the harvest. Our belts held up the pails while we picked the fruit. We ate as much as we picked, but the pails always came home filled to the brim. It was a carefree and happy time in our lives. Some of the wild fruits that made it home to my mother were preserved in jars for the winter. We also picked the petals of the Alberta roses that abounded in the open fields. The petals were dried and put away to be used in the winter to make a wonderful tea.

The Shandro pioneers celebrated Bohorodytsia (St. Mary's Day) as one of their more important religious holidays, usually on the twenty-eighth of August. This was also known as *Khram* Day in Andrew, Shandro, Boian, and Willingdon. That

Overflow Crowd at St. Mary's Russo Greek Orthodox Church at Shandro

Fine Crop of Garlic Dried Before Storage in the Attic

day had been set aside for this purpose by the parishioners who built St. Mary's Russo Greek Orthodox Church in 1904. A special service was celebrated at the church in the morning, and some of the larger families would then invite people over for meals and festivities. Not all parishioners would prepare feasts, as not everyone could afford the expense. No one was left out, however, as everyone who came to the church service received an invitation. Many were invited to more than one home, and they went from one place to the next. Traditional, sumptuous meals were served fresh out of *pich* ovens. Guests and hosts toasted each other, and everyone took part in joyous conversation, singing, and dancing. Such celebrations continued late into the night, with everyone leaving early the next morning.

Autumn

Storing food for the long winter ahead was the focus of autumn activities. Mushrooms of various kinds abounded in the woods, and each species grew at different times. Some were visible before the leaves were out; others were summer-ripening, fall varieties. Any surplus of puffball mushrooms was sliced into strips, dried, and placed in paper bags or jars in the attic for use in special Christmas and Easter feast dishes. A large wooden barrel served as a hamper for sauerkraut. Rows of jars of jams, jellies, and fruit lined cellar shelves. Blueberries and cranberries were canned whole, to be used later in pies. Eggs were stored in brine for winter consumption. *Buz* (a soft summer cheese) was hung in cotton bags to dry and was then prepared with salt as a processed cheese known as *brynza* and stored in crocks for the winter. A hog and a steer would be

butchered and the meat placed in cold storage in the *burdei* for the winter supply. Sometimes the meat was placed in a bucket and lowered into a deep well for storage. A trap door in the wooden floor led down a ladder into a dug cellar where potatoes, vegetables, preserved eggs, fruits, and meat were stored. Hanging from the roof beams in the attic would be rows of onions and garlic, bunches of herbs, and native, aromatic flowers used for cooking, dyeing cloth, or making cough medicine.

Canada geese, ducks, and partridge supplemented the domestic larder in the fall. Rabbits were hunted in fall and snared in winter when their fur coats turned white and made them easily visible. Goose and duck feathers were carefully plucked, cleaned, and then used in pillows and *peryny* (feather beds).

Rose hips were also picked in the fall and dried to be used for brews and herbal teas in winter. Some herbs were used to prepare dyes and a mordant for homemade clothing, tea, and medicines. One settlers' descendant (Anastasia Shandro Zazula, interviewed by the author in 1958) remembers that "in later years … mother would sell one can of cream, and then the next one would be made into butter for the winter. It was put away in earthen crocks." Young boys made whistles and slingshots from willow, and its bark was used as a purgative "tea" and was a good source of vitamins D and C, as well as a painkiller (a natural substitute for aspirin).

The threshing feast was another social highlight of the year. It held special significance as a thanksgiving gesture for nature's bounty at the end of the harvest season. It was the role of the lady of the house to supervise, cook, and serve the supper with assistance from the visiting ladies, who would pitch in with the preparation and then help serve. The women only sat down to dinner after the men at the main table finished eating.

Nickon and Anna Shandro Celebrating their Jubilee Anniversary   A Shandro Pioneers' Get-together

Children were fed at the kitchen table in the next room, away from the bantering men folk!

The threshing feast was laid out on a long table set on temporary "saw horses" or on two tables brought together to accommodate the crews. The tables were set out in the living room (the largest room in the house) and spread with worn linen cloths and an assortment of plates and eating utensils. The men and older boys made up the first sitting, squeezing together on benches, chairs, and upturned boxes.

There were fat roast chickens and borsch, both cabbage and beet leaf (stuffed with bread crumb filling and garlic), freshly baked rounds of hearth-baked bread glazed with egg yolk and fresh milk and sprinkled with salt, new potatoes garnished in parsley and cream sauce, and sometimes, corn on the cob and green beans. Fresh picked cucumbers and beets added variety. Cucumbers sliced fine and mixed with white turnip and onions in oil and vinegar dressing provided a salad. Freshly picked greens were the garnish. Dried apples, prunes, and apricots were prepared in syrup for dessert, and gallons of milk were consumed. Strawberry, rhubarb, and saskatoon pies, cakes, and loads of coffee put everyone in a festive mood.

After the meal, tables were cleared, and the men adjourned to the other side of the room while the next sitting was taken care of. The men would then gather around a grizzled story teller, who would light his pipe and tell stories of the days of the Cossacks on the steppe, the attack of Asian warriors on horseback, and how the small brave group outfought and ingeniously outmanoeuvred the invading hordes, to live another day and fight once more. The stories were embellished with anecdotes about each of the characters and their love affairs. The richness of the historical saga often brought tears to the eyes of

the older men who had left their homeland forever. The youngsters listened with wide eyes, enthralled with the adventure and the heroic grandeur of it all. Their imaginations took over in the flickering fire light from the hearth, and they looked over their shoulders into the darkness of the open door to check for lurking enemies that might creep up on them.

Later, one of the old-timers would bring out his flute and sit on the outside porch playing a medley of love songs and folk tunes from the Carpathian Mountains of the homeland. My grandfather loved to play folk songs and dances on the flute in the evenings after a long day of harvesting. In the early days, the darkening evenings were still and you could hear the trill and the melancholy melodies for miles around. Slowly, tired youngsters would be packed off to bed and older men would adjourn to the barn to lay out their bedrolls and sleep in the loft.[1]

Winter

In early December, the men would go to the lakes in Northern Alberta with their teams and sleighs and return with sleigh boxes laden with whitefish and pickerel. Jack fish or suckers were not collected or eaten because all preferred the bone-free flesh of whitefish. On the trek home, the men would stop at each settler's home and barter or sell fresh frozen fish, stacked like firewood in the sleigh box. Frozen fish were kept in the *komora*. A generous supply of fish was now available for Lenten meals and special Christmas or New Year's feasts, important holiday periods that distinctly marked the end of the old and the beginning of the new.

The upcoming holiday season was replete with special festive, sumptuous foods used to celebrate the time of sharing, not only with neighbours and relatives, but also with domesticated animals and nature. In the early years, feasts did not always include the traditional range of dishes, as not all foods were available to the newcomers. There was also concern regarding whether the ingredients used in some of the traditional dishes, such as *kutia*, could be spared from what was required for seeding next year's crop on the newly broken acreages, but with the help of neighbours and the custom of sharing, this was not usually a problem.

Christmas Eve was particularly significant. The settlers later adopted the Christmas tree as a symbol from western Europe, but for many years the Christmas holidays included a *triitsia*, a nicely braided sheaf of grain that was carefully placed around a small wooden cross on a stand located in a spot of veneration, either on the main table or in the east room under the wall with the saints and icons. Candles were lit at the appropriate time and either stuck into this *triitsia* or placed on either side. This solemn tradition marked the beginning of the feast meal on each of the important holidays during the Christmas/New Year's celebrations.

Wives would try to obtain a small jar of hemp-seed oil from one of the more established settlers for cooking the Lenten meal. Much of this preparation was done beforehand, as the pleasure of preparation was very much a part of the initiation of the feast. Cabbage leaves were thawed from the sauerkraut barrel for *holubtsi*. Buckwheat and wheat were crushed with a *stupa* in the storage shed. Poppy seed was soaked and then ground to a fine paste with a mortar and pestle. Fish was thawed, cleaned, and stuffed – then roasted whole in the oven. Everyone looked forward to sharing all of these tasks and to the leisurely, holy days of rest afterward.

Even the animals in the barn were given a token taste of the main dishes to be eaten that evening by their human counterparts. Children could hardly wait for the supper. It was a day of Lent, thus by dinnertime, all were famished. The smells of *holubtsi*, *pyrohy*, and baked fish swimming in a rich onion and oil sauce were enough to cause an occasional morsel to disappear when mother wasn't looking. There was a sumptuous feast of twelve dishes. Two round braided loaves (*kalachi*) were placed on the table along with two or three garlic heads with a candle in the centre for the duration of the festive season. If a member of the family had passed away during the year, a place setting was reserved for the departed soul.

With the first rising star in the sky, Father would bring in a sheaf of wheat (*didukh*) saved specifically for this event and spread some straw (*soloma*) under the table (*pidstilla*). This tradition originated in ancient times. Hay was also thinly spread under the tablecloth. Some believe that Venus, the first rising star, was the guiding star that led the wise men to the birthplace of Jesus. Capping this ritual, Father would quietly meditate on the bounty of the past year and give thanks for all of the pleasures and good things in life. Everyone then sat around the table and, with a blessing, the Christmas supper began. After supper, the children would search for a few nuts and candies that Father had secretly strewn in the straw under the table, and then they would go off to bed.

The twelve dishes of this feast were cooked in sufficient quantity in the *pich* to supply enough for the next three days, as no cooking was to be done during the Christmas holidays. There was also ample food to share with neighbours and carollers dropping in. The arrival of happy singers by sleigh the next day gave occasion for rejoicing. As best wishes for the New Year were exchanged, so were bits of news and some of the best snacks mother had to offer. Father brought out his gallon of port wine and a bottle of whiskey to help the singers on towards their next visit. Each caroller downed a shot before they were sent merrily on their way.

All of this cooking and preparation required, of course, a number of kitchen tools and utensils. A collection of traditional kitchen tools from the farm kitchen of Mrs. Lynkowski (the grandmother of Adeline Youzwyshyn Fodchuk, whom I married in 1957) is depicted in figures 6:1 and 6:2. This heirloom collection of wooden kitchen utensils is displayed on the atrium wall of our Cochrane home, a wonderful exhibit of craftsmen's art from the turn of the century.

Table Set for Incoming Guests

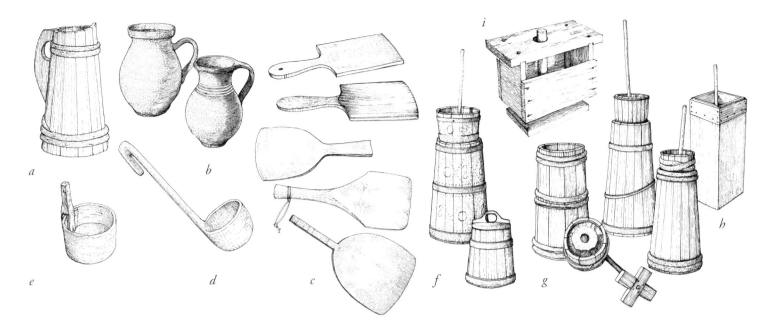

Kitchen Wooden Utensils: Adeline Fodchuk's heirloom collection of Wooden Kitchen Utensils inherited from her Baba Lynkowski (see the story of maister carpenter Prokip Lynkowski, Baba Lynkowski's husband, in the Tools and Specialty Services segment of chapter 2).

    a. Wooden Milk Pitcher (*konovka*)

    b. Clay-fired Pottery Food Jars (*horschok*); thought to have been brought over from Halychyna in the early 1900s

    c. Series of Wooden Paddles (*lopatka/lopatky/kruzhky*); used for removing hot food containers and pots from the *pich*

    d. Wooden Ladle (*dereviánna lozhka*); for mixing and serving hot food

    e. Wooden Grain or Seed Measure (*hornets*); commonly used in the homeland

    f. Wooden Bucket with cover *vidro*

    g. Wooden Butter Churns (*masnychka/maslynka*); made by a maister craftsman

    h. Square Butter Churn (*maznytsi/masnychka*)

    i. Wooden Butter Form (*forma*)

January

The next community occasion, the "Blessing of the Waters" on the nearby river, marked the end of the old year and the beginning of the new. It was celebrated shortly after Christmas on the nineteenth of January. Also known as Jordan Day or the Epiphany, it commemorated Christ's baptism by John the Baptist in the Jordan River. Johnny Shandro, in an interview with the author in 1958, described the tradition:

At Shandro, this was a significant religious celebration, as everyone in the community would go down to the Saskatchewan River where the "blessing of the waters" took place. The day prior, the church elders would cut a hole in the ice with an ice saw in the shape of a cross. The cross was lifted and placed at the end of the open water cross, to stand free. In the cold winter night, it would freeze solid and present an impressive setting for the service.

After the ceremony, everyone would take their jars or containers, dip them into the open channel of the cross, take a drink, and fill their receptacle with the blessed water. Next, everyone would chant the appropriate hymns in unison with the priest and then take their container of holy water to their sleighs.

Johnny Shandro recalls marvelling at the long line of horse-drawn sleighs with runners squealing in the sharp, ice-cold snow going up the embankment and on their way home. This would form a circuitous, snake-like line approximately a mile long. Some of the horses had fancy harnesses, with dancing percherons and ringing sleigh bells creating a wonderful winter postcard scene never to be experienced on the same grand scale again.[2]

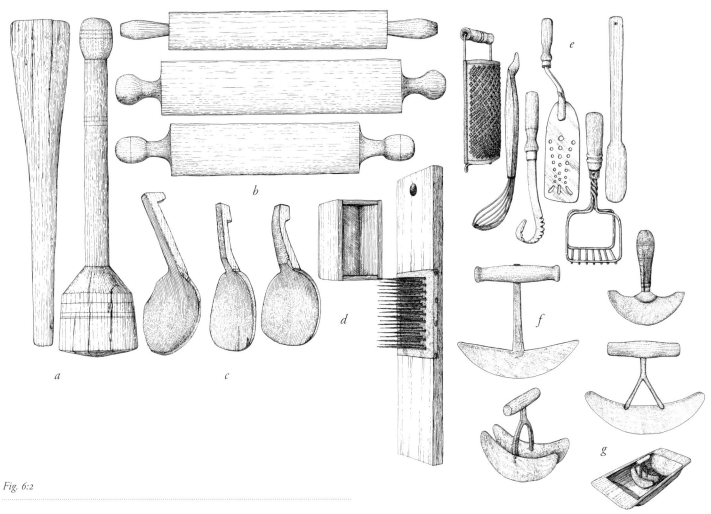

Fig. 6:2

**Butter Churns and Attendant Utensils: More of the Collection
from the Home of Baba Lynkowski in Myrnam, Alberta**

a. Two Wooden Mallets (*dovbni*); one hand-carved that may
have been used as a mortar for crushing seed; the other, a
Turned Mallet, sometimes waved threateningly by housewives
at children and husbands, referred to as a *makohin*

b. Series of Wooden Rolling Pins (*tachilky*)

c. Carved Ladle Paddles (*dereviani; lozhky*); used to stir
hot liquids, *holubtsi*, fruit, and other boiled foods

d. A Fine Comb (*hrebin*); used to straighten flax fibres

e. A series of 1920s wooden-handled kitchen tools (*posudy*)

f. Chopping and Butchering Knives

g. Wooden, Carved Bread Trough; with a
slicing knife for chopping salads

Provody at Shandro – Sadochok

"Sadochok" – Kalach – Provody at Shandro – Table Setting

Miscellaneous Rituals

When I was a young teenager, my maternal grandmother hosted an elaborate dinner celebration at her home to commemorate the passing of her husband Wasyl. This was usually on the same day *Provody*, the blessing of graves that took place the week after Easter was celebrated. The entire family was invited. I remember the long tables set outside in the sun, decked out with all kinds of delicious food. At each plate setting was a *kalach* (pictured below, at left) with an apple, an orange, and a candle. Special decorative pieces were set at each end. These had substantial, hearth-baked *kalachi*, each with a series of five long stakes impaled with a variety of fruits and baked sweets. A bright red apple was anchored immediately onto the bread. Each stake was about two feet long and had a repository of cookies, marshmallows, prunes, and jello candies. The center was upright and held a prominent position within four others at angles to each other and firmly secured in a quadrant with a bit of bright red yarn (this was called a *sadochok*, pictured above, at left). The entire creation gave the impression of a colourfully-masted sailing ship. Two of these impressive food sculptures gave rise to the thought of some lucky person having a most sumptuous lunch. Since there were many adults at this momentous occasion, and we younger folk would not be seated till the second or third setting, we would soon find out. A short blessing and a prayer, and the guests sat down to a hot meal of *pich*-baked dishes. The first seating was my uncles, my aunts, and my mother and my grandmother, along with her elder brother. The elaborate centerpieces dressed with sweets (*solodoschi*) were commemoratively (*pomianuty*) presented to two of grandfather Wasyl's best friends who were also at this first seating. Now it was our turn, and each got a *pomana*[3] of a small *kalach* with an apple, an orange, and a coloured, hardboiled egg. The candle was lit for the short prayer before we sat down to enjoy our meal.

Today, we go to the church between *Paskha* (Easter) and Pentecost – the Green Holidays (*Zelenii Sviata*) – to celebrate through Christ the ultimate resurrection of our ancestors, who are considered to be very much with us on these momentous occasions. The living progeny and relatives coming from the cities would meet in the outlying country churches for morning worship, and then go on to the cemetery where they would set out a blessed meal for each one coming to the gravesite itself. The Apostolic custom of leaving an empty place for the departed was the usual practice. *Kalachi* (with the customary apple, orange, Easter egg, and candle) made up each of the place settings. One *kalach* was handed out as a *pomana* at the grave-site by the lady of the house. There was always extra, in case a friend of the departed should stop by. The crowds at these events in this modern day far exceed the seating available in the small country churches, and many arrivals spend their time outside, visiting with acquaintances from the rural past.

Used only occasionally, these country churches and cemeteries draw many Ukrainian Canadians back to their roots and their ancestors every spring. To this day, these momentous occasions take place at St. Mary's Shandro Russo Greek Orthodox Church; at St. Pokrova Ukrainian Orthodox Church, Borowich; at St. Peter and Paul Ukrainian Orthodox Church of Kaleland; St. Mary's Church at Szypenitz, and at the Holy Trinity Ukrainian-Orthodox Church of Two Hills. These events take place from time to time at other churches in the Ukrainian bloc as well.

These gatherings embody a strong sense of community, of shared traditions and origins, of humble prairie beginnings, and strong ties with their ancestors; an ongoing spiritual relationship between the living and the dead. As the population increased owing to further immigration and natural increase, the pioneers' houses soon filled up during social events, and people spilled outside due to the lack of space. Social activities were thus stymied despite the homeowners' generosity. In response, they would organize a *toloka* to build a community hall. Neighbours would get together and donate materials, cut logs, and gather suitable lumber. The hall arose amidst hustle and bustle under the guidance of a carpenter community member who had the intricate tools required to properly fit the steps and to notch beams and make frames for doors, windows, and window sashes. The building would soon be

completed, and a blessing ceremony initiated the first function. Meanwhile, women prepared a rich and sumptuous variety of dishes in the freshly built *pich* next to the new hall, and everyone would enjoy a thanksgiving feast. Such events were community functions. Everyone participated and was welcome. Drama societies, libraries, and reading/debating societies formed at the height of the pioneering era, primarily from the 1900s to 1920s.

These rural halls that served so many functions were slowly dismantled, the old grey siding used to refurbish family rooms in Edmonton, among other uses. Today, if you sit quietly across from one of the country churches, relics of past richness, you can almost hear in the sighing winds the resounding echoes of concerts and plays, weddings and dances, bazaars and parties, through their broken and ghostly framed halls.

Assumption of the Blessed Virgin Mary Ukrainian Catholic Church in Skaro

St. Mary's at Shandro in the 1950s

Conclusion

Much is written about the socio-economic, religious, and political history of the Ukrainian people, but information about their material culture is sparse. Classic cultural aspects such as dancing and music, literature, poetry, Easter eggs, and art are all well covered. The things that were used in everyday life, the material culture of country folk, are not the subject of much study. Not only are these the real tools of living, functional in design and expressive of the uses they were put to, but they are also symbolic of the Ukrainian cultural identity. These tools illustrate how the pioneers lived, their close relationship to the earth and with nature, and their spiritual make-up.

The principal crafts practised were carpentry, weaving, and cooperage. The cooper made wooden containers and vessels using staves of wood formed by hoops of wood or iron, an art reaching far back into antiquity. Cooperage was practised in southern Ukraine from Grecian times forward. Large wooden barrels were needed for storing wine in that era. The Ukrainian pioneers needed numerous types of household and farming containers: buckets; milk churns; wash tubs; cattle-feeding tubs; and last (though certainly not least), home brewing vessels. These crafts reach back to Ukraine's prehistoric times. The tree-covered provinces of western Ukraine were made up of foothills and the Carpathian Mountains. Woodsmen had access to ample resources for practicing carpentry and the making of wood-based utensils, containers, dishes, platters, cups, tubs, and shovels. Cooperage, a respected trade, was widespread throughout the provinces of Chernihiv, Volynia, Hutsulschyna, Bukovyna, and Halychyna. Lovely wooden churches with shingle cupolas and carved beams are found throughout the region.

The immigrants who came to Canada from these regions were skilled in woodcrafts of all kinds, and they quickly produced useful tools, utensils, and complex machines used to process food and clothing on their homesteads. They were able to make and assemble exacting machines such as *zhorna* to grind grain, a hempseed oil press, complex looms, carpentry and agricultural utensils, and much more. Some could also forge iron and practice blacksmithing, tackling carriage making and producing the metal components of a carriage or wagon. Of them all, it is *zhorna* that best reflects the pioneer spirit your forbears brought to the task of carving out a new and better life in Canada a hundred years ago.

It is no wonder these pioneers survived and flourished under the most trying and dire conditions in the natural landscape of western Canada. I have gone back a century to Tulova, a small rural community five kilometres southwest of Sniatyn in Halychyna, to retrace the pioneer's journey. I asked a friend, Nick Topolnisky, to visit Tulova on his recent trip to western Ukraine, and he was able to spend an afternoon in the village.[1] I gave him a copy of Peter Svarich's plan and a layout of the town of Tulova as it was then. Mr. Topolnisky took photographs of most of the remaining buildings, including the Orthodox Church (still a dominant feature overlooking the green commons in the center of the village). The school was also there, another of the institutional buildings of a century ago. With the help of a local individual known as "the keeper of the history" in the village, Nick located my grandfather's former village holdings. The original home had been replaced by a recently-built brick home. He stated "there are no Fodchuk's living in today's Tulova." However, as recently as 2002, Roy Fodchuk (whose grandfather Ivan was my grandfather's brother) made a special trip to Tulova and located the descendants of Matvii and Helen Fodchuk, who remained behind in Ukraine. The open green space of the commons remains as it is shown on Peter Svarich's documents. A regional roadway still cuts through the park diagonally, passing a central mound that draws attention to a memorial to Taras Shevchenko, a national poet, in the center of the commons. Tulova had not changed much from the town my grandfather Paul left behind on his way to Canada in 1907. Some of the institutional buildings were still important landmarks in the town after more than a hundred years.

I believe these people saw nature as sacred; they lived in voluntary simplicity, and their way of life and their agrarian roots were the basis of living in harmony with the earth. Their lives were lived in association with their neighbours, their community, and the larger matrix of their ethnic group, rich in an exotic cultural and spiritual milieu of the ancient Byzantine religion (a connection that began in the year 911 with the First Treaty of Rus' between Ukraine and the Byzantine Greeks). The Ukrainian pioneers possessed a wealth of knowledge regarding plants and their use, a body of knowledge that will be lost if it is not passed along. They had the courage and stamina to not only survive, but to flourish despite all kinds of hardships, and they had the creative ingenuity to convert natural materials into useful and functional objects that were also expressions of beauty, a process exemplified by the *zhorna*.

Epilogue
A Letter to my Grandchildren

Mason and Spencer & Lewis and Jasmine

As long as I can remember, I have had a keen interest in discovering my roots. Like many others, I wanted answers to questions such as: Who am I? Where did I come from? What is my relationship to the "family of man"? What role do my psyche and my spiritual make-up play in my life? The answers weren't urgently required, and I kept putting off the detailed research needed to find them. When I did finally set out to learn more about my roots, many ready sources of knowledge no longer existed. My grandfathers and grandmothers, my mother and father, and most of my uncles and aunts were gone. I should have begun this task much earlier in life. Believing that you will also be looking to your roots at some future date, I write this to make your task easier. Of course, the whole story is not here. You will find many gaps and missing details that need exploration. This would depend on the specific interests of your own personal search. I have focused on the material folk culture of a people.

I want you to know your genetic base is richly endowed with the hardy characteristics of these pioneers. You have the ability to persevere under the most trying of conditions. You have the ability to use and to give your creative resources free reign in resolving diverse problems and unforeseen events. You have the ability to overcome catastrophic events, to survive and to flourish within the expression of your rich cultural heritage. I say this in the context of a rapidly changing world. Over the span of a single lifetime, we have gone from the pioneer experience of complete self-sufficiency to today's luxurious, consumer-oriented lifestyle, where everything is highly processed, from the way televisions and computers run our lives to a society where tasteless tomatoes are grown square to fit shipping containers and where beef is ground, cooked, and frozen in ready-to-eat patties full of unhealthy fatty acids. Let me suggest to you that everything can change very quickly, almost overnight, as has happened in my lifetime.

Your creativity will enable you to flourish. Your inner resources are potent and without bounds. Only you set the limits. Be flexible. Explore life to the fullest. Enjoy! You have a priceless heritage that will be the basis of your future survival. You also have my enduring love.

Roman Fodchuk, your humble Granddad.

Appendix 1:
From Idea to Concept to Reality: The Planning and Design of the Ukrainian Cultural Heritage Village

Presented at the Learned Societies Meetings, University of Alberta, Edmonton, 28 May 2000.

This project was begun in 1971. In April of that year, William Hawrelak and Frank Lakusta came to Ottawa to initiate financial assistance from the federal government. The Privy Council Office[1] advised them to contact me and Robert Klymasz of the Canadian Centre for Folk Culture to review their project. At the time, I was head of Landscape Architecture with the National Capital Commission. I knew both of these gentlemen,[2] having served as a district agriculturalist in the Municipal District of Eagle with offices at Myrnam and Two Hills from 1954 to 1959.

I spent three days with the group visiting various historic restorations and theme parks in the Ottawa area as well as visiting Upper Canada Village[3] in the Cornwall area and Black Creek Village in Toronto. They then went on to see Kings Landing in Nova Scotia and other such developments as Sturbridge Village in Massachusetts and the Henry Ford Village in Upper New York State. My professional work had been with National Parks and the National Historic Sites. I had an opportunity to work on various historic sites in the Atlantic provinces as well as Ontario and Quebec. Some of our projects were based on the "Living Museum" concept.

Their first plan proposal was somewhat rudimentary, consisting of a single row of restored buildings, a restaurant, and a motel with a commercial theme. This was not acceptable for the kind of grant they desired. Their original society board soon realized that a comprehensive planning approach would be beneficial if they were to succeed in obtaining government funding. They requested professional help. The office of the Secretary of State agreed to secure technical and professional assistance through Parks Canada. In November of 1971, I, as the senior planner in the Western Region, was asked to provide the initial programming design, layout, and planning advisory services. I encouraged the President and his Board to go for the "Big Concept," an *Agricultural Living Museum*.

Dr. Robert Klymasz was also an enthusiastic supporter of this approach. In March of 1972, the society's board approved the suggested overall plan[4] and the submission was finalized. Upon submission to the federal government, they received a grant of $177,000.

In May 1972, I was appointed by Parks Canada to represent them on the board of the Ukrainian Cultural Heritage Village in an ex-officio capacity. I acted in the federal government's interest on behalf of the Regional Director, Ron Malis. This was in addition to my regular duties as Senior Planner, Western Region. The project was then well underway with rural buildings being bought and moved to begin to form the 1920s town with early 1890s–1900s pioneer farms depicting the rich material culture of this pioneering community. Most of the people involved in this early stage were volunteers from the farming communities in the Ukrainian bloc settlement, pitching in and doing whatever was necessary to develop this project. The hours were long, there was no recompense, and it was a labour of love.

Public meetings were held throughout the Lakeland region with town and country councils and with the public in general. The support for the project was unanimous. I recall attending meetings in Vegreville, Two Hills, and Lamont to present the concept plan. The "concept plan" became a reality because of the involvement of many people. Some of them were old timers who provided their know-how and pioneering skills. When it came to thatching or mixing and plastering clay mud on to log buildings, or repairing hand-crafted beams and rafters, they showed us how. They had worked with their pioneer parents and had even personally experienced the last vestiges of the pioneering era. They knew why, when, what, and how things were done. It was a pleasure to work with these people who drew upon their rich heritage to carve out a living from the wilderness, for they were the true experts.

We found that the volunteers' support, both labour and financial, could not be maintained at the desired levels. Many of the buildings were in place and restoration of the log structures had commenced. Pioneer furnishings and some of the early farm equipment was brought in. Special events[5] at harvest and in the spring were well attended. The project was just too big to be maintained under private sector sponsorship, and eventually discussions were undertaken with the Alberta government.

Alberta Government Minister of the Environment (subsequently the Minister of Public Works) Wm. J. Yurko and Cultural Minister Horst Schmid played a significant role in the evolution of the Cultural Heritage Village at this stage. Les Usher, then Deputy Minister for Alberta Culture, asked me to undertake the preparation of detailed documentation of the project including field research studies and the preparation of a comprehensive master plan. This was to be presented to a cabinet committee of Alberta ministers who were particularly interested in the project. At the time, Alberta Culture did not have research staff or museum staff particularly concerned with Ukrainian culture.

In 1975, I had established a private practice in landscape architecture with offices in Edmonton and Calgary. We established a small team with expertise in agro-ecology, local history, planning, and design. Measured drawings were prepared in the field of various farmsteads depicting the many faceted elements of the Ukrainian settlement, and these provided a basis for the master plan.[6] Our problem was to try and squeeze all of this onto fifty-five acres. Our documentation was completed, consisting of a Master Plan Report, a series of drawings showing the staging of development, a farmstead inventory report with building selection criteria based on field studies, including measured drawings of select pioneer buildings. This first stage was to make up the rural community component and complete the five exemplar early farmsteads. This was presented to the select ministers' committee,[7] and the plans and program were approved.

Roman Fodchuk and Associates, Ltd. were then retained by Alberta Culture and Alberta Housing and Public Works to carry out the necessary research and develop a series of layout and working drawings incorporating a proposed visitors' centre, a day-use picnic area, and a museum/administrative/interpretive complex. This was connected with a causeway across a small lake which conveniently and naturally separated the modern facility from the pioneer village and historic farmsteads. The project site and the program were a natural fit. The concept was now complete but for the details that would give it the richness of a living museum.

In 1977, Alberta Culture named Roman Ostashevsky as director of the program and project construction was undertaken. The buildings for the five typical farm complexes were brought in and established on site. This project's objectives were to place a strong emphasis on the early rural communities and pioneer life in agriculture. Utilities, roads, and services were installed and the visitor services complex was built.[8] We completed the overall landscape development, including the planting of hundreds of indigenous trees supplied by the Alberta Provincial Nursery. The main stages, the physical skeleton of the project with major buildings and the layout of the total complex, were now in place. There was now the need for finishing touches so necessary to clothe it with an antique patina and with people activities. A program for interpretation and presentation, the basis for a living museum, had yet to be developed.

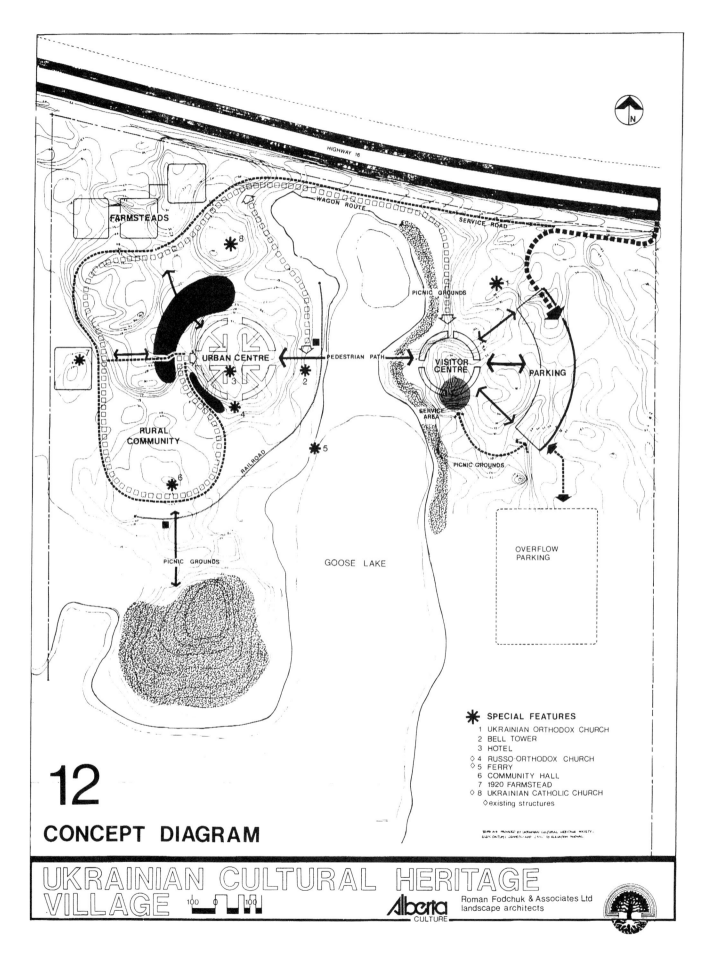

12
CONCEPT DIAGRAM

SPECIAL FEATURES
1 UKRAINIAN ORTHODOX CHURCH
2 BELL TOWER
3 HOTEL
◇ 4 RUSSO-ORTHODOX CHURCH
◇ 5 FERRY
6 COMMUNITY HALL
7 1920 FARMSTEAD
◇ 8 UKRAINIAN CATHOLIC CHURCH
◇ existing structures

UKRAINIAN CULTURAL HERITAGE VILLAGE

Roman Fodchuk & Associates Ltd
landscape architects

Alberta CULTURE

Appendix 1: From Idea to Concept to Reality: The Planning and Design of the Ukrainian Cultural Heritage Village

Comprehensive and detailed plans for landscape development for each of the components were completed in 1978. A large portion of this site development work was carried out that summer. The remainder was to be phased as funds permitted. Alberta Culture chose to place the initial emphasis on staff training and research. This was an important first step and is very evident when one examines the 1977 Master Plan in light of actual project completion as of that date.

The Development Plan for the project completed in 1977 called for a village of the 1920s complete in the many services available, on the scale of Heritage Park in Calgary. The early farms depicting the pioneer era of 1890s–1900s were to be rich in their cultural expression and horticultural variety. The pioneers had brought various fruits, seeds, and corms with them. They introduced various varieties of the potato, buckwheat, orach, apple, cherry, and plum, beets, onions, garlic, vinca minor, poppies, and various herbs and cereal grains to their new homeland. They were good at farming, growing a large variety of crops and some oil seed crops, then considered exotic by other settlers. They had "green thumbs" and they knew how to use these plants for everyday living. Their landscape was not to remain virgin and sterile for very long, but was quickly converted into rich gardens.[9] Any suggestion otherwise is wrong.

In retrospect, very few of the people who conceived of the project in its earliest stages and ensured that it was accepted and supported by the public (who had also put endless effort into the many facets of its overall and detailed development) have yet to be recognized and thanked. Here I would like to mention William Hawrelak (d), Frank Lakusta (d), and his wife Lena (d), Tony Mokry, Dan Lutzak and his wife Marian (d), Paul Youzwyshyn (d), the Right Reverend Myroslav Kryschuk, and other members of the early Board of Directors.[10] All the volunteers who had put in endless hours of work also deserve our sincerest thanks. Without their perseverance, hard-headed stubbornness in seeing it through the many complex problems, and long hours of work, this project would not have been achieved.

I also wish to mention the capable members of our project staff: Murray Allen, Hugh Harwell, Denice Wagner, Linda Irvine, and Noreen Chibuk,[11] among others who were directly involved in field studies and the important aspects of planning. They prepared reports and design studies, co-ordinated the field studies, and brought sense and style to complete this important formative stage and bring this project to reality.

Roman Fodchuk, 31 May 2000

(*previous page*) Master Plan, reports, and various documents from the Ukrainian Cultural Heritage Village, 1977 and 1978.

(*opposite page*) "Site Development" Plate from the 1977 Master Plan for the Development of the Ukrainian Cultural Heritage Village prepared by Roman Fodchuk and Associates

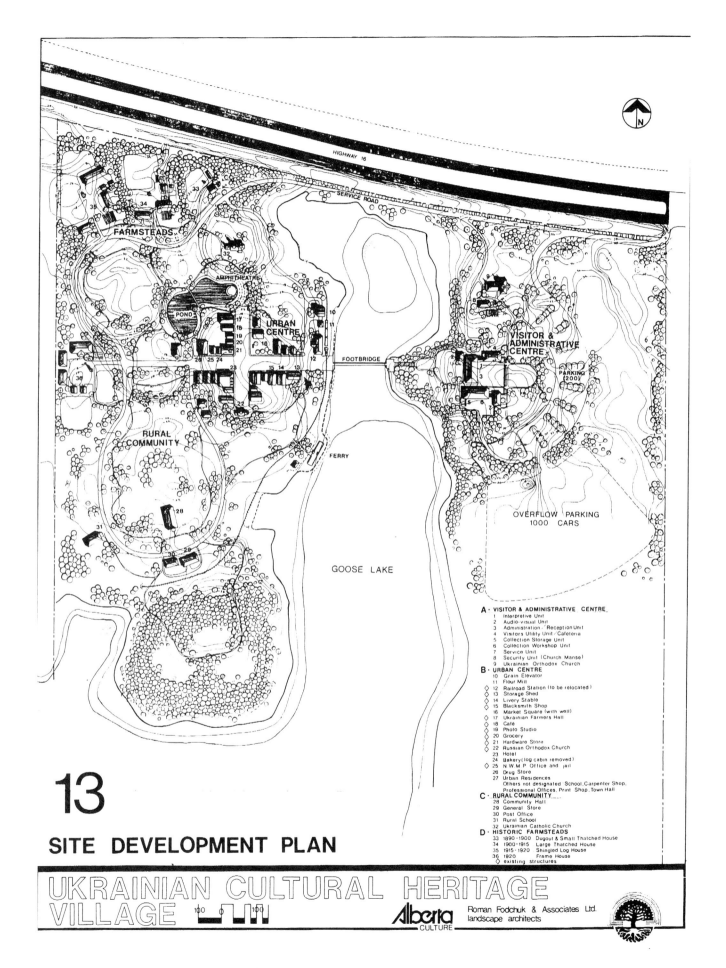

13

SITE DEVELOPMENT PLAN

UKRAINIAN CULTURAL HERITAGE VILLAGE

Alberta CULTURE

Roman Fodchuk & Associates Ltd.
landscape architects

Appendix 2:
Religious History Pertinent to the Ukrainian Settlers in Canada

by Stan Humenuk, Ph.D.

Settlers from Halychyna

A momentous event in the religious history of Ukraine was the adoption of Christianity in 988 by the political leader of the state, Volodymyr the Great. The church recognized him to be a saint of importance equal to that of the Apostles of Christ. Many converts from paganism to Christianity were attributed to his endeavors when he made Christianity the state religion within his vast domain. The church in Ukraine was in communion with the church of Byzantium. When the Roman church separated in 1054 from the other Christian churches located in the lands around the Mediterranean Sea, the Kyivan metropolitan remained loyal to the patriarch of Constantinople. Like the other Christian churches in the east, the church in Ukraine became known as an Orthodox church. The term, Orthodox, distinguished the Christian churches in the east from the Roman Catholic churches in the west.

The Polish kings remained loyal to the popes of Rome. When Ukrainian lands came under the governance of the Polish state, the Polish kings assumed patronage in 1498 over the Orthodox Church in Ukraine. However, Polish state officials applied political and economic pressure to the hierarchy and clergy to convert the Orthodox Church to Roman Catholicism. After the Orthodox Church lost its traditional support from the state under the Polish kings, brotherhoods of Ukrainian lay people became organized to support it.

Many of the lay Orthodox Brotherhoods received charters from the patriarchs of either Jerusalem or Constantinople. These are known as Stavropihian Charters (from the Greek for erecting a cross), and they were issued to the brotherhoods with ceremonies of erecting crosses of the three bar type with a sloping lower bar for St. Andrew, the apostle who first brought Christianity to Ukraine during his missionary travels. Such crosses, properly called Stavropihian Crosses, were erected on those churches where Orthodox Brotherhoods were active. The charters gave the lay Orthodox Brotherhoods rights equal to the rights of bishops in matters of church administration.

Subsequently, with the Sobor (Council) of Berestia in 1596, when the metropolitan of Kyiv, Mykhailo Rohoza, and all but two of his bishops, Bishop Hedeon Balaban of L'viv and Bishop Mykhailo Kopystens'kyi of Peremyshyl', joined the Church of Rome, the lay Orthodox Brotherhoods were able to keep the Orthodox Church alive within the Polish common-wealth with help from many lower status, local clergy. In 1620, the kozak host of Zaporizhia, under Hetman Sahaidachnyi, joined the Orthodox Brotherhoods and protected the patri-arch of Jerusalem from Polish intervention during his visit to Ukraine so he could restore a hierarchy of new bishops for the Orthodox faithful in Ukraine under a new metropolitan of Kyiv, Iov Borets'kyi.

In the ancient kingdom of Halychyna, the Orthodox Brotherhood associated with the Dormition Church in L'viv was among the most active. The strong arm of the Polish state eventually wore down the resistance of that brother-hood to Catholicism such that, in 1708, the L'viv Orthodox Brotherhood joined the Church that was in union with Rome. Today, that church is known as the Ukrainian Greek Catholic Church. A year later, the L'viv Brotherhood received a Stavropihian Charter from the pope. It should be noted that, according to the documents generated during its negotiations for unification with Rome, the Ukrainian Greek Catholic Church had the right to maintain traditional orthodox rites, services, and practices. However, it recognized the pope as its head as a part of his role as primate over the Catholic Church as a whole.

After the first partition of Poland in 1792, Halychyna re-tained its status as a kingdom within Austria, known by the German word, Galicia, in the Austro-Hungarian Empire. The area of the former kingdom of Halychyna was expanded west-ward within Austria to include the Polish city of Krakow and the surrounding areas settled by ethnic Poles. Austrian politi-cal strategy was to ferment animosity between the Poles and the Ukrainians. The principle of divide and conquer was used to rule them. Nevertheless, the Roman Catholic Hapsburg emperors favoured the position of the Roman Catholic poli-ticians of Polish descent over the Ukrainian politicians in matters of religion within Austrian Galicia. However, the Ukrainian Greek Catholics were somewhat tolerated in Austria because they recognized the pope as the head of their church. Consequently, by the time Ukrainians began coming to Canada from Halychyna, most considered themselves Greek Catholics.

In Canada, the Greek Catholic Ukrainian settlers were pressured to assimilate by the Roman Catholic Church. Their Greek Catholic hierarchy acquiesced to pressure to have their churches served by non-married clergy and to adopt other Roman Catholic practices intended to assimilate the Ukrainians of Canada gradually into Roman Catholicism. However, among some of the Ukrainian settlers in Canada, there remained a strong perception of their religious lay rights from the historical traditions generated by the Orthodox Brotherhoods in Ukraine. Those frustrated by the romaniza-tion practices organized an Orthodox Brotherhood in 1918 and formed the autocephalic Ukrainian Greek Orthodox Church of Canada. The Orthodox Ukrainians in Canada from Bukovyna and other parts of Ukraine supported and joined that church. It is known today as the Ukrainian Orthodox Church of Canada. Stavropihian Crosses, symbolic of the Orthodox Brotherhood churches in Ukraine, can be seen on Orthodox churches in Canada built by Ukrainian settlers. However, the Ukrainian Orthodox Church of Canada is no longer a self-reliant, autocephalic church, having joined the pa-triarchate of Constantinople in 1990. That patriarch considers the patriarchate of Constantinople to be ecumenical in nature and oversees the Ukrainian Orthodox Church of Canada as only one eparchy (diocese) among many within his claimed scope of authority.

When the Roman Catholic hierarchy in Canada realized that Ukrainian lay people were capable of establishing their own church, they reduced their pressure on the Ukrainian Greek Catholic Church. They began to tolerate its existence in Canada and allowed it to develop more freely on its own initiatives. Consequently, one can conclude that the Ukrainian Greek Catholic Church survived in Canada largely because of the establishment of the Ukrainian Greek Orthodox Church of Canada.

Nevertheless, with Ukrainian Greek Catholic children pres-sured to attend Roman Catholic schools, many Greek Catholic youth adopted some Roman Catholic practices, which were brought with them into the Greek Catholic Church. Individually, others have espoused Roman Catholicism en-tirely. Today, they attend Roman Catholic churches and continue to associate with former classmates with whom they went to confession, partook of communion, and attended re-ligious services and other activities organized by their schools. The assimilation process from Ukrainian Greek Catholic rites (Orthodox in content) to Roman Catholic rites among youth has ended, but only to the extent that separate Ukrainian lan-guage schools within the provincial school systems were estab-lished in some communities in Canada.

Settlers from Bukovyna

Bukovyna became a duchy under the Austro-Hungarian Empire. The area was annexed by Austria in 1774 from Moldavia, a principality within the Turkish Ottoman Empire. In 1781, the Radovytsi Eparchy in Bukovyna was reorganized into a group of three eparchies, one for Bukovyna and two for Dalmatia. In 1865, the eparchy of Bukovyna joined the metropolitanate of Transylvania, a principality of the Hungarian kingdom within the Austro-Hungarian Empire, rather than join the Orthodox Church being formed at that time in Romania within the Ottoman Empire. In 1873, the Austrian emperor elevated the eparchy of Bukovyna into an independent, autocephalic metropolitanate which included the two eparchies in Dalmatia. Yevhenyi Hakman is the first Bukovyna-based metropolitan. He was succeeded by Metropolitan Sylvester Andriievych-Morar during the period 1880–95, then by Metropolitan Volodymyr Repta, 1902–25. Many Bukovynians came to Canada and the United States during these last two metropolitanships.

Meanwhile, the Romanians in the principalities of Wallachia and Moldavia within the Ottoman Empire united to form a united Romania in 1859 under a common ruler, Prince Alexander Cuza. During the Russian war on Turkey in 1877, Romania was invaded by the Russians, and the Romanians joined the Russians in their war on the Ottoman Empire. To be at war with the Turkish suzerain meant de facto that Romania had declared its independence. That independence was recognized with the *Treaty of Berlin* in 1878. During World War I, Romania joined Russia in 1916 in the war against the Austro-Hungarian empire, the Russians having promised that Romania could annex Bukovyna, Transylvania, and the Banat if the Austro-Hungarians were defeated. Indeed, Romania occupied Bukovyna in 1918 when the Austro-Hungarian Empire collapsed. Consequently, with the *Treaty of Sevres* in 1920, Bukovyna became an integral part of Romania. Ukrainians in Bukovyna were pressured to become Romanianized. Services in the churches also were Romanianized. The Romanianization movement followed many of the Ukrainian immigrants to Canada. Many Canadians with obvious Ukrainian names speak Romanian and consider themselves Romanian.

After the union of Wallachia and Moldavia in 1859, the Romanians organized their Orthodox Church into an autocephalic church in 1865. Their autocephalic status was recognized by the patriarch of Constantinople in 1885. In 1925, the Romanians consecrated their own patriarch. At that time the Orthodox in Bukovyna became administered by the patri-arch of Romania. But not until after the *Molotov-Ribbentrop Pact* in 1939 and the Soviet occupation of Bukovyna in 1940 were Orthodox Ukrainians there placed under the patriarch of Moscow in 1941. Church history in Bukovyna after the German and Romanian invasion of the Soviet Union in 1941 and after World War II had no significant carryover effect on settlers from Bukovyna who were already in Canada. Considerably earlier, some had joined and have remained loyal to the Russian Orthodox Church (established by Russian missionaries in Canada before World War I with money received from the sale of Alaska to the United States). Many of these people today are members of the Canadian branch of the Orthodox Church in America, the progeny of the Russian Orthodox Church in North America. But that is another story.

Glossary[1]

Note: On 19 April 1996, an official Ukrainian-English transliteration system was adopted by the Ukrainian Legal Terminology Commission (Decision No. 9). This system is used to transliterate all Ukrainian words, dialectal or otherwise, from Cyrillic letters to Roman letters, and has been used for the Ukrainian terms in this book. Other resources used in the preparation of this glossary include the following:

Akademiia Nauk Ukrains'koi RSR, Instytut Movoznavstva im. O.O. Potebni. 1970–1980. *Slovnyk Ukrains'koi Movy*. Kyiv: Vydavnytstvo, "Ukrains'ka Dumka."

Holoskevych, H. 1977. *Pravopysnyi Slovny*, Desiate vydannia {10th edition}. London: Vydavnytstvo Soiuzu Ukraintsiv u Velykii Britanii, 452 pp.

Podvez'ko, M.L. 1967. *Ukrains'ko-Anhliis'kyi Slovnyk [Ukrainian-English Dictionary]*, Vydannia druhe, vypravlene i dopovnene {2nd edition, corrected and expanded with additional material}. Kyiv: Derzhavne Uchbovo-Pedahohichne Vydavnytstvo "Radians'ka Shkola," 1019 pp.

Podvez'ko, M.L., and Hryhorenko, K.I. 1963. *English-Ukrainian Dictionary, Anhlo-Ukrains'kyi Slovnyk*. Reprinted in the United States by Saphrograph Company, 792 pp.

Words in square brackets in the text indicate corrections made to words quoted by other authors (in order to render all Ukrainian terms consistently). Transliterated Ukrainian terms are italicized in the glossary, and dialectal terms are noted as such in the definitions.

ban'ka (pl. *ban'ky*)
  jar, can, small tin container

banta (pl. *banty*)
  transom beam

Banyliv
  Ukrainian village in the upper Carpathians, formerly Rus'kyi Banyliv, officially renamed Banyliv in 1947

barvinok (pl. *barvinky*)
  blue myrtle (*vinca minor*)

berdo (pl. *berdy*)
  comb for spreading waft threads

bochka (pl. *bochky*)
  barrel, wooden barrel

Bohorodytsia
  religious holiday honouring St. Mary; literally, the mother of God (Jesus)

bondars'kyi ohnutyi nizh
  cooper's hollowing knife

bondars'kyi struh
  cooper's drawing knife

borona (pl. *borony*)
  harrow, harrows

borsch
  beet and vegetable soup

brusok (diminutive of *brus*)
  whet stone sharpener

brynza
  processed cheese made from goat milk

Bukovyna
  name given to a duchy within the Austrian part of the Austro-Hungarian
  Empire; literally an area where beech trees grow in Ukrainian

Bukovynian
  adjective in English usage for Bukovyna

burdei (pl. *burdei*)
  first shelter, a primitive earthen dugout with an A-
  frame roof of logs covered with sod or clay

buz
  dialectal for a soft summer cheese

bylen'
  that part of a flail that swings from the flail's handle

Carpathia
  area of the Carpathian Mountains settled by Ukrainians, politically today
  the Transcarpathian Oblast' (province) of Ukraine, *Zakarpats'ka Oblast'*

chasivnetsia
  long-toothed comb to remove seed pods from a sheaf
  of grain to be used for thatching roofs

cheliust
  mouth (opening) of an oven

Chernivtsi
  capital city of Bukovyna, politically today the capital city
  of the Chernivtsi Oblast' (province) of Ukraine

Chernihiv
  Oblast' (province) in northern Ukraine, named
  after its capital city, *Chernihiv*

chornozem
  chernozem is used when transliterated from Russian, which
  is pronounced in Russian as it is spelled in Ukrainian,
  i.e., *chornozem*, the black loam of Ukraine

chil'na storona
  on buildings, the main façade facing south; literally,
  the primary direction, or the brightest side

chip
  spigot or a bung for a barrel

chotyryskhyl'nyi dakh
  roof with four slopes

chysta khata
  clean room/smaller room in a two-roomed house; literally, a clean house

Dazhboh
  pagan sun god

dereviana lozhka (pl. *dereviani lozhky*)
  wooden spoon, spoons

didukh
  sheaf of wheat braided and brought indoors for the Christmas celebration

dishka (pl. *dizhky*)
  dialectal for *posud*, meaning dishes

dizha (pl. *dizhky*)
  wooden or metal bowl often used for kneading bread dough

dovbnia (pl. *dovbni*)
  wooden hammer, mallet, beater, pestle

drabyna
  ladder

dranytsia (pl. *dranytsi*);
also *dranka* (pl. *dranky*)
  lath, shingle

dveri
  door

dvertsi, dvertsiata
  little door

dvir; also *podviria*
  yard (enclosure around the house), courtyard, or homestead

dymar
  chimney flue

forma
  mould

Galicia
  Galicia is the German word for the land known in Ukrainian as *Halychyna*

ganok; also *hanok*
  porch

garnyts'
  see *konovka* below

gazda
  dialectal for the owner or head of a household, farmstead, or cottage industry

gralia (pl. *grali*)
  steel pitch forks

grazhda
  dialectal for *sadyba*, a grange, a homestead; used
  also for a farm yard; see *hrazhda* below

greblia (pl. *grebli*)
  dialectal for edging tool; the related word, *hreblia*,
  dam, weir, dike, or embankment

gyrdan
  short, choker-style necklace beaded on horsehair

halereia
  portico, entrance way, gallery

Halychanka
  variety of wheat demonstrating significant hardiness and other
  qualities that made it an excellent choice for prairie farmers, who
  adopted it when it was brought to Canada from Halychyna

Halychyna (Galicia)
  Halychyna is the name of a Ukrainian historic kingdom within
  the Ukrainian empire of *Kyivan Rus'*; the name comes from its
  former capital city, Halych, located today in the Ivano-Frankivs'k
  Oblast' (province) of Ukraine; also see Galicia above

hlynobyta khata

    earthen-walled house

holubtsi

    cabbage rolls with fillings of buckwheat, rice, or other

    grains, sometimes mixed with meat pieces or ground meat,

    then rolled within large leaves of cabbage and baked

homsha't

    home grown tobacco

horbotka (pl. *horbotky*)

    piece of material wrapped around a female's waist to form a skirt

hornets' (pl. *hornytsi*)

    dialectal for *horschyk*, small pot or cup

horod (pl. *horody*)

    yard, enclosed area used for garden plants, coming

    from the word for a walled city

horschok; also *horschyk*

    pot made from clay

hrablia (pl. *hrabli*)

    rake

hradka (pl. *hradky*)

    small garden plot of vegetables

hrazhda

    dialectal for a yard enclosed by fencing, a courtyard, or

    an isolated farmstead, a grange; see *grazhda* above

hrebin' (pl. *hrebni*)

    comb, as for card raddles with spikes for textiles

    or for combing cotton, wool, or flax

huhlia

    another name for *mantiia*, manta, mantle, mantua, manteau

Hutsul (pl. *Hutsuly*)

    person or (pl.) people having a distinctive ethnographic identity

    who live in the hills of the Carpathian Mountains of Ukraine

Hutsul'schyna

    common name for the homeland area of the *Hutsuly*

hybel' (pl. *hybli*)

    dialectal for *rubanok*, plane for working or smoothing wood

hybel' na vikonnu ramu

    window framing plane

hymbel' (pl. *hymbli*)

    Austrian plane

kabinet

    case or cupboard of drawers or shelves

kahla

    opening in the flue of a chimney

kalach (pl. *kalachi*)

    round, braided loaves often used at Thanksgiving and other

    religious ceremonies, or in services for the deceased

kal'dub

    wooden base that holds a millstone in place

kaminna plyta

    millstone, stone slab

kapusniak

    sauerkraut soup, cabbage soup

khata (pl. *khaty*)

    house made up of two rooms, for example, a vestibule and a large living room

khatchyna, khatka

    small house used as a summer kitchen; if in a dialect,

    khatchyna referred specifically to a cottage built of logs,

    properly it should have been called a *kolodna khatyna*

khatyna

    small house, usually having only one room

khram

    refers to a church or temple as a place of protection

Khram Day

    community holiday celebrating the namesake day for the

    saint after whom the local church was named

kiptar

    sheepskin vest with the hair facing the inside

kirat

    horse-powered rig consisting of a large, six-foot-diameter bull-

    wheel that transferred rotary energy to a drive-shaft that powered

    early threshing machines before the arrival of steam engines

kizla

    cross-piece placed over the ridge of a thatched roof to secure the thatch

kliamka

    door latch

klynok

    wedge-shaped rod that adjusts the space between grinding stones

kocherha

    fire iron, poker hook, see also *kotsiuba* below

kolach (pl. *kolachi*)

    see *kalach* (pl. *kalachi*) above

koloshi

    black woolen pants tied at the waist with a belt of braided thread

kolyska

    baby's cradle

komora

    pantry, store room, or granary for grain with a drive-through

    corridor; also multi-use storage building that served as a summer

    kitchen and unheated cold storage during the winter

komyn

    chimney

konovka, konivka

    small pail, cream can, or wooden milk pitcher

korm (pl. *kormy*)

    food for people or forage, fodder, and provender for animals *koromyslo* (pl. *koromesla*)

yoke-like scale beam for balancing two pails of water on one's shoulder while carrying them, as from the well to the house

koryto (pl. *koryta*)

elongated wooden trough or basin

kosa (pl. *kosy*)

scythe

koshara

enclosure for livestock; pen, especially for sheep and goats

koshka

wooden pouch for carrying a sharpening stone; small basket

kotsiuba

wooden, hoe-like oven cleaning tool

kovznyi zamok

sliding lock

kozhukh

sheepskin overcoat with the hair facing the inside

kozlova pyla

bucksaw, dialectal for *luchkova pylka*

krokva

rafter-truss

krosna

weaving loom

krovlia

rafter-minor truss

kruzhok (pl. *kruzhky*)

disk; round lid as for a stove or a barrel; bread board; hot pot holder

ktelsok

stump or block

kucha

pig barn

kuchma

cap made of woolen fleece, usually black

kudelia

spun thread holder, tow of hemp

kukhlia (also *kukhol'*)

mug or pitcher from which to drink or pour liquids

kurnyk

chicken barn, chicken coop

kushka (pl. *kushky*)

wooden mug or pitcher in which a scythesman would carry his *brusok*, whet stone sharpener

kutia

wheat, honey, and poppy seed dish prepared for Christmas

kuznia

blacksmith shop

lata

dialectal for a wash tub, a *vanna*

lava

bench adjacent to wall

lavka

small, freestanding bench

lopata

spatula, a shovel or spade

lopatka (pl. *lopatky*)

small spatula

lozhka, dereviana

wooden spoon, see *dereviana lozhka* above

magli vnytsia; also *magil'nytsia*

dialectal for washboard, *rubel'*, clothes beater or ruffler

maister

master craftsman, such as a cooper, a carpenter, or a tradesman

makohin (pl. *makohony*)

wooden pestle or pounder

makykh

basin for crushing or washing small seed such as poppy seed, a *makitra*

mantiia; also *mantel'ia* (pl. *manty*)

manta, mantle, mantua, manteau

mashyna

machine or a motor car

maslynka

dialectal for a butter churn, a *maslorobka*

masnychka

churn, also called *maznytsia*

mechok

small blade

mirka

measuring device

mistechko

small town

mitla

long handled broom

mlyn

mill

molotok

hammer, mallet, gavel, or a hammer-shaped millwright's specialty tool for dressing the working face of a millstone; called a mill bill and thrift

molotyty

to thresh

motovylo

skein winder

myska (pl. *mysky*)

bowl or dish

mysnyk

cupboard for dishes

napilna stina

back wall of room where the *pich* or plank bed would be located

nastinnyi rozpys
design for decorating a wall

Nebyliv
town in Halychyna

nizh do sina
hay-cutting knife, also used for cutting straw, *nizh do solomy*

nozhytsi
scissors

nytka (pl. *nytky*)
thread, the warp threads in a loom

nyty
the weft or woof threads in a loom

obtochuval'na pyla
turning saw

okesna
dialectal for window sash, *vikonna rama*

okolot, okolit
truss of straw

oliia
oil, often made from hemp or sunflowers and used
for Christmas and Easter Lenten cooking.

oliinyk
expert oil press journeyman

oliinytsia
hemp seed oil press

oliinytsia klynova
wooden wedge oil press

orach
ploughman

oslin do priadyva
bench for spinning

ostrishok
low edge of thatched roof; literally, next to the *strikha*, roof eaves

paluba
wooden protective trough on the ridge of a thatched roof; a deck

pan
large area landowner, lord of the manor

parkan
fence

Paskha
Easter, Passover

perednia stina
main façade; literally the front wall

perekhid
passage way

peremitka
headpiece, a women's headdress, wound around the head

perepichka
small loaf of sourdough bread

pereplit
window sash, transom

pereveslo
plait of straw with which to tie a bundle (sheaf) of grain

peryna (pl. *peryny*)
feather-filled quilt, a feather bed, a fluffy feather pillow or
quilt containing wild goose down and duck feathers

pich
earthen clay stove used for heating and cooking;
the top could be used for sleeping

pich na priazhennia
stove for roasting seed, *zerna,* such as oilseed

pid
dialectal for attic, loft, upstairs, *horysche*

piddashok
veranda, porch

pidkurna khata
semi smoke house, smoke enters attic

pidstillia
underneath the table

pil
plank bed (a rough, sawn-plank bed for sleeping),
wooden shelf used for sleeping

platva
roof sill, top plate

pletinka (pl. *pletinky*)
wicker baskets (*koshyky*)

plit, plitro
wicker fence, wattle fence, woven willow fence

pluh
plough

podilia
lower plains relative to higher or mountainous plains, specifically
in Ukraine, *Podilia* refers to the area of the Dnister River Basin

podilian boots
boots worn by those living in *Podilia* of Ukraine

pohrib
cellar, lower vault *pohrits, pidval, l'okh*

pokut'
wall adorned with icons, area for dining or guests, corner of honour

pole (pl. *polia*)
farm field

polotno
linen or hemp cloth

pomana
gift in reference to food from heaven, as in "manna"
from the biblical story in *Exodus,* 16: 1 36

pomianuty
to speak well of someone in memory

porih

threshold

portkynytsi

baggy pyjama-type pants, *portky*

poshyta

adjective; as in *poshyta khata* (feminine), thatched house,

or *poshytyi dakh* (masculine), thatched roof

poshyvnyk (pl. *poshyval'nyky*)

thatcher

postil'

bed, bedding, bed linens

posud (pl. *posudy*)

a collective noun for dishes and plates, kitchenware,

including earthenware, glassware, and china

potachok

opening at the bottom of an oven

predava

bench used for spinning

priadka

spinning wheel

provody

the blessing of graves that took place the week following Easter

prut

dialectal for a length of land; one *prut* equals one

hectare; otherwise, a rod or a twig

prychilka

small side of building

prychilok

side of building

prychipok

the front opening of the stove or oven

prysinok (pl. *prysinky*)

lean-to, attachment, porch

pryz'ba

bench-like structure of densely pressed clay that reinforced

the outer walls and foundation of the structure

puky na strikhu

bundles for the protruding edges of a thatched roof

pyilo (pl. *pyila*)

Ukrainianized version of English word for pail, *vidro* in Ukrainian

pyla, pylka

frame saw, hand saw, crosscut saw

pyrohy

thin dough, dumplings, with various fillings, sometimes

mashed potatoes with cheese and onions

quern

small round millstone, *zhorna*

resheto

sieve used in winnowing or cleaning grain

reshitka

wire netting, grating, grill

rosil

juice of sauerkraut

rubel'

a clothes beater or ruffler

rublena khata

log house

Rus'kyi-Banyliv

see *Banyliv* above

Ruthenians

Anglicized term from the Latin name given to the

descendants of Kyivan Rus', today's Ukrainians

sad

orchard

sadochok

small orchard; also a decorative planting into a *kalach* of prongs

onto which confections and fruits are attached, used to celebrate

Christmas at the festive table or a memorial dinner

salitra

salty

sardak; also *serdak*

warm, short, felt jacket

Scythians

Skify in Ukrainian. Rulers over Ukrainian lands from 1150 to

750 BC and in a smaller area in the south until AD 200

selo

village

serdak

see *sardak* above

serp (pl. *serpy*)

sickle

shandar (pl. *shandari*)

policeman (pl. police)

sharvarok

Ukrainian word adopted in Canada for "share work." In Ukraine, *sharvarok*

referred to a serf's obligation to do public service work for his master,

such as road building, dam construction, or other construction work

shekivnetsia

cabbage shredder

shely

posts, this word comes from *sheliuha*, a sand willow tree

shkola

school

shparhut

cast-iron plate with either three eight-inch [20 cm] lids, or concave

hollow in the cooking surface which fit over the firebox of a *pich*

shpykhlir

granary

shtakhety

stakes in a board fence

shukhlia

grain shovel, *shukhlia* is a Canadian Ukrainianization via

shuflia; as for a shovel in English, *sovok* in Ukrainian

shyba (pl. *shyby*)

glass pane

Sich Kolomea

name for a place in Alberta that was named after

places in Ukraine, *Sich* and *Kolomyia*

sichkarnia

straw cutter

sikach

chopping knife, cleaver, chopper

siny

entrance hall, passageway, vestibule

skhody

steps

skrynia

chest

Sniatyn

town in Ukraine

snip

sheaf

sobor

church of importance, a cathedral, a gathering of people, a council

soim; also *seim*

parliament, legislative council

solodoschi

sweets, confection

soloma

straw

solomianyi dakh

straw roof

sopilka

flute – metal or wooden

sorochka

shirt or a blouse

spomyn (pl. *spomyny*)

recollection (pl.) memoirs

stainia

stable barn

stelyna

dialectal for a ceiling, *stelia*

stil

table

stodola

threshing barn

strikha

eaves of a roof

stupa

grain crusher, stamp mill, mortar and pestle type of grain huller

and crusher that used foot power to increase efficiency

sverdel'; also *sverdlo* (pl. *sverdli*)

drill, borer

svitlytsia

living room, parlour, sitting room, east room, sometimes a

small room in the attic; also *velyka kimnata*, great room

svoloka (pl. *svoloky*)

cross-tie beam, girder, transform, or ceiling support

tachilka (pl. *tachilky*)

rolling pin

terlytsia, or *ternytsia*, or *tipalka*

flax or hemp fibre crusher; scutch or scutching machine

tesliars'kyi struh

spokeshave; literally, carpenter's drawblade

tkats'kyi verstat

weaving loom

toloka

community pasture, an open gathering place in a village

square, or a gathering of people to accomplish a major task

collectively, as in constructing a building quickly

topir or *topor*

axe

torbyna (pl. *torbyny*)

bag, pouch

tovkach (pl. *tovkachi*)

pestle for a mortar made of hard wood for crushing grain

Transcarpathia

common name for an ethnically Ukrainian settled area having

had a variety of official political names historically; today, that

area is called the *Zakarpats'ka Oblast'* (province) in Ukraine

triitsia

the Trinity, a triple candle holder, a Christmas table centrepiece

tsebryk

small wash tub, a large one being a *tseber*

tsip

flail

tsisars'ka doroha

imperial or national highway; literally, Caesar's Road

tsymbaly

multi-string hammer dulcimer

Tulova

village in Halychyna; today, in the *Ivano-*

Frankivsk Oblast' (province) of Ukraine

tybel' (pl. *tybli*)

wooden pin (nail), wooden peg, wooden dowel

vavka

skein winder

velyka kimnata

literally, the great room, the sitting room, the parlour, the living

room, the east room in a Ukrainian house, a *svitlytsia*

verena (pl. *vereny*)

dialectal for a bedcover, a very thick blanket, a *vereta*

vereta (pl. *verety*)

cover for a bed or furniture

vereteno (pl. *vereteny*)

spinning spindle

verstat

work bench (*tkats'kyi verstat* is a weaver's loom)

vertliuh

swivel, pivot yoke; also a pivot swivel that balances the rock in the quern mill

viazy

dialectal for a scythe handle, the nape of the neck;

literally, a bond, link, brace, or tie

vidro

pail, bucket

vikno (pl. *vikna*)

window

vilni zemli

free lands

vinyk

whisk, small broom

vkryval'nyk

roofer

Volynia

name of a Ukrainian historic kingdom within the Ukrainian empire of

Kyivan Rus', a part of which is within the *Volyns'ka Oblast'* (province)

of Ukraine today; the name comes from the area's former capital

city, Volodymyr. Today, the capital city for the *Oblast'* is *Luts'k*.

vtsivku

from a compounding of the words, *u tsivku*, referring to a saddle

joint, cylindrical hole for a pin; literally, in the rivet hole

vyimchastyi hybel'

hollowed-out, grooved plane

vykrutok or *vykrutka*

flat-blade screwdriver

vyretnok

Archimedian drill with a chuck

vzamok

from a compounding of the words, *u zamok*, referring

to a dovetail joint; literally, locked in

vzrub

from a compounding of the words, *u zrub*, referring to a framework,

as in logs cut to fit into each other on the corner of a building

yalyna

pine or spruce tree

yarmo

oxen yoke, *koromyslo dlia voliv*, or *yarmo dlia voliv*

yarno

dialectal for a yoke on top of a thatched roof, probably related to a yoke,

yarmo, for harnessing horned cattle such as oxen to do pulling work

zahata

dialectal for a protective outdoor insulation, could be reinforced

with a willow matrix; literally, a dam, dyke, or solid fence

zamkaiuchyi zarub (pl. *zamkaiuchi zaruby*)

interlocking cuts into logs such as dovetail or u-channel joints

zatyskach

clamp

Zelenii Sviata

Green Holidays, Ascension of our Lord Day

zemlianka

sod house; turf blocks built up to form walls

zhorno (pl. *zhorna*)

millstone when used in the singular; quern or

stone mill when used in the plural

References

Numerous field interviews were conducted by the author in preparing this material, and written notes were recorded directly following.

List of Interviews

Boychuk, Helen Solowan. Interviewed in 1977 by author in Edmonton.

Magera, Fred. 1978. Interviewed multiple times by author in Willingdon, AB. Magera was the district agriculturist in the Willingdon region and was thoroughly acquainted with the early pioneering practices of the Bukovynian and Galician settlers in the area.

Orleski, Steve. 1957–1997. Interviewed by author on a number of occasions in Two Hills concerning the Szypenitz settlement and hemp seed oil production.

Pawlowsky, Sidney. 2002. Interviewed by author in Mallaig, 22 December.

Pidruchney, Anna Rycheba. 1987. Interviewed by author in Edmonton. Pidruchney was a long-time resident of Vegreville, AB, and knew Peter Svarich. She translated his written materials that were stored at the Provincial Archives.

Shandro, Johnny. 1957–1978. Interviewed by author in Andrew regarding home construction, thatching, and community social and religious events in the Shandro district.

Shandro, Martha. Regularly interviewed by author in Shandro on occasions too numerous to count, as she is the author's grandmother.

Salamandyk, Pearl Svarich. 1950–1954. Interviewed by author in Edmonton. Pearl was Peter Svarich's youngest sister, and she came to homestead in Alberta via wagon from Strathcona.

Stanko, John. 1956. Interviewed at his home in Edmonton about thatching houses.

Zazula, Wasyl. 1977, 1978. Interviewed multiple times by author in Shandro. Zazula was thoroughly acquainted with traditional thatching practices, having thatched several homes in the Shandro and Willingdon districts of east central Alberta.

Zukiwsky, Harry. July 1998. Interviewed multiple times by author in Willingdon, AB. Zukiwsky is the elder son of a pioneer family; his father was a carpenter. Much of the detailed information regarding construction practices in Chapter 3 came from his interviews.

List of Works Cited

Currelly, Charles Trick. 1956. *I Brought the Ages Home*. Toronto: Royal Ontario Museum.

Darlington, James W. 1991. "The Ukrainian impress on the Canadian west." In *Canada's Ukrainians: Negotiating an Identity*, ed. Lubomyr Y. Luciuk and Stella Hryniuk, 53–80. Toronto: University of Toronto Press.

Dowsett, Gwen. 1986. "Folk housing: The vernacular architecture of the Ukrainian people in Manitoba." *Border Crossings* 5, no. 4: 12–20.

Elston, Miriam. 1915. "The Russian in our midst." *Westminster*: 532.

Ewanchuk, Michael. 1977. *Spruce, Swamp and Stone: A History of the Pioneer Ukrainian Settlements in the Gimli Area*. Steinbach: Self-published.

———. 1981. *Pioneer Profiles: Ukrainian Settlers in Manitoba*. Steinbach: Self-published.

Fedorak, Michael, ed. 1990. *Early Foundations: Willingdon and Area History*. Edmonton: Willingdon History Book Committee.

Fodchuk, Roman. May 1977. "The Ukrainian Cultural Heritage Village Master Site Plan – 1977." Report produced by Roman Fodchuk and Associates, Ltd., for Alberta Culture.

———. July 1978. "Master Plan – Ukrainian Cultural Heritage Village: Farmstead Group Building Selection Report." Unpublished report in three volumes prepared by Roman Fodchuk and Associates for Alberta's Department of Culture and the Department of Housing and Public Works.

———. Spring 1989. "Building the little house on the prairies: Ukrainian technology, Canadian resources." In *Material History Bulletin*, ed. Robert Klymasz, 89–97. Ottawa: Canadian Museum of Civilization and the National Museum of Science and Technology; also published as a series of consecutive articles in Winnipeg's *Ukrainian Voice* newspaper, Sept. 2001.

Gregorovich, Andrew. 2001. "Scythia of Scythian gold." *Forum: A Ukrainian Review* 103–104: n/a.

Himka, John Paul. 1988. *Galician Villagers and the Ukrainian National Movement in the Nineteenth Century*. Edmonton: Canadian Institute of Ukrainian Studies Press.

Hohn, Hubert, ed. 1976. *Byzantine Churches of Alberta* (Photographs by Orest Semchishen). Edmonton: Edmonton Art Gallery.

Hohol, Demjan. 1985. "The Grekul house: A land use and structural history," Historic Sites Service paper, no. 14. Edmonton: Alberta Department of Culture and Multiculturalism.

Hryniuk, Stella. 1991a. "Sifton's pets: Who were they?" In *Canada's Ukrainians: Negotiating an Identity*, ed. Lubomyr Y. Luciuk and Stella Hryniuk, 3–16. Toronto: University of Toronto Press.

———. 1991b. *Peasants with Promise*. Edmonton: Canadian Institute of Ukrainian Studies Press.

Hryniuk, Stella, and Jeffrey Picknicki. 1995. *The Land They Left Behind: Canada's Ukrainians in the Homeland*. Winnipeg: Watson Dwyer.

Kaye, Vladimir J. 1964. *Early Ukrainian Settlement in Canada, 1895–1900*. Toronto: University of Toronto Press.

Kostek, Mike, ed. 1986. *Down Memory Trails: A History of Two Hills and Surrounding Area*. Winnipeg: Two Hills Historical Society.

Kurelek, William. 1980. *The Ukrainian Pioneers*. Niagara Falls, ON: Niagara Falls Art Gallery.

Landsman, Pearl Shandro. 1999. "Shandro, Andrew S. His Memoirs and Reminiscing." In *The Shandros – Our Story*. Edmonton: Shandro Heritage Society, 226–41.

Lehr, John C. 1976. "Ukrainian vernacular architecture in Alberta." Occasional paper no. 1, Historic Sites Service, Edmonton.

———. 1991. "Peopling the prairies with Ukrainians." In *Canada's Ukrainians: Negotiating an Identity*, ed. Lubomyr Y. Luciuk and Stella Hryniuk, 30–52. Toronto: University of Toronto Press.

———. 2002. "The geographical background to church union in Canada," *Prairie Forum* 27, no. 2: 199–208.

Lehr John C., and Jeffrey Picknicki Morski. 1999. "Family matters and global concerns: The origins of the Ukrainian pioneer diaspora, 1891–1914." *Journal of Historical Geography* 25, no. 3: 349–66.

Lehr, John C., and Serge Cipko. 2000. "Contested identities: Competing articulations of the national heritage of pioneer settlers in Misiones, Argentina." In *Prairie Perspectives: Geographical Essays*, ed. J. Romanowski, 165–80. Winnipeg: University of Manitoba Press.

Lesoway, Marie. 1989. *Out of the Peasant Mold: A Structural History of the M. Hawreliak Home in Shandro, Alberta*. Edmonton: Alberta Culture and Multiculturalism, Historical Resources Division.

Luciuk, Lubomyr Y., and Bohdan S. Kordan. 1989. *Creating a Landscape: A Geography of Ukrainians in Canada*. Toronto: University of Toronto Press.

Jordan, Terry G. 1978. *Texas Log Buildings. A Folk Architecture*. Austin/London: University of Texas Press.

Macgregor J.G. 1969. *Vilni Zemli (Freelands): The Ukrainian settlement of Alberta*. Toronto: McClelland & Stewart.

Martynowych, Orest T. 1991. *Ukrainians in Canada: The Formative Period, 1891–1924*. Edmonton: Canadian Institute of Ukrainian Studies, University of Alberta.

Maylon, T., and A. Henman. 1980. Name of article NA. *New Scientist* 13 (November): 433–35.

Melchizedek, Drunvalo. 1998. *The Ancient Secret of the Flower of Life*. Flagstaff: Sight Technology.

Melnyky, Peter. 1988. "Mashyna: Ukrainians and agricultural technology in Alberta to 1930." In *Continuity and Change: The Cultural Life of Alberta's First Ukrainians*, ed. Manoly R. Lupul, 1. Edmonton: Canadian Institute of Ukrainian Studies, University of Alberta, and Historic Sites Service, Alberta Culture and Multiculturalism.

Nahachewsky, Andriy. 1985. "Ukrainian Dug-out Dwellings in East-central Alberta." Historic Sites Service, occasional paper no. 11, Edmonton, Alberta Culture.

Orshinsky, Peter. *Traditional Bukovynian Skirts and Jewellery for Women as Found in Canada*. Fenwick, ON: Self-published, 1974.

Potrebenko, Helen. 1977. *No Streets of Gold: A Social History of Ukrainians in Alberta*. Vancouver: New Star Books.

Romaniuk, Gus. 1954. *Taking Root in Canada*. Winnipeg: Columbia Printers.

Rotoff, Basil, Roman Yereniuk, and Stella Hryniuk. 1990. *Monuments to Faith: Ukrainian Churches in Manitoba*. Winnipeg: University of Manitoba Press.

Semeniuk, Lilian, ed. 1980. *Dreams and Destinies; Andrew and District*. Edmonton: Andrew Historical Society.

Shandro Heritage Society. 1999. *The Shandros – Our Story*. Edmonton: Shandro Heritage Society.

Shostak, Peter. *For Our Children: A Book Commemorating Ukrainian Settlement in Western Canada*. Victoria: Yalenka Books, 1991.

Stashyn, Mykhailo. 1981. "Memoirs." In *Pioneer Profiles: Ukrainian Settlers in Manitoba*, ed. Michael Ewanchuk, 11–16. Steinbach: Self-published.

Svarich, Peter. 1934. Peter Svarich Collection (1891–1964), translated by Anna Rycheba Pidruchney. Edmonton: PAA Collection no. 75.74; document no. 82.225. (An English translation of Ukrainian material in the Peter Svarich Collection; Provincial Archives of Alberta, no page numbers assigned).

Thomas-Kordan, Diana. 1988. "Tradition in a new world: Ukrainian-Canadian churches in Alberta." *Society for the Study of Architecture in Canada, Bulletin 13*: 3–7.

Tomyn, Mike. 1980. "Harry and Annie Tomyn family." In *Our Crossing: Rivers to Roads. A History of Brosseau, Duvernay and Surrounding Area*, ed. Hector Coutu, 544–48. Edmonton: Brosseay and Duvernay Historical Book Committee.

Turkewich, Joseph. 1981 [1927]. "Stonebreaker turned farmer." In *Pioneer Profiles: Ukrainian Settlers in Manitoba*, ed. Michael Ewanchuk, 77–79. Steinbach: Self-published.

Zazula, Wasyl. 1983. *Pioneer Memories*. Edmonton: Self-published biography.

Notes

Notes to Preface

1 Lake Eliza is located directly north of Myrnam and across the bridge on the North Saskatchewan River.

2 I subsequently learned this was the home of Peter Tymchuk.

3 Commonly referred to as the "Ukrainian Bloc" in contemporary literature about ethnicity on the prairies.

4 My maternal, Bukovynian grandparents lived in the Shandro district, but have long since passed on.

5 "*Pan*" is a common Ukrainian term for the "Lord of the Manor," the major landholder in the eastern European feudal social system before the Second World War.

6 It is now available in paperback, having been translated and printed by Trident Press in 1976. Work has begun on the second half, which deals with the Svarich family's immigration and resettlement experiences from 1904 on.

7 St. John's served as "home" for many Ukrainian-Canadian students at the University of Alberta.

8 I served as the Myrnam region's district agriculturist from 1954 to 1957.

9 When I began preparing this manuscript, Svarich's memoirs were available only in Ukrainian. I was granted special permission by St. John's Institute to translate and reference segments of his written work, and I have quoted from this translation extensively. Ms. Anna Rycheba Pidruchney was retained to produce an English translation of selected writings from the original Ukrainian, now housed in the Provincial Archives of Alberta. Page numbers are not assigned, as the translated materials are not available to the public.

10 The author was the principal consultant for the Ukrainian Cultural Heritage Village project, first to the society that started the project and then to the Government of Alberta. Several planning documents were prepared, including the master plan for the U.C.H. Village, the basis for the development of the historical complex. The major component of this work was carried out from 1976 to 1979. Appendix 1 is the text of a talk I prepared for the Learned Societies Meetings (held at the University of Alberta in May of 2000). It describes the project in some detail, including the development of the museum from concept to completion, in addition to noting the contributions made by other individuals involved.

11 A brief essay describes the settlers' religious background in more detail in Appendix 2.

12 Terry Jordan was a cultural geographer who studied the log structures of Germans, Swedes, and other people from the Carpathians who settled in east Texas. His comments regarding the interconnection of cultural and structural matters are applicable to the Ukrainian pioneers, as well.

Notes to Introduction Part One, by Dr. Robert Klymasz

1 A hammer dulcimer *tsymbaly* is an old Ukrainian instrument consisting of a series of strings stretched across a sound box. On top are twelve or more groups of four strings, tuned vertically, usually with two bridges. The instrument is played with a wooden hammer and has a range of two or three octaves in basses and treble. The instrument was a favourite with country orchestras who entertained at weddings, showers, and other events.

Notes to Introduction Part Two, by Dr. John C. Lehr

1 For an overview of Ukrainian settlement in Canada, see V.J. Kaye, *Early Ukrainian Settlement in Canada, 1895–1900* (Toronto: University of Toronto Press, 1964); and Orest T. Martynowych, *Ukrainians in Canada: The Formative Period 1891–1924* (Edmonton: Canadian Institute of Ukrainian Studies, University of Alberta Press, 1991).

2 On the Ukrainian settlements in Brazil, see John C. Lehr and Jeffrey Picknicki Morski, "Family matters and global concerns: The origins of the Ukrainian pioneer diaspora, 1891–1914," *Journal of Historical Geography* 25, no. 3 (1999): 349–66. Ukrainian emigration to Argentina is described briefly in John C. Lehr and Serge Cipko, "Contested identities: Competing articulations of the national heritage of pioneer settlers in Misiones, Argentina" in *Prairie Perspectives: Geographical Essays*, ed. J. Romanowski (Winnipeg: University of Manitoba, 2000), 165–80.

3 Again, see Appendix 2 for a brief overview of the Ukrainian settlers' religious history.

4 C.W. Speers, colonization officer in Winnipeg, to W.F. McCreary, Commissioner of Immigration (Winnipeg, 9 July 1897, National Archives of Canada [LAC], Record Group 76, Vol. 144, File 34214, part 1).

5 For an excellent depiction of western Ukraine at the time of the Ukrainian emigration to Canada, see Stella Hryniuk and Jeffrey Picknicki, *The Land They Left Behind: Canada's Ukrainians in the Homeland* (Winnipeg: Watson Dwyer, 1995).

6 See John C. Lehr, "Government perceptions of Ukrainian immigrants to western Canada, 1896–1902," *Canadian Ethnic Studies/Études ethniques au Canada* 19, no. 2 (1987): 1–12.

7 See, for example, James W. Darlington, "The Ukrainian impress on the Canadian west," in *Canada's Ukrainians*, 53–80; Lubomyr Y. Luciuk and Bohdan S. Kordan, *Creating a Landscape: A Geography of Ukrainians in Canada* (Toronto: University of Toronto Press, 1989): John C. Lehr, "Ukrainian houses in Alberta," *Alberta Historical Review* 21 (1973): 9–15; "Colour preferences and building decoration among Ukrainians in western Canada," *Prairie Forum* 6 (1981): 203–06; "The Ukrainian sacred landscape: A metaphor of survival and acculturation," *Material History Bulletin* 29 (1989): 3–11; Demjan Hohol, "The Grekul house: A land use and structural history" (Historic Sites Service, no. 14, Edmonton, 1985); Diana Thomas-Kordan, "Tradition in a new world: Ukrainian-Canadian churches in Alberta," Society for the Study of Architecture in Canada, *Bulletin 13*, 1988: 3–7; and Basil Rotoff, Roman Yereniuk, and Stella Hryniuk, *Monuments to Faith: Ukrainian Churches in Manitoba* (Winnipeg: University of Manitoba Press, 1990).

8 The agricultural technology of the pioneer era receives passing attention in many pioneer memoirs, and it has been the subject of some scholarly enquiry. See, for example, Peter Melnyky, "Mashyna: Ukrainians and agricultural technology in Alberta to 1930," in *Continuity and Change: The Cultural Life of Alberta's First Ukrainians*, ed. Manoly R. Lupul, 100–118 (Edmonton: Canadian Institute of Ukrainian Studies, and Historic Sites Service, Alberta Culture and Multiculturalism, 1988), 1.

Notes to Chapter 1 The Journey

1 The people in the Romanian settlement in Alberta just east of Willingdon came from the province of Bukovyna, which was under Romanian jurisdiction. Most have Ukrainian surnames such as Cucheron, Porozny, Hutzkol, and Yurko. Their immigrant grandparents spoke both languages, but considered themselves Romanian. Their children, if they spoke a second language, spoke Romanian.

2 Wasyl and Martha Shandro are the author's maternal grandparents. Martha Megley came to Canada with her parents, Michailo and Anna Megley, in 1904.

3 Peter Svarich crossed the Atlantic Ocean three times and the Pacific twice and was never ill.

4 Fort William marked the halfway point of the long journey.

5 These friends were the Nicholas Gregoraschuk family from Tulova, Halychyna. Nicholas was the brother of my grandmother, Marie Fodchuk.

6 This Romanian settlement consisted primarily of families from Romanian Bukovyna, an area that was occupied by Romania for approximately fifty years under the Austria-Hungarian Empire. Most of these settlers came to Canada 100 years ago at about the same time as the Ukrainian immigration. See *Romanians in Alberta* (Zawadiuk et al., eds., Edmonton: Canadian Romanian Society of Alberta 1898–1998); also see Appendix 2 for more information.

7 This is the "official" spelling of the place name today, but it had a number of spellings in this area in the past. Szypenitz is the Germanic spelling of the Bukovynian name "Shypyntsi" (a town in western Ukraine from whence the settlers in this area came). A map in MacGregor's *Vilni Zemli* of the "Star Colony about 1910," shows Szypenitz as a school, and very close by is Shepenge, an early post office that was part of an early general store operated by Wasyl Weranka on his homestead. The Szypenitz School was the first school district to be established in 1906 in the Two Hills area. The school and the post office were within half a mile of the Ukrainian Orthodox Church of St. Mary, which is the only landmark still standing. The school, hall, and post office are long gone.

8 At least thirty place names listed on the Bloc Historical Development chart on p. 9 were transplanted from the homeland.

9 The town of Andrew was named after its first Postmaster, Andrew Shandro (Lesoway, 1989), 46.

10 This developmental material is paraphrased from a series of occasional papers prepared for the Historic Sites Services and published by the Historical Resources Division of the Government of Aberta's Department of Culture and Multiculturalism and from the Andrew Historical Society's publication *Dreams and Destinies; Andrew and District*.

11 At that time, it was referred to as the Canadian Northern Railroad, but it was later changed to Canadian National.

Notes to Chapter 2 Surviving

1 This beautiful, common flower, or prickly rose, is the floral emblem of Alberta.

2 Such symbols are found in old Egyptian temples dated to the time of the God Thoth, and are timeless. Some of Leonardo da Vinci's original drawings depict an understanding of sacred geometry, and the "Flower of Life" is said to originate in the pre-historic, Atlantian period (Melchizedek 1998, 38–30).

3 It is encouraging to note that a new interest in antique tools is developing owing to collectors and others with an interest in material culture.

4 For more information regarding the Cultural Village development, refer to Appendix 1.

5 The Peter Svarich Collection includes drawings by Peter Svarich as part of the collection of documents. An English translation of the Ukrainian materials accompanying the drawings was completed by Anna Rycheba Pidruchney. The original Ukrainian version is with the Peter Svarich Collection (1891–1964) housed by the Provincial Archives of Alberta in Edmonton (PAA collection no. 75, document no. 82.225 (1934)).

6 Martha Megley Shandro is the author's grandmother.

Notes to Chapter 3 Building the Little House on the Prairies

1 Chapter 3 is an expanded and less technical version of an article published in the spring of 1989 in the *Material History Bulletin*, a twice-yearly publication of the Canadian Museum of Civilization and the National Museum of Science and Technology. (Roman Fodchuk, "Building the Little House on the Prairies: Ukrainian Technology, Canadian Resources"), 89–97. Robert Klymasz was the guest editor of that issue.

2 The information about home building comes from such numerous sources that, rather than break the narrative up frequently in order to cite individual authors regarding matters that each addressed to some extent in their published materials or during interviews, I have listed them instead, and suggest that the reader consult the bibliography for further information.

3 This being but one in a series of hardships, it is appropriate to note here that these immigrants survived, and indeed thrived, against all odds.

4 "Master Plan – Ukrainian Cultural Heritage Village: Farmstead Group Building Selection Report" (Calgary: Roman Fodchuk and Associates, Ltd., July 1978). All the houses in this unpublished field survey of nineteen early homesteads were found to be facing south. Most of the observations and data in the present report were confirmed by Fodchuk's field study.

5 Svarich headed up the Committee of the Association of Ukrainian Pioneers of Alberta who built the Ukrainian Pioneers House in Elk Island National Park in 1951 in honour of Dr. Archer, a pioneer doctor from Lamont, Alberta, who served the Ukrainian community.

6 It is noteworthy that mud plastering in Ukraine was usually men's work. However, my own experience, the experiences of many of the pioneers interviewed, and much of the literature written on the subject suggests women played a major role in this aspect of home construction in Canada.

7 Magera was the District Agriculturist in the Willingdon region and was thoroughly acquainted with the early pioneering practices of the settlers in this area from Bukovyna and Halychyna.

8 A historical account of the Stepanski family describes their pioneer home with clay floors.

9 The author made a field trip to verify the construction of two existing examples of a pich with a shparhut in the Willingdon area with Harry Zukiwsky in 1988.

10 Based on field studies by Roman Fodchuk and Associates in the Shandro-Smoky Lake and Szypenitz area of Alberta. See also "Master Plan – Ukrainian Cultural Heritage Village."

Notes to Chapter 4 One Hundred and Sixty Acres

1 When these pioneers came to Canada, the season was well-on. Before they could even begin to clear land, they had to find and register their homestead. They did not have much time to clear and plough before winter would set in. The estimate is an average of five acres; however some were able to accomplish more depending on availability of equipment and local conditions.

2 See http://res2.agr.gc.ca/publications/marquis/page05_e.htm#halychanka for Dr. Charles Saunders' (of Ottawa's Central Experimental Farms; Federal Department of Agriculture) description of how "Red Fife" wheat actually originated from a shipment of Hirka wheat from Southern Ukraine. It was sent to Scotland, then forwarded by a friend to the renowned Mr. Fife in Cobourg, Ontario about 1842. It was found to be a superior spring wheat that grew well on the prairies and became the genetic foundation of such outstanding wheat varieties as Marquis, Saunders, and Thatcher. By 1928 about 85% of all spring wheat seeded on the prairies was a strain of this original Ukrainian seed. The wheat known as Halychanka (originating in Halychyna, the home of Peter Svarich and Paul Fodchuk), or Red Fife, became a western Canadian staple by sheer happenstance.

3 The finest hay produced was the result of knowing when the plants were at the ideal stage for producing easily digested forage. The grass floral organs are usually encased in a leaf covering called a "boot." These are usually clustered panicles that, once extended out of the "boot," mature quickly and increase lignin content. The older the grass beyond the "bloom" stage, the coarser and less nutritious the hay.

4 Gregorovich, 2001.

5 The power sweep, or kirat, was an early method to transfer horse-power into a motive power drive for threshing before the steam engine. Teams of horses up to as many as six would walk around a central large cast iron gear. This was mounted on a sturdy wagon frame and the motive power was transferred via drive shaft and universal joints to the main drive on the threshing machine. Horse power was erratic with much variability in energy generated, and it was not sustainable over the long work day. Horses were quickly replaced by engine powered drive belts.

Notes to Chapter 5 Other Tasks

1 The lands of Ukraine were the home of the Scythians, who lived as nomads on the steppes. They ruled over the farmers living in villages who grew wheat, barley, millet, buckwheat, rye, poppies, and hemp. Archaeological findings show that the Scythians used hemp for its fibre, the oil and seed as food, and its THC content for medicinal purposes. See the Gregorovich, 2001, bibliographic entry for more information.

2 Most Ukrainian immigrants came from the south-western provinces of Bukovyna and Halychyna of Ukraine, where grapes, pears, apples, and hard-wood trees grew with the warmer climate, which resembled Canada's Okanogan Valley.

3 The oliinyk was highly valued by the community. The term "oliinyk" became the surname of those who undertook this profession some centuries in the past.

4 Steve Orleski recalls having gone with his father, Dmitro, to their neighbours near Kaleland School who had a "screw" press. He remembers having a hand in applying pressure to the screw press. They had brought with them a half-bushel bag full of garden hemp seed and proceeded to extract hemp oil, which was then used in the fine art of cooking Lenten, Christmas, and Easter meals. The screw press is a smaller and more modern version of the old wooden block and wedge press. It is a metal container with a wooden handle on top of a "screw" that tightens a piston and presses oil from the seed cakes.

5 Harry Zukiwski of Willingdon, Alberta, recalled the use of the Shandro press in the late 1930s and early 1940s in an interview. People from the surrounding area brought their hemp and poppy seed for oil extraction.

6 As a grandchild, I was lucky enough to have one such heirloom; a woolen blanket for my bed.

7 Hemp, *Cannabis Sativa*, is a close relative to the marijuana family, *C. Indic and C. Ruderalia*. Some varieties of hemp are known to produce the same intoxicating drugs as marijuana and are a prohibited plant in Canada.

8 The American hemp industry was virtually destroyed by the *Marihuana Tax Act* of 1937. Farmers in China, India, Russia, Romania, Ukraine, Hungary, and France have continued to grow hemp for fibre and oil. Cultivars have been developed that produce less than the legal limit of 0.3 percent THC, thus enabling the development of a fibre mash without the possibility of diversion for drug use (Maylon and Henman 1980, 433–35).

Notes to Chapter 6 Food/Celebrations

1 The threshing feast as it is here described occurred only during the early years of settlement (pre-WWI) during the flail, kirat and steam threshing phases. When the original wave of pioneers passed on, there was no one left to recount the "historical fables" of the Turkomen on horseback.

2 This description is paraphrased by the author, but a full description of the tradition is included on page 70 of Fedorak's *The Shandros – Our Story*.

3 *Pomana* refers to a gift, food from heaven, in reference to "manna" from a biblical story, sometimes confused with the word, *pomianuty*, meaning to mention in memory.

Notes to Conclusion

1 I would have made the trip myself, but at the time, my wife was ill, and I was her primary caregiver.

Notes to Appendix 1 From Idea to Concept to Reality: The Planning and Design of the Ukrainian Cultural Heritage Village

1 The Clerk of the Privy Council was Gordon Robertson. Prior to this, he was Deputy Minister of Indian and Northern Affairs looking after Parks Canada. He knew of my work in Parks and Historic Sites.

2 I knew Frank Lakusta, because he lived in the vicinity of Hairy Hill, where I went to high school. William Hawrelak was married to a Shandro. My mother was a Shandro. I knew William Hawrelak very well.

3 Upper Canada Village is an excellent example of an early agricultural "living museum," consisting of a collection of early Upper Canada buildings from the St. Lawrence Seaway Floodway.

4 I developed this plan, together with a program for their use in making a submission.

5 Frank Lakusta and his board had special events and days during the years 1973, 1974, 1975, and 1976. In 1976 the land was sold to Alberta Environment, under the auspices of Minister Wm. J. Yurko.

6 The master plan consisted of fifteen panels, all drawings taking you through the process of explaining the concept to that of staged phases and development. All of this was supported by a report and supporting documents.

7 The Select Ministers' Committee consisted of Wm. J. Yurko, Horst Schmidt, John Batiuk, Bert Hohol, and George Topolnisky. Anatholy Lupul was advisor to Dr. Lunn, who chaired the meeting. I, Roman Fodchuk, as consultant, made the presentation. The project was accepted and approved.

8 Roman Fodchuk and Associates, Ltd. supervised the siting of each of the buildings brought in as well as that of the landscape development. The remainder of the work under contract was completed in 1978 and 1979.

9 This was planned as a rural agricultural theme park, and the concept placed a very strong emphasis on the farmsteads. Historically, the farming community, the country churches, schools, and post-offices developed before the townsite, which only came after the railways were built. The rural communities were there first, and that should be emphasized.

10 Although Frank Lakusta owned the land and the buildings, the early board members provided much stability to the evolution of the project. Dan Lutzak was a hotel owner, as was Paul Youzwyshyn. They had an excellent business sense, and Frank Lakusta, also a former hotel owner, respected their input. Their wives had the brains and were an excellent stabilizing influence. Without these people this project would not have succeeded. Most of them are gone by now. They should and need to be remembered, for without their stamina and hard work, this project would not exist.

11 I had the opportunity to study rural agricultural theme parks at the Graduate School of Design at Harvard University in Massachusetts from 1963 to 1964. My staff who worked on this project were very conscientious and hard working and put in a lot of effort to ensure that we had a successful project.

Notes to Glossary

1 The official Ukrainian-English transliteration system was adopted by
   the Ukrainian Legal Terminology Commission (Decision 9). That table
   was approved by the Supreme Council, Verkhovna Rada (Parliament) for
   Ukraine. The United Nations follows the practice of accepting only the
   spellings of geographic names, other names, and transliterations of names,
   if required, that are provided by the governments of its member nations
   for words whose source is in each member's country. That practice fosters
   a universal standardization process for the spelling of words, and is a very
   useful principle, especially for searching on the Internet.

Index

a

b

c

d

e

a. Set of Wooden Planes as found on a pioneer farm or in an early Carpenters Chest. Note that two planes have prominent "horn-like handles", a characteristic of Austrian and east European origin. This set also includes two smoothing planes and a set of various interchangeable blades, more commonly used in grooving and plow planes.

b. A set of two Jointer Planes , a heavy duty tool used in the leveling of floor boards, and a Trying Plane.

c. Two woven storage baskets; made of native willow or hazel nut branching in its fine pliable and green state, foraged in the fields in the early spring.

d. Child's Cradle, would also be made of similar flexible thin branches. not uncommon in the newly settled lands.

e. Hand-made wooden straw fork, hearth cleaning wooden hoe and carved grain shovel.

Photos by Myron Bodnaruk

a

b

c

d

e

a. A rasher of hand-built Wooden Butter
   Churns; with no metal connectors.

b. A series of wooden Wash Boards and ribbed Ironing Boards; a special
   tool for detailed setting of pleats in linen and hemp clothing.

c. Various Carding Paddles and spiked Boards for processing
   wool, flax and hemp fibers in preparation for cloth making.

d. Hand carved wooden "troughs" used in kneeding
   and preparing dough in bread making.

e. Two ceramic pots of local clays, fired and used
   as containers for fresh milk and cream.
   Photos by Myron Bodnaruk

a

b

d

c

a. A handsomely carved measuring container
used for determining seed quantity.

b. Basket of woven willow or other native shrub
species that were used in basket making.

c. An excellent collection of combs or "berdos", the key
component of a loom in guiding threads in the weaving process.
These were in most instances brought from the pioneers'
homeland and were the basis for building the loom.

d. Large Clothing "Suit Case" or travel case made of woven willow.
Photos by Myron Bodnaruk

Excellent examples of two wooden spinning wheels, found
throughout the households in Ukrainian Settlement Bloc.
Photos by Myron Bodnaruk

The Kupchenko family, all dressed up for the Shandro Reunion
Rosaline, Lena, Natalka and Mike Kupchenko

Martha Shandro, the "Head of the Wasyl Shandro family" and her kin
Nancy Fodchuk, Grace Shandro, Sophie Shandro, Barbie Orleskis, Darin
Cherniwchan, Natalka Kupchenko,. Kosten Menzak , Elizabeth Shandro,
Martha Shandro, Lena Kupchenko, Mike Kupchenko, and Anne Mitanski

Fodchuks, Lutzaks, Orleskis and Yurkos at the Lutzak Family plot

Fodchuks, Yurkos and Orleskis at the Fodchuk Family plot at Szypenitz

A gathering of people amongst the graves , all in reverence of
their departed ancestors, This ceremony takes place every year,
a week or two after Orthodox Easter at the grave sites

Lena and Mike Kupchenko

Seniors; Kosten Menzak, Mike Kupchenko, Lena Kupchenko,
Grandmother Martha Shandro, Sharlene Cherniwchan,
Anne Mitanski, Pearl Shandro and Sam Shandro

The youngsters all in costume; Rosaline Kupchenko,
Darin Cherniwchan, and Natalka Kupchenko

Blessing of the Graves procession at Szypenitz

Russo Orthodox Church at Wasel, overlooking the North Saskatchewan River Valley

Hempseed oil press at the Shandro Museum

Blessing of the Easter baskets

An example of an old outdoor *pich*

A parking lot full of horses and sleighs at the Ukrainian Orthodox Church of St. Peter and St. Paul, Dickie Bush

Two pioneers stop to chat and exchange news as they pass each other on the way to town and back

Funeral procession to a country grave site near Willingdon

Structural framing showing the chimney structure and the flue within a thatched attic

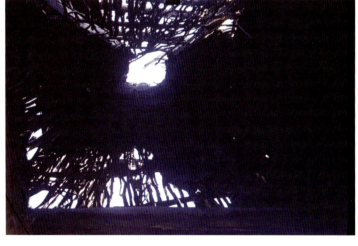

Structural framing looking up through the chimney structure and the flue within a thatched attic

Nichon and Anna Shandro celebrate their Anniversary

Provody at Luzan; a family honours their ancestors

Provody at Borowich; a family honours their ancestors

A new grave site in preparation for the Provody celebrations at
St. Pokrova Ukrainian Orthodox Church at Borowich

Thatching crew in the partially completed house in Elk Island National Park

A modern Pich in the Author's boyhood home on the farm at Hairy Hill

Fine old *Khata* showing the protective leak-proof structure
on a thatched roof that is badly deteriorated

An original settler's home in the Andrew district - serves as a model
for the "Replica" to be built at Elk Island National Park

Fine old thatched homes in the Zawale area south of Andrew

Disappearing folk heritage in the Smoky Lake Area;
old homes decaying and falling apart

Structural integrity of a distressed thatched roof

Disappearing folk heritage in the Smoky Lake Area;
old homes decaying and falling apart

Nick Mandryk home in the Szypenitz area

A typical Bokovynian's settlers home in the Szypenitz district

Outer structural linear wall of a series of joined narrow
buildings forming an enclosed farm courtyard

Attendee's arrive by Model T's and Model A's as well as 1950's cars
at St. Demitrius Ruthenian Greek Orthodox Church at Luzan

Homestead in the Szypenitz area

Winrows of green Oat hay - Scything by hand

Fine old thatched *Khata* near Musidora

Disappearing folk heritage in the Smoky Lake Area;
old homes decaying and falling apart

Thanksgiving service at Willingdon

Shandros celebrate a century in Canada